morning**glories**
volume**six**
demerits

*This is a gift from
the Friends of the
Pleasant Hill Library*

WORDS
NICK SPENCER

ART
JOE EISMA

RODIN ESQUEJO
COVERS

PAUL LITTLE - JASON LEWIS
COLORS

JOHNNY LOWE - TIM DANIEL
LETTERS   DESIGN

IMAGE COMICS, INC.
Robert Kirkman - chief operating officer
Erik Larsen - chief financial officer
Todd McFarlane - president
Marc Silvestri - chief executive officer
Jim Valentino - vice-president

Eric Stephenson - publisher
Ron Richards - director of business development
Jennifer de Guzman - pr & marketing director
Branwyn Bigglestone - accounts manager
Emily Miller - accounting assistant
Jamie Parreno - marketing assistant
Emilio Bautista - sales assistant
Jaimie Dudas - administrative assistant
Kevin Yuen - digital rights coordinator
Tyler Shainline - events coordinator
David Brothers - content manager
Jonathan Chan - production manager
Drew Gill - art director
Monica Garcia - senior production artist
Vincent Kukua - production artist
Jenna Savage - production artist
Addison Duke - production artist
www.imagecomics.com

thirty

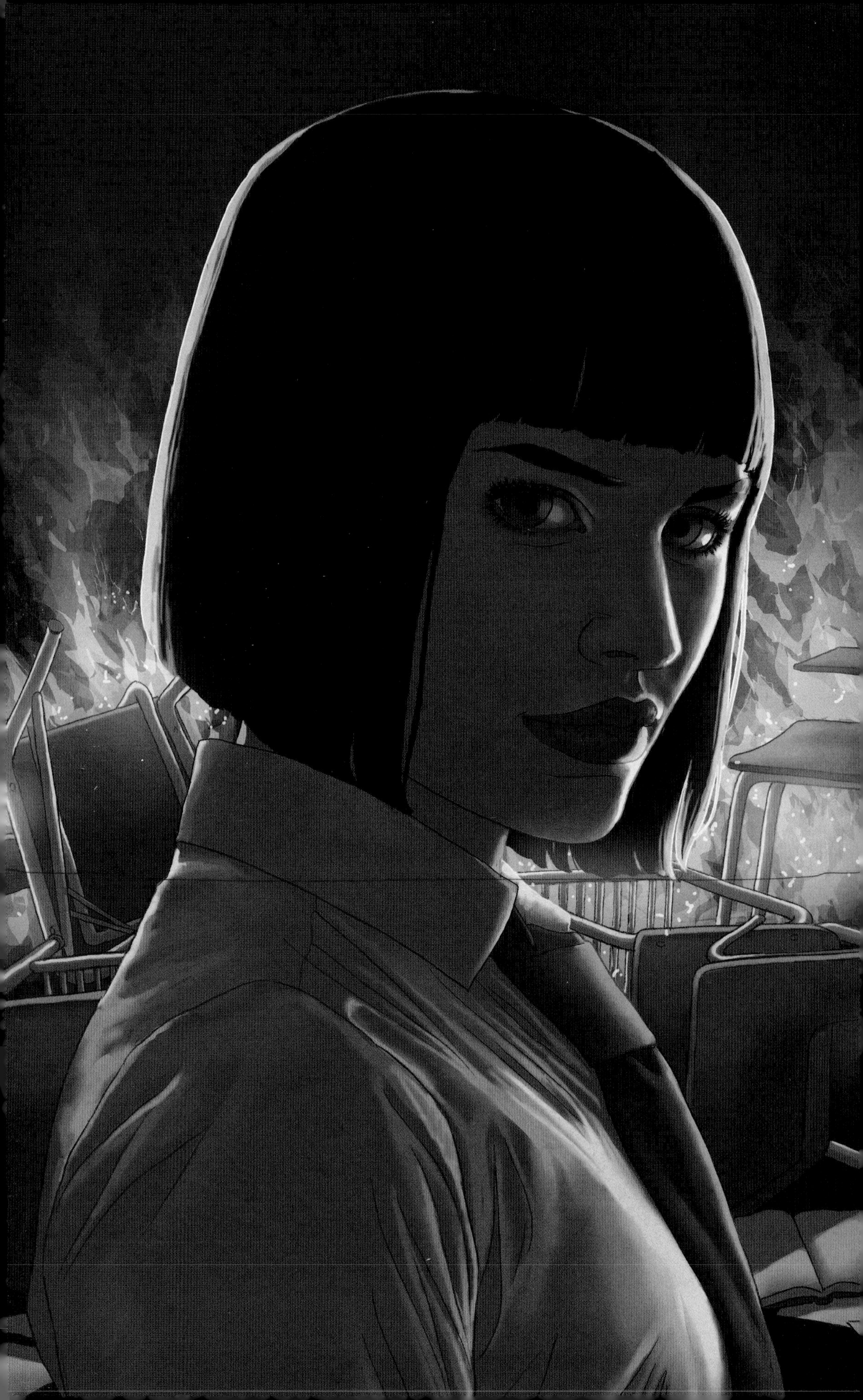

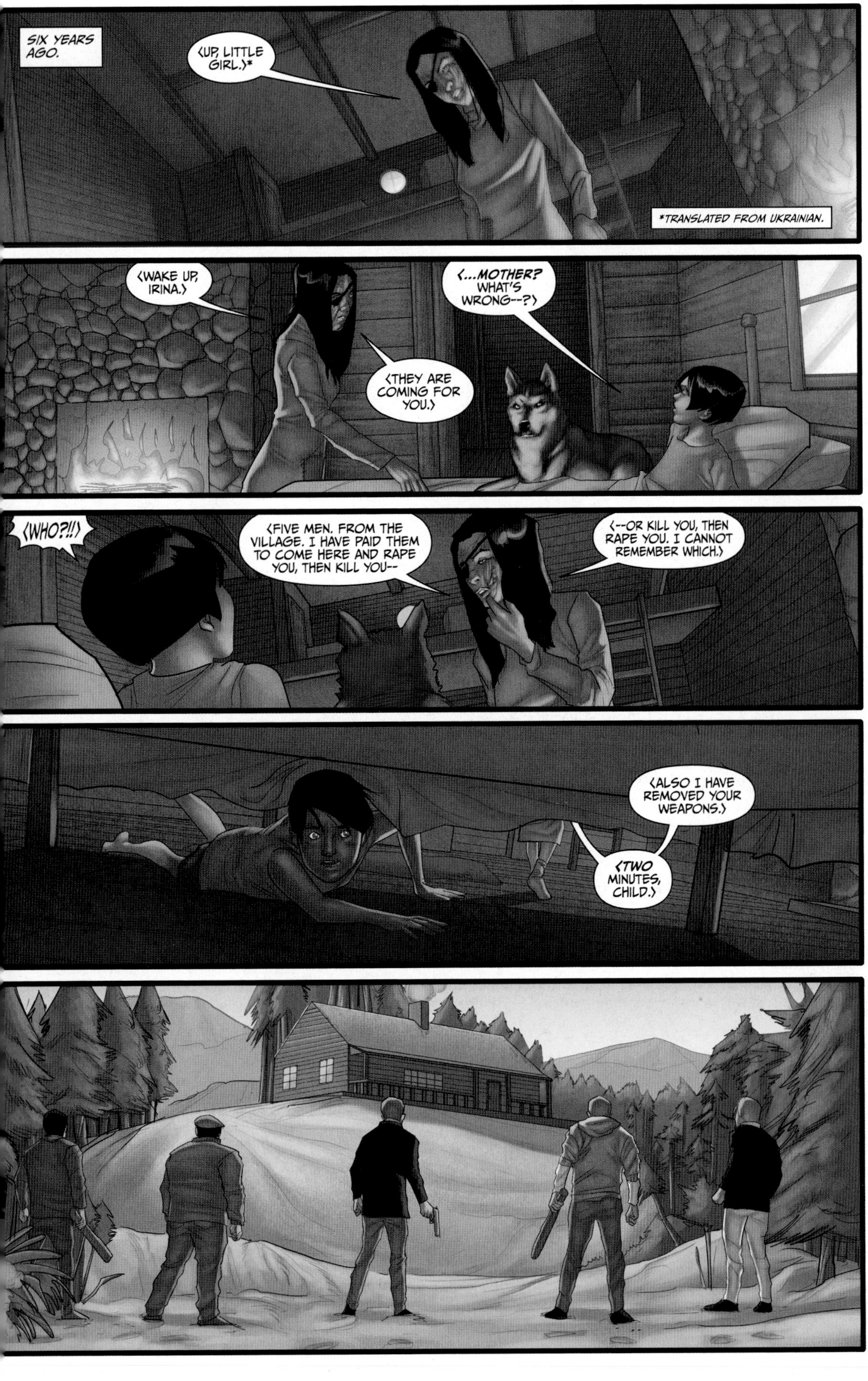

SIX YEARS AGO.
‹UP, LITTLE GIRL.›*
*TRANSLATED FROM UKRAINIAN.
‹WAKE UP, IRINA.›
‹...MOTHER? WHAT'S WRONG--?›
‹THEY ARE COMING FOR YOU.›
‹WHO?!!›
‹FIVE MEN. FROM THE VILLAGE. I HAVE PAID THEM TO COME HERE AND RAPE YOU, THEN KILL YOU--
‹--OR KILL YOU, THEN RAPE YOU. I CANNOT REMEMBER WHICH.›
‹ALSO I HAVE REMOVED YOUR WEAPONS.›
‹TWO MINUTES, CHILD.›

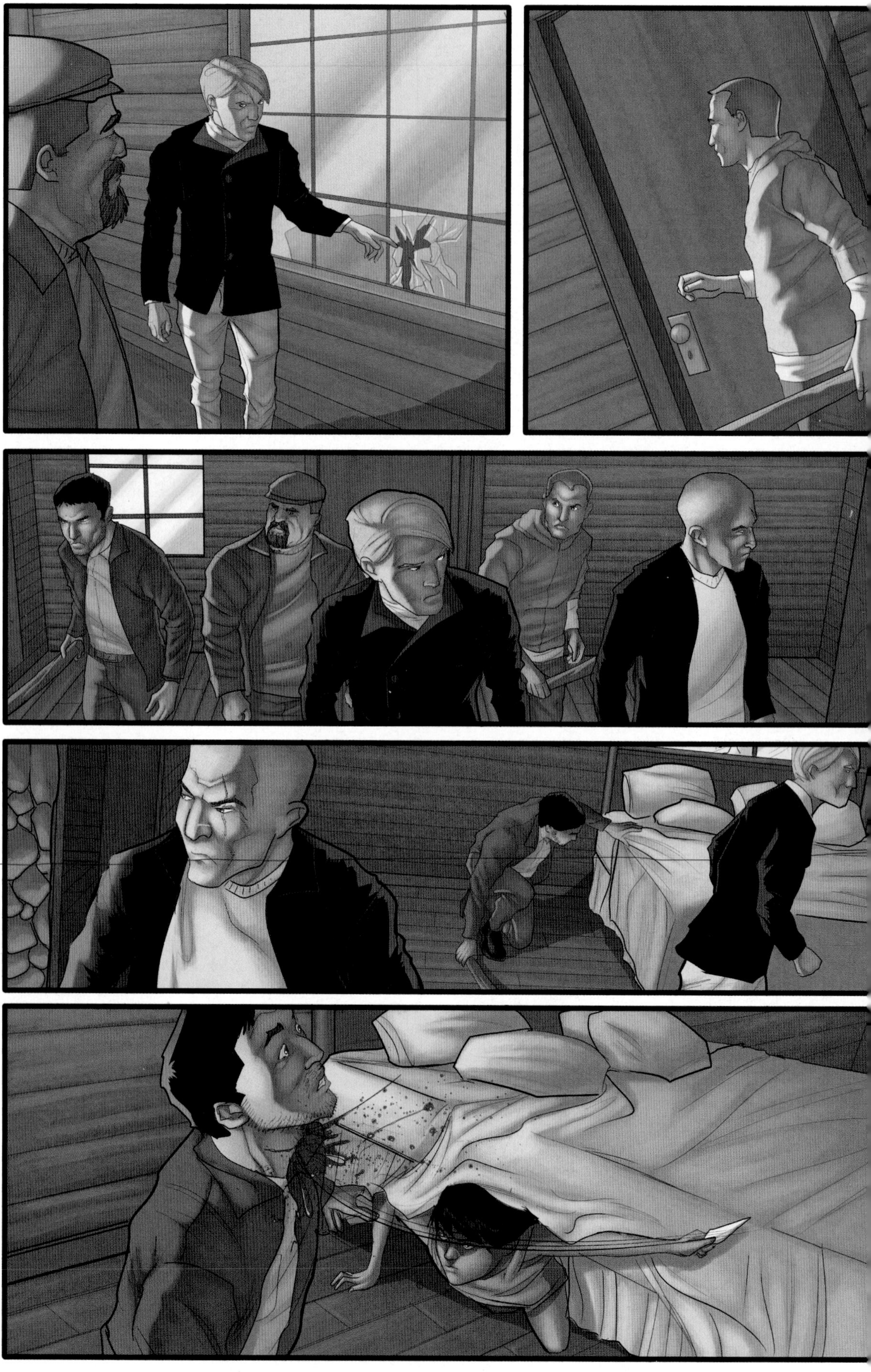

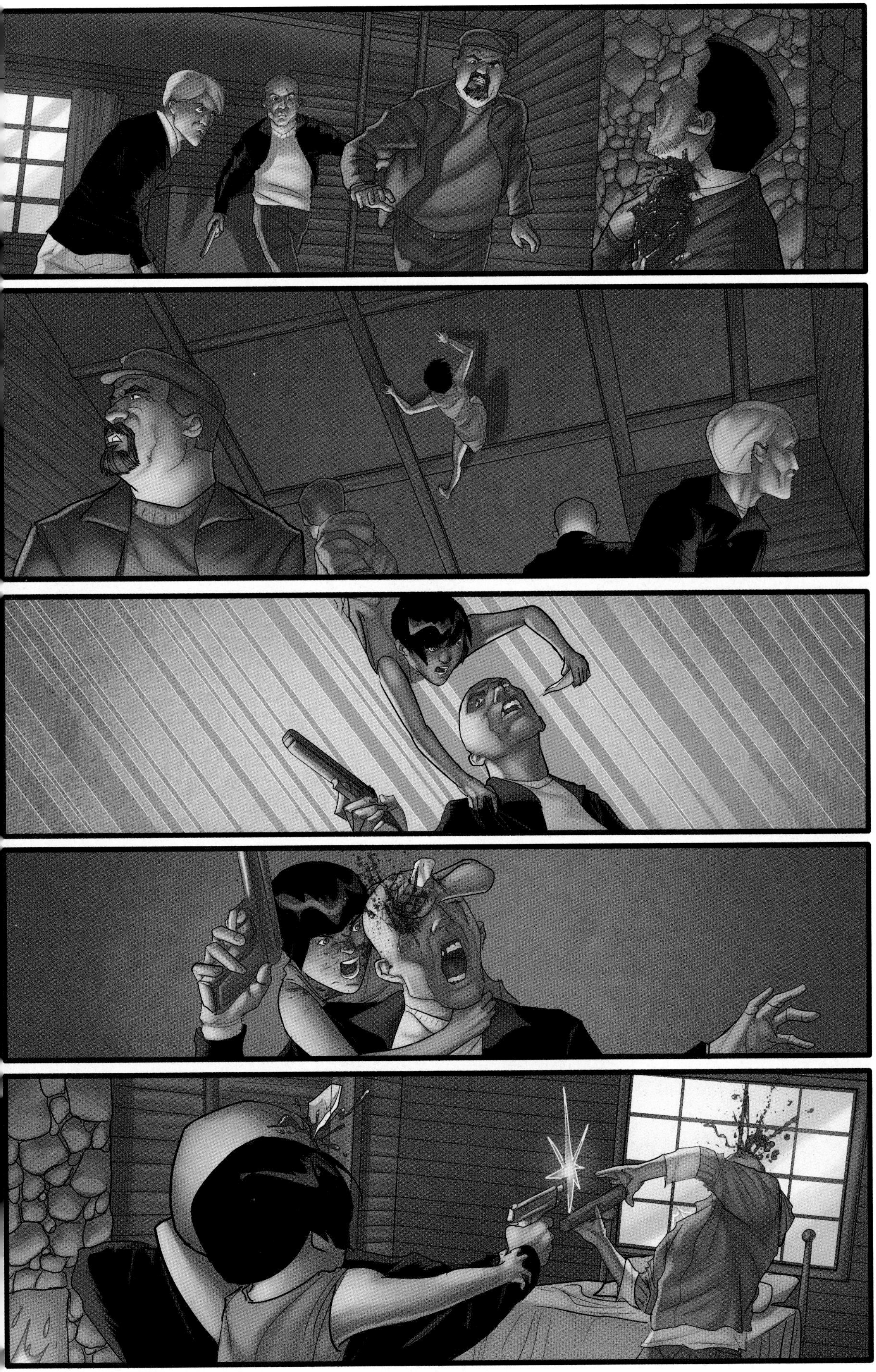

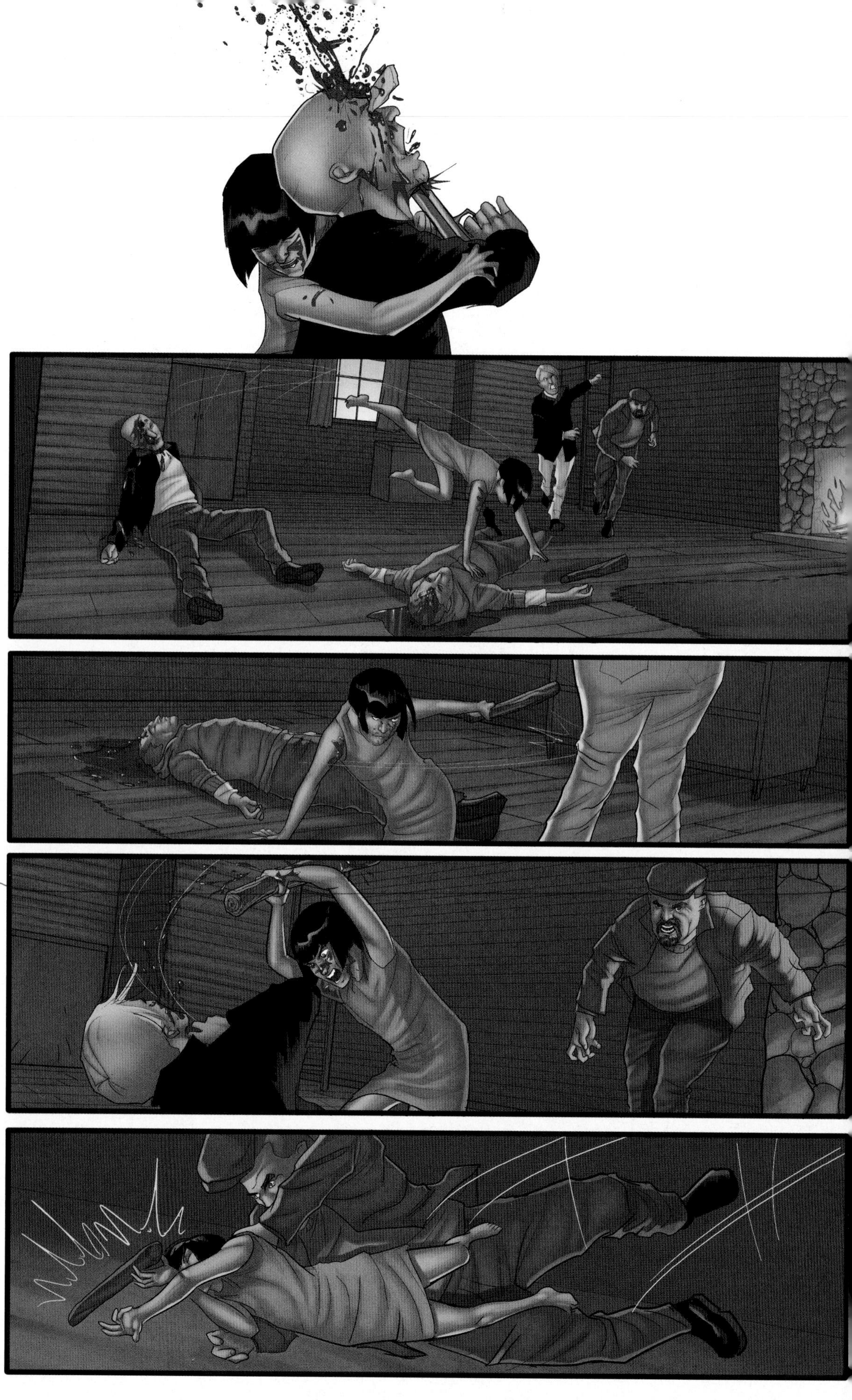

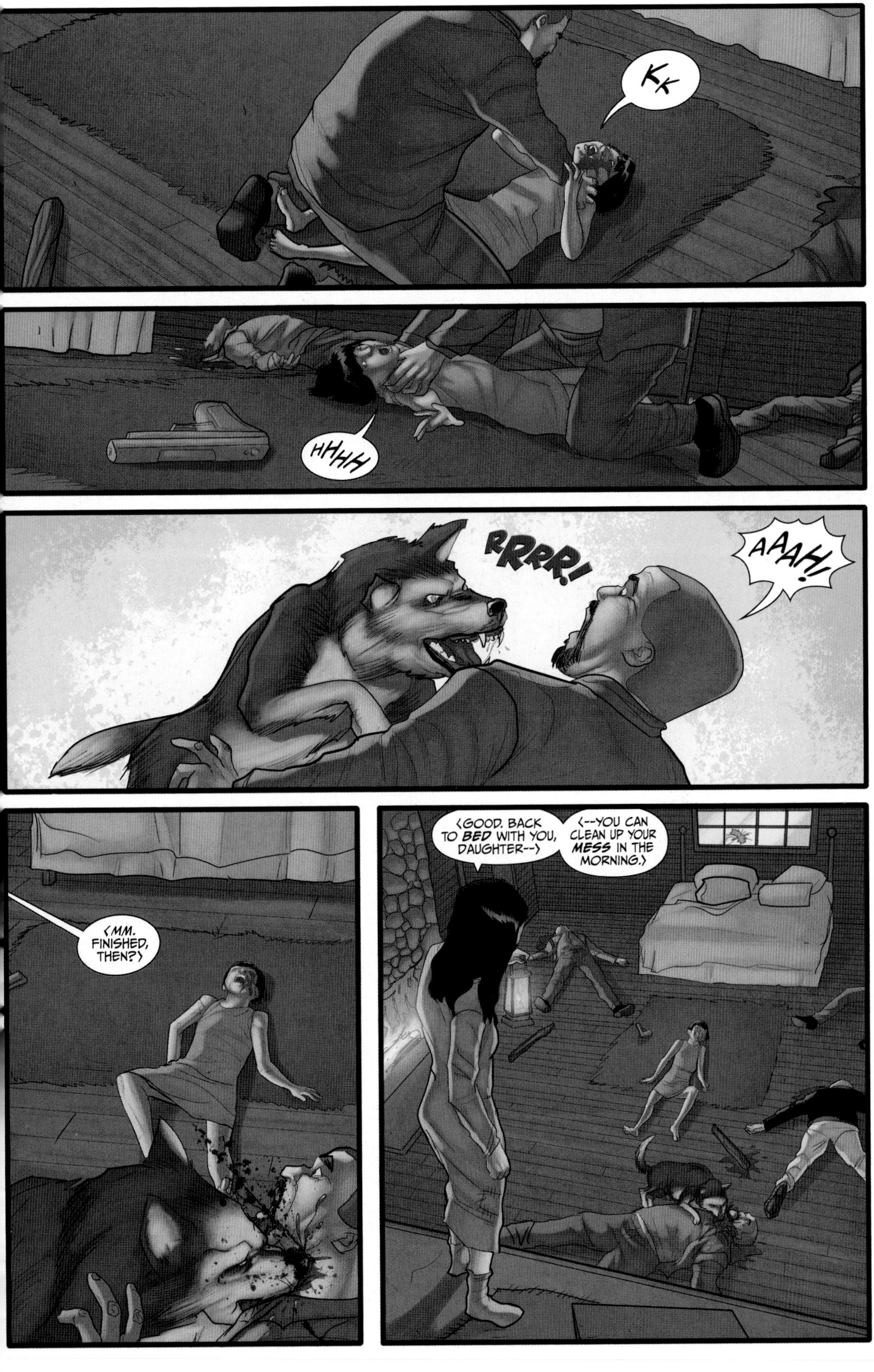
KK
HHHH
RRRR!
AAAH!
⟨MM. FINISHED, THEN?⟩
⟨GOOD. BACK TO BED WITH YOU, DAUGHTER--⟩
⟨--YOU CAN CLEAN UP YOUR MESS IN THE MORNING.⟩

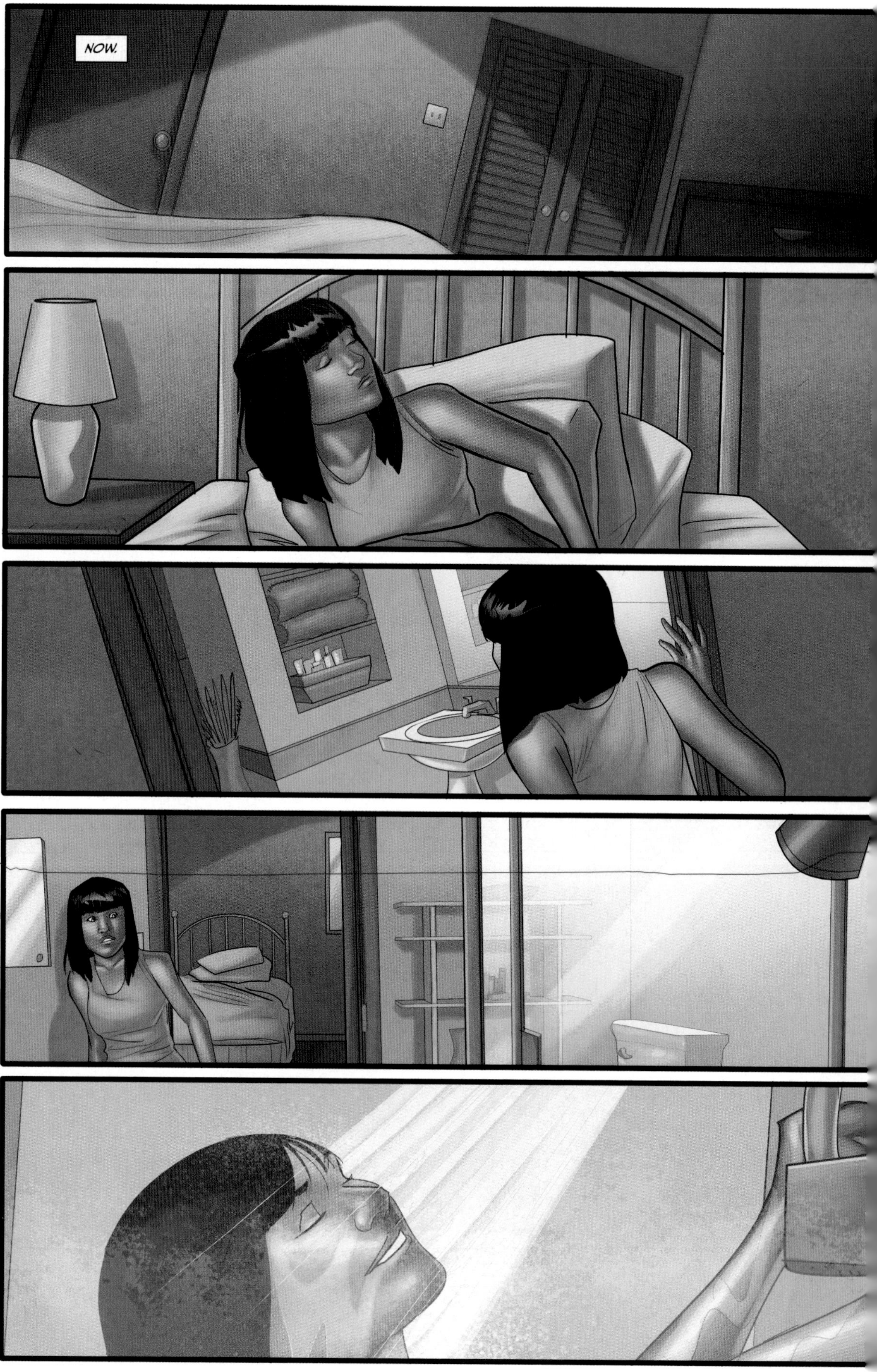
NOW.

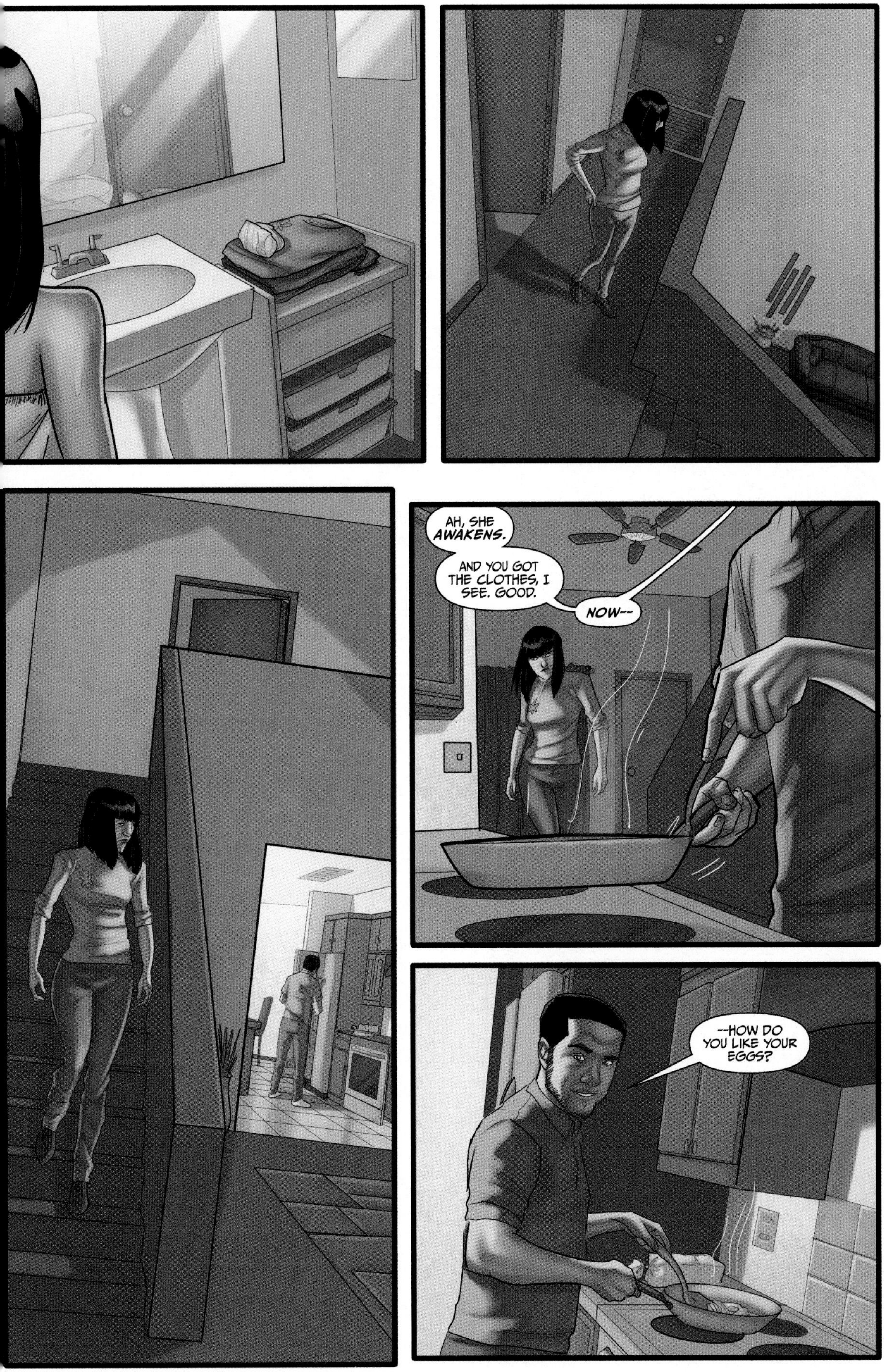
AH, SHE AWAKENS.
AND YOU GOT THE CLOTHES, I SEE. GOOD.
NOW--
--HOW DO YOU LIKE YOUR EGGS?

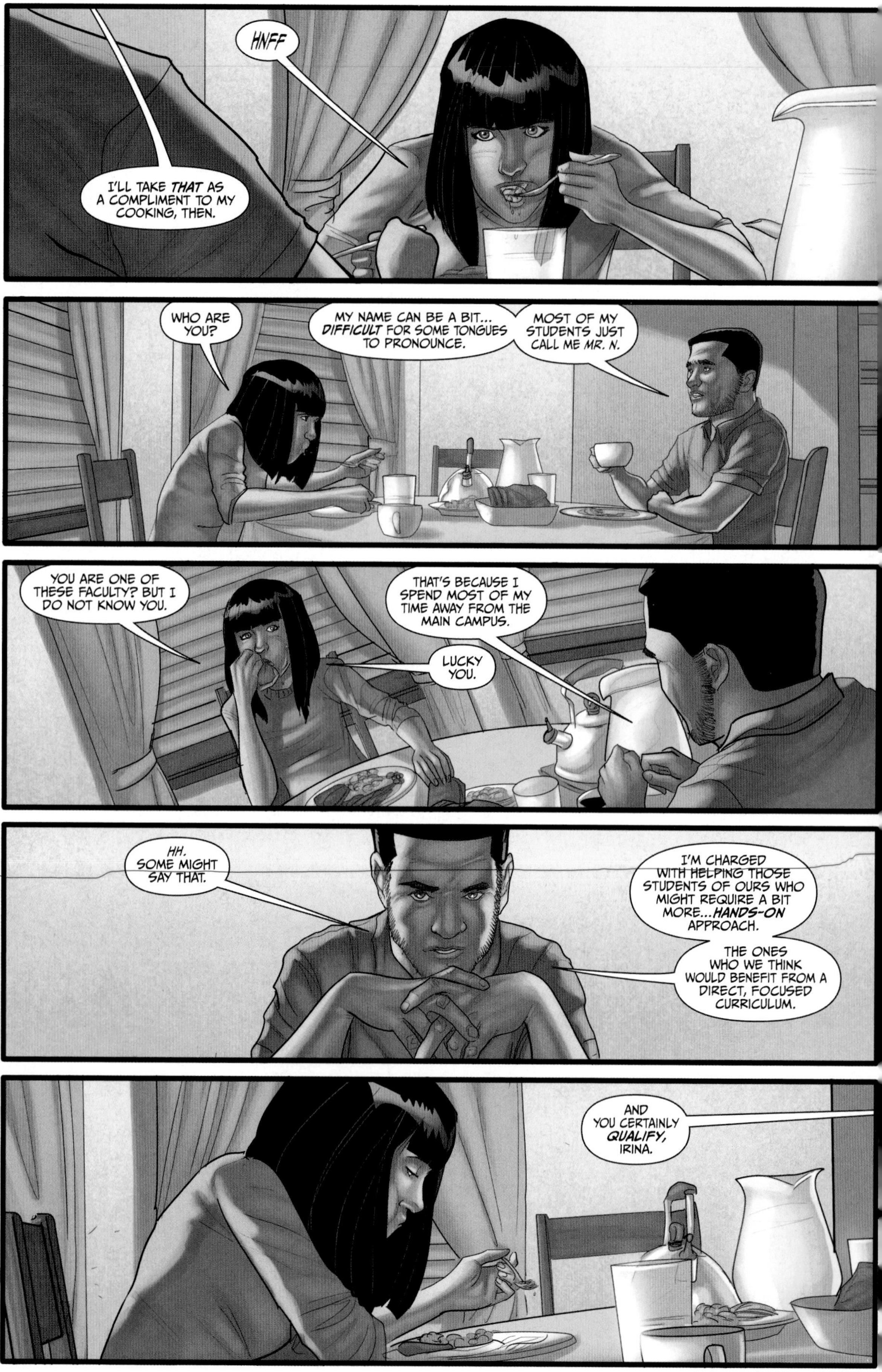
HNFF
I'LL TAKE THAT AS A COMPLIMENT TO MY COOKING, THEN.
WHO ARE YOU?
MY NAME CAN BE A BIT... DIFFICULT FOR SOME TONGUES TO PRONOUNCE.
MOST OF MY STUDENTS JUST CALL ME MR. N.
YOU ARE ONE OF THESE FACULTY? BUT I DO NOT KNOW YOU.
THAT'S BECAUSE I SPEND MOST OF MY TIME AWAY FROM THE MAIN CAMPUS.
LUCKY YOU.
HH. SOME MIGHT SAY THAT.
I'M CHARGED WITH HELPING THOSE STUDENTS OF OURS WHO MIGHT REQUIRE A BIT MORE...HANDS-ON APPROACH.
THE ONES WHO WE THINK WOULD BENEFIT FROM A DIRECT, FOCUSED CURRICULUM.
AND YOU CERTAINLY QUALIFY, IRINA.

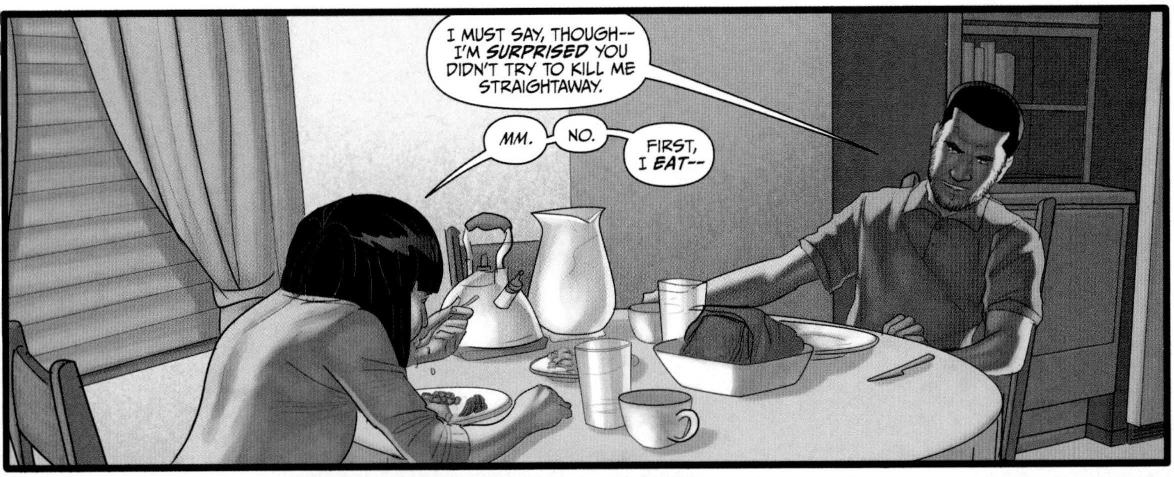
I MUST SAY, THOUGH-- I'M SURPRISED YOU DIDN'T TRY TO KILL ME STRAIGHTAWAY.
MM.
NO.
FIRST, I EAT--

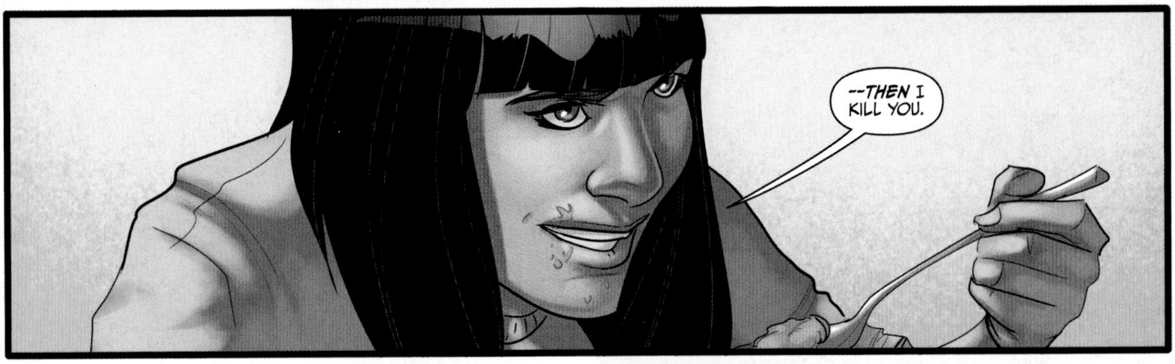
--THEN I KILL YOU.

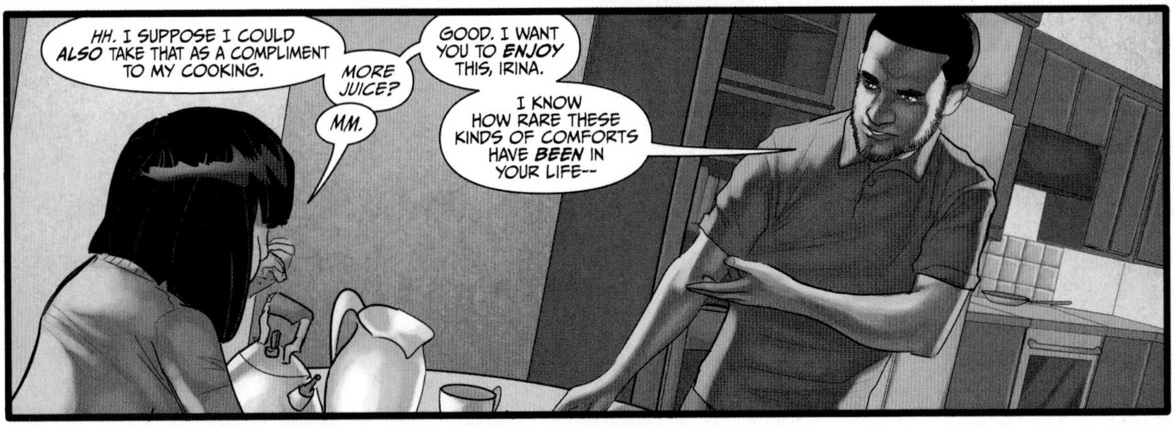
HH. I SUPPOSE I COULD ALSO TAKE THAT AS A COMPLIMENT TO MY COOKING.
MORE JUICE?
MM.
GOOD. I WANT YOU TO ENJOY THIS, IRINA.
I KNOW HOW RARE THESE KINDS OF COMFORTS HAVE BEEN IN YOUR LIFE--

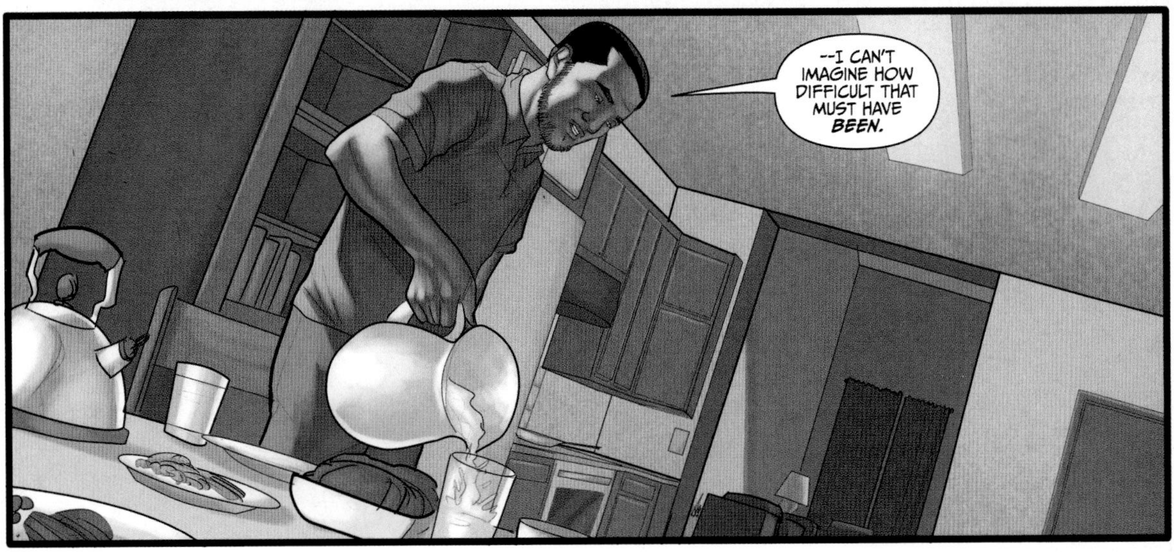
--I CAN'T IMAGINE HOW DIFFICULT THAT MUST HAVE BEEN.

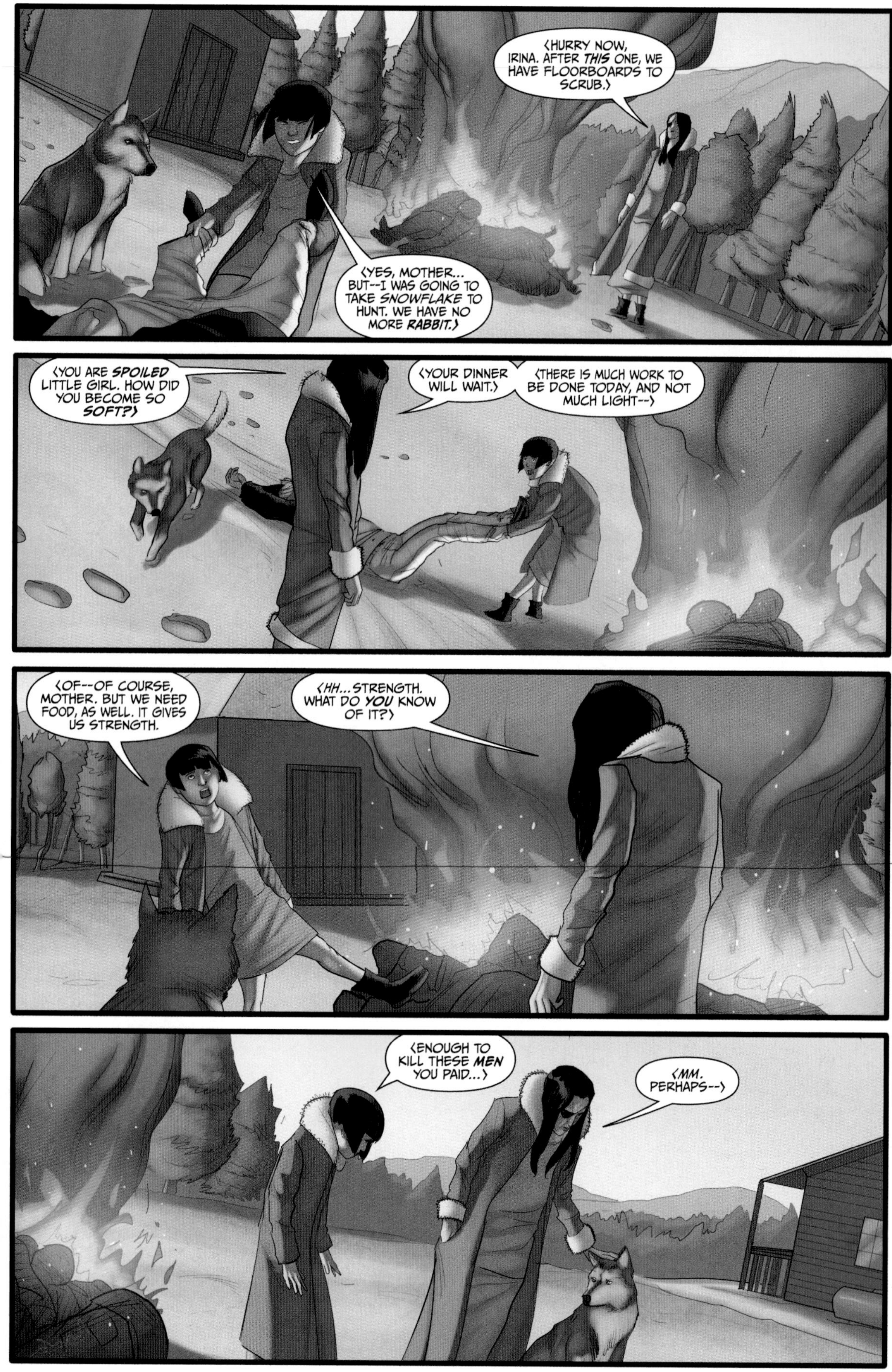

‹HURRY NOW, IRINA. AFTER *THIS* ONE, WE HAVE FLOORBOARDS TO SCRUB.›
‹YES, MOTHER... BUT--I WAS GOING TO TAKE *SNOWFLAKE* TO HUNT. WE HAVE NO MORE *RABBIT.*›
‹YOU ARE *SPOILED* LITTLE GIRL. HOW DID YOU BECOME SO *SOFT?*›
‹YOUR DINNER WILL WAIT.›
‹THERE IS MUCH WORK TO BE DONE TODAY, AND NOT MUCH LIGHT--›
‹OF--OF COURSE, MOTHER. BUT WE NEED FOOD, AS WELL. IT GIVES US STRENGTH.
‹*HH...* STRENGTH. WHAT DO *YOU* KNOW OF IT?›
‹ENOUGH TO KILL THESE *MEN* YOU PAID...›
‹MM. PERHAPS--›

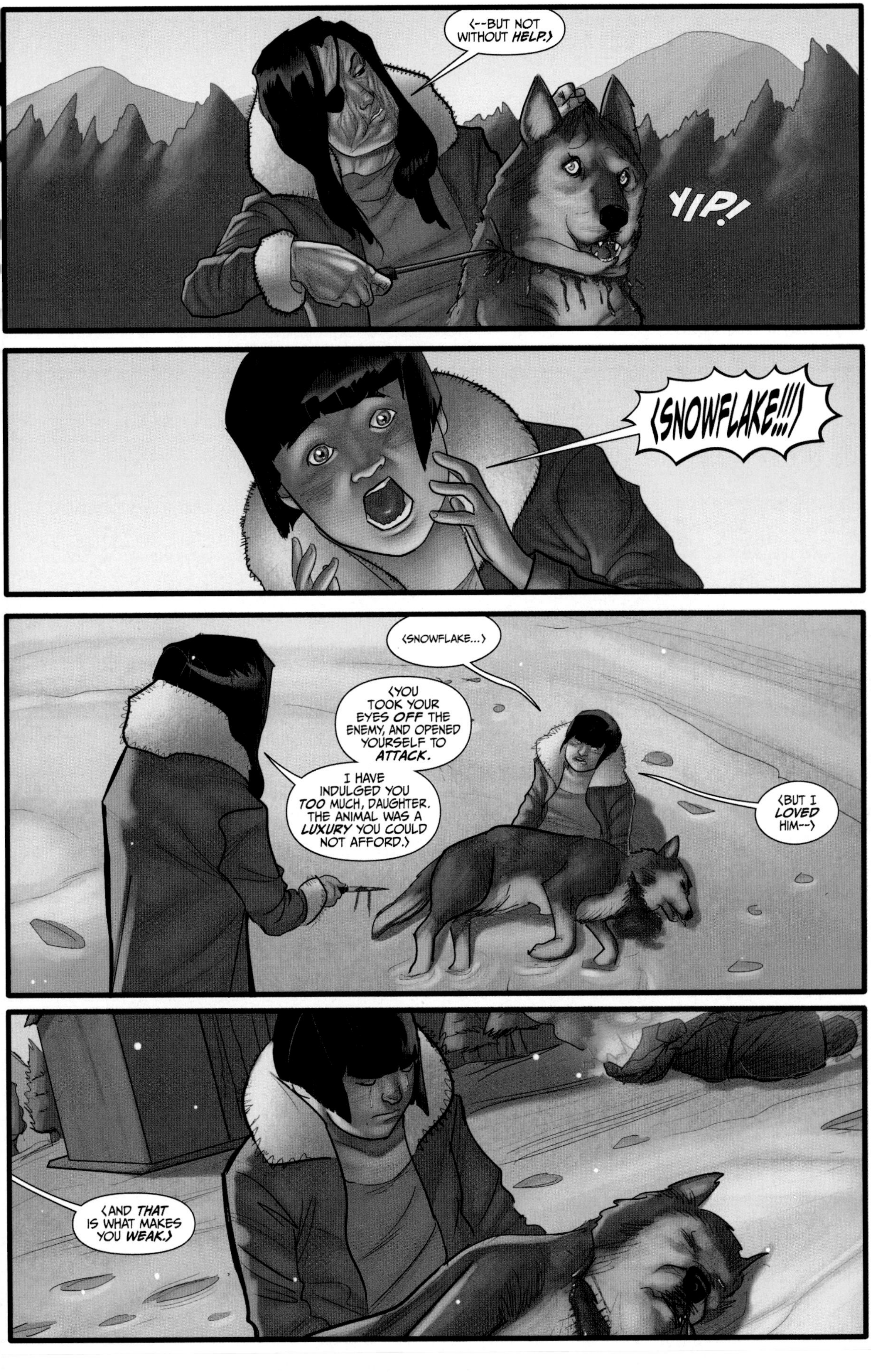
‹--BUT NOT WITHOUT HELP.›
YIP!
‹SNOWFLAKE!!!›
‹SNOWFLAKE...›
‹YOU TOOK YOUR EYES OFF THE ENEMY, AND OPENED YOURSELF TO ATTACK.
I HAVE INDULGED YOU TOO MUCH, DAUGHTER. THE ANIMAL WAS A LUXURY YOU COULD NOT AFFORD.›
‹BUT I LOVED HIM--›
‹AND THAT IS WHAT MAKES YOU WEAK.›

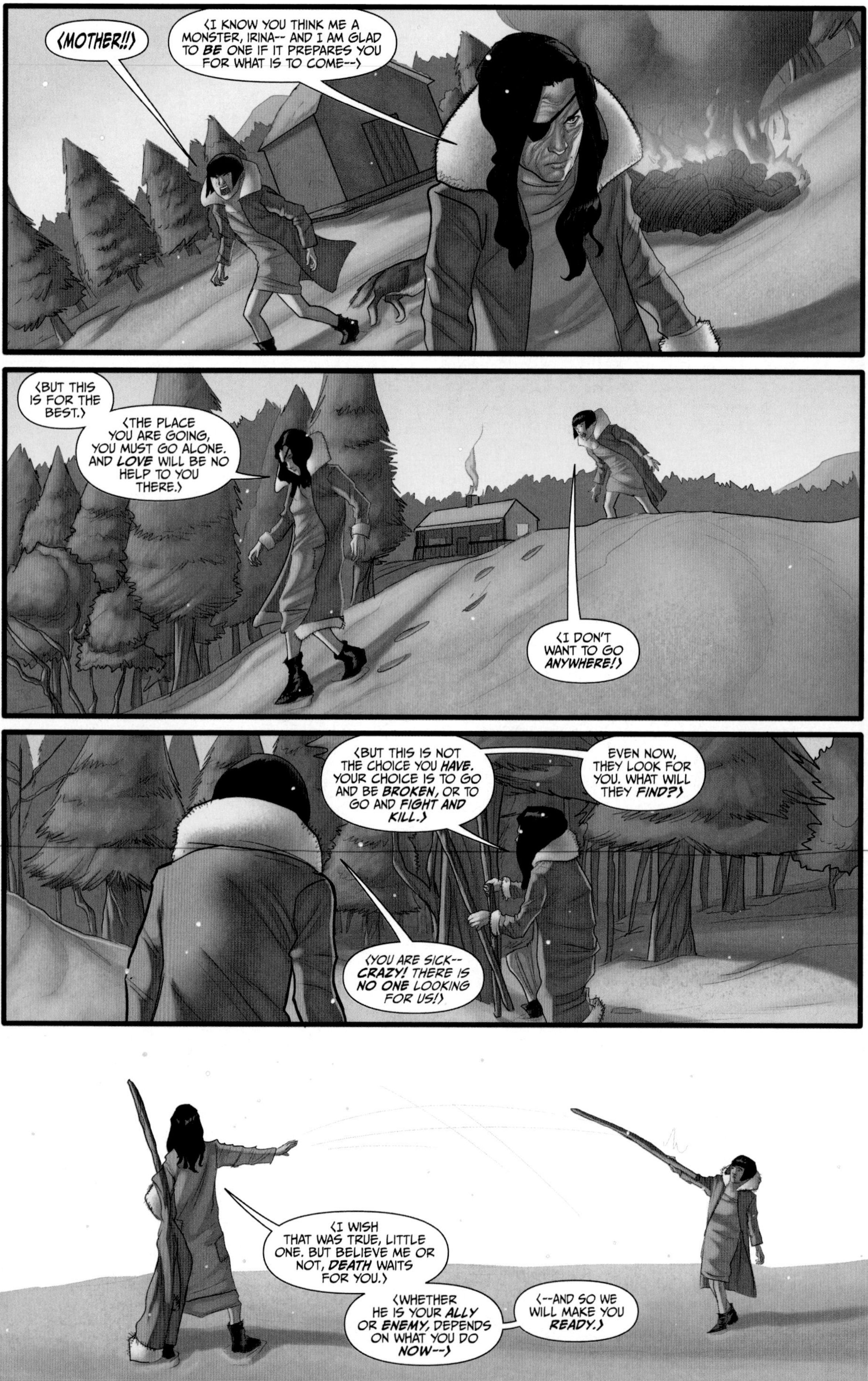
⟨MOTHER!!⟩
⟨I KNOW YOU THINK ME A MONSTER, IRINA-- AND I AM GLAD TO BE ONE IF IT PREPARES YOU FOR WHAT IS TO COME--⟩
⟨BUT THIS IS FOR THE BEST.⟩
⟨THE PLACE YOU ARE GOING, YOU MUST GO ALONE. AND LOVE WILL BE NO HELP TO YOU THERE.⟩
⟨I DON'T WANT TO GO ANYWHERE!⟩
⟨BUT THIS IS NOT THE CHOICE YOU HAVE. YOUR CHOICE IS TO GO AND BE BROKEN, OR TO GO AND FIGHT AND KILL.⟩
EVEN NOW, THEY LOOK FOR YOU. WHAT WILL THEY FIND?⟩
⟨YOU ARE SICK-- CRAZY! THERE IS NO ONE LOOKING FOR US!⟩
⟨I WISH THAT WAS TRUE, LITTLE ONE. BUT BELIEVE ME OR NOT, DEATH WAITS FOR YOU.⟩
⟨WHETHER HE IS YOUR ALLY OR ENEMY, DEPENDS ON WHAT YOU DO NOW--⟩
⟨--AND SO WE WILL MAKE YOU READY.⟩

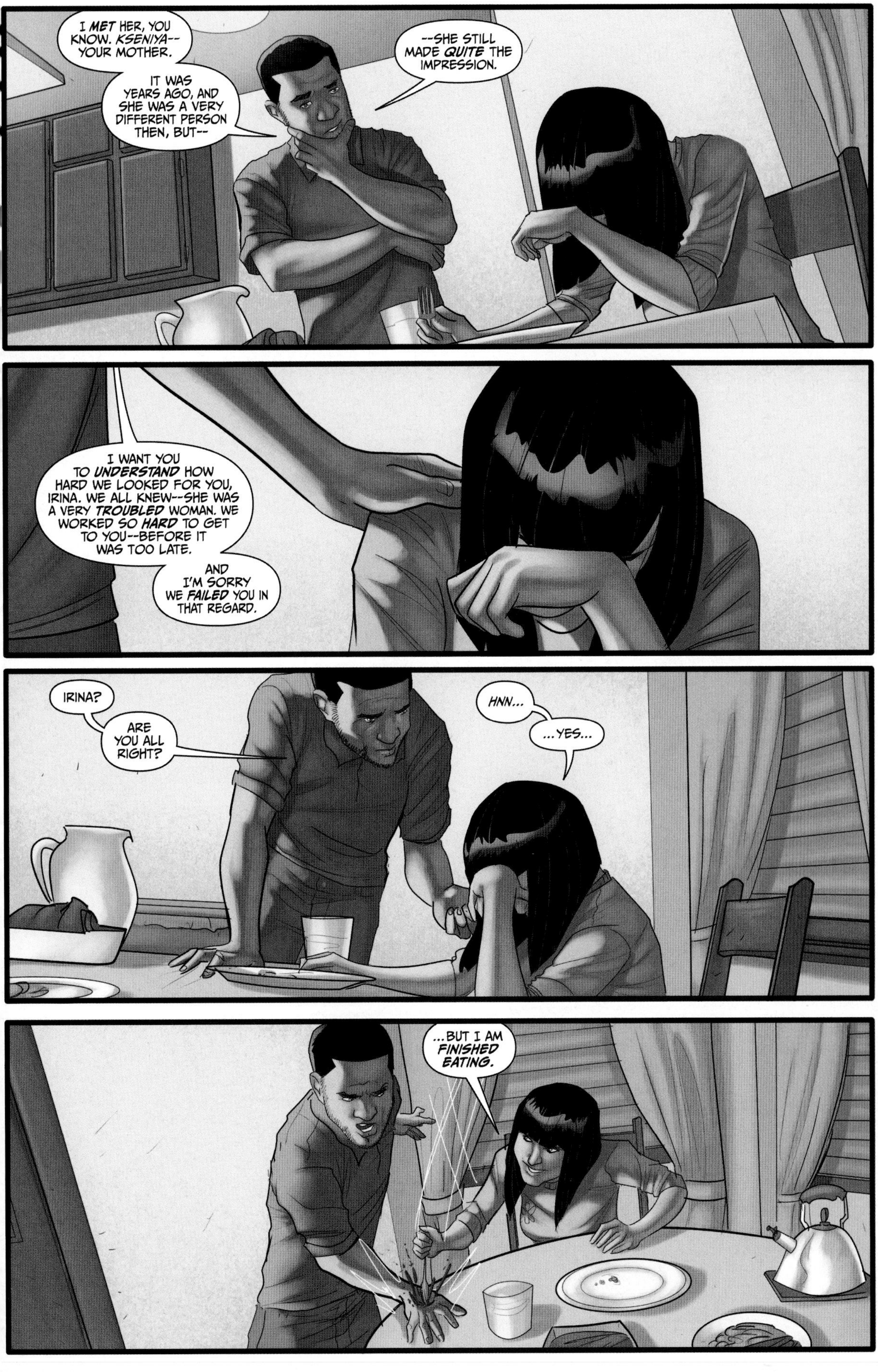

I MET HER, YOU KNOW. KSENIYA-- YOUR MOTHER.
IT WAS YEARS AGO, AND SHE WAS A VERY DIFFERENT PERSON THEN, BUT--
--SHE STILL MADE QUITE THE IMPRESSION.
I WANT YOU TO UNDERSTAND HOW HARD WE LOOKED FOR YOU, IRINA. WE ALL KNEW--SHE WAS A VERY TROUBLED WOMAN. WE WORKED SO HARD TO GET TO YOU--BEFORE IT WAS TOO LATE.
AND I'M SORRY WE FAILED YOU IN THAT REGARD.
IRINA?
ARE YOU ALL RIGHT?
HNN...
...YES...
...BUT I AM FINISHED EATING.

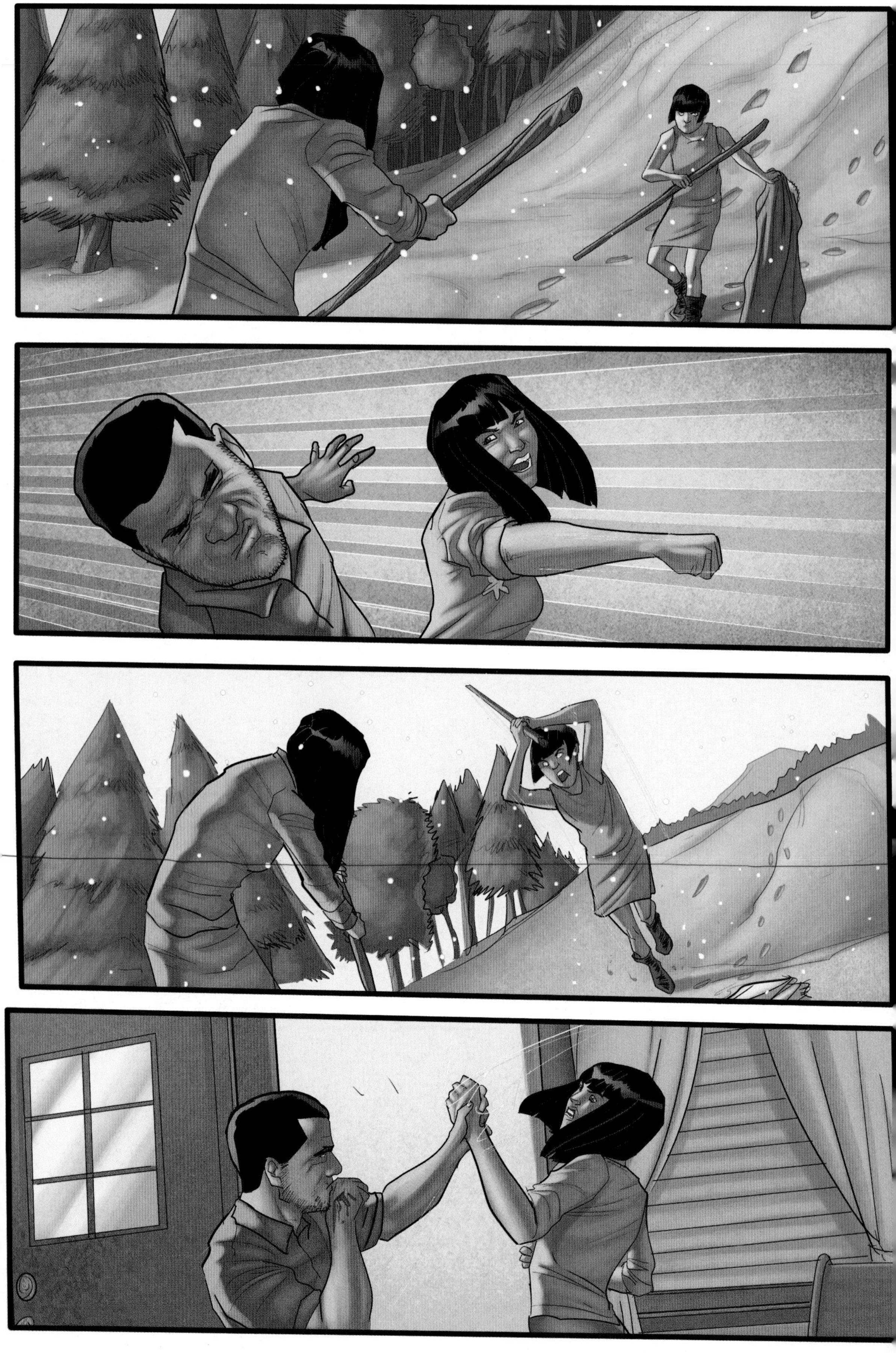

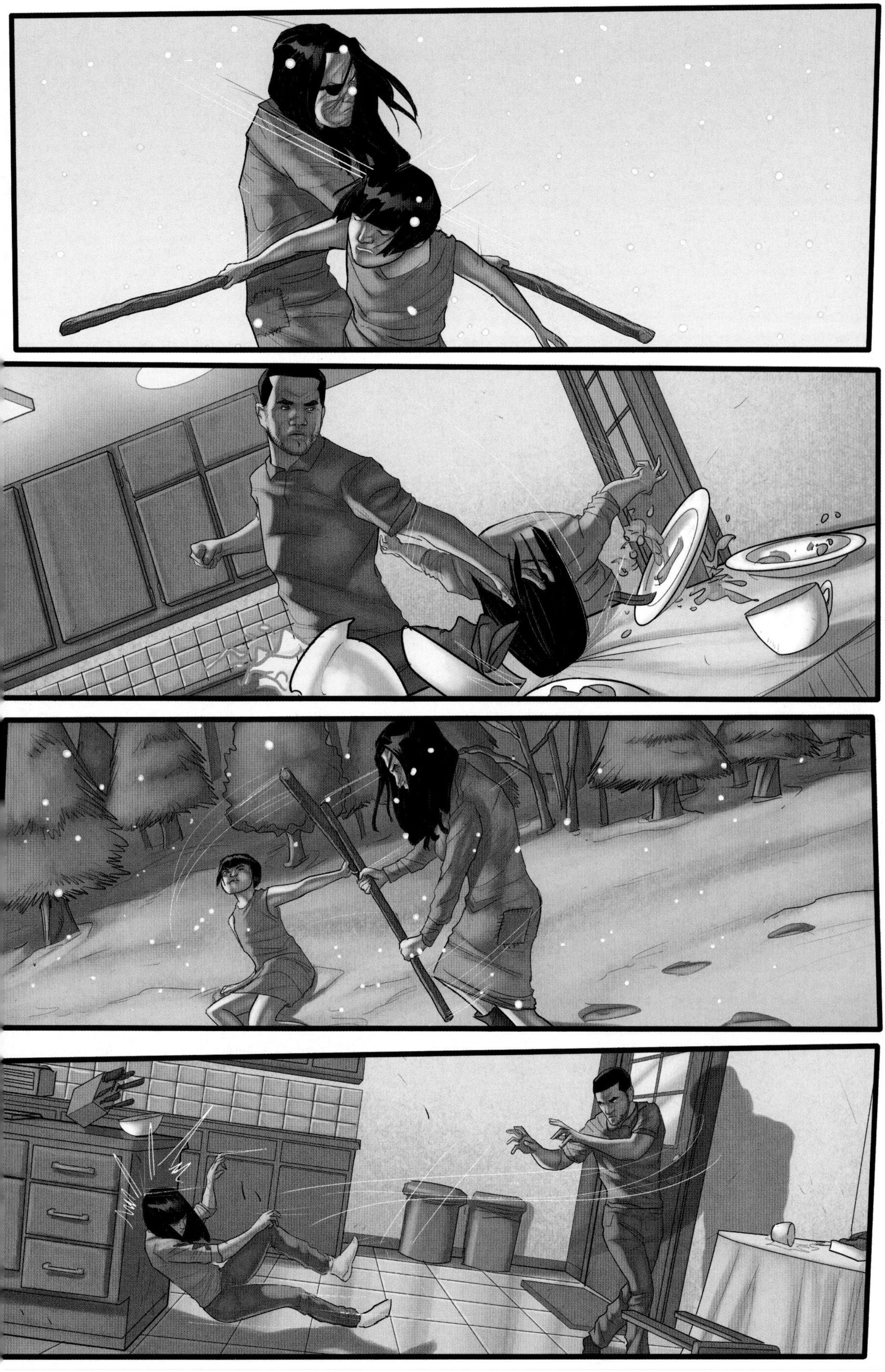

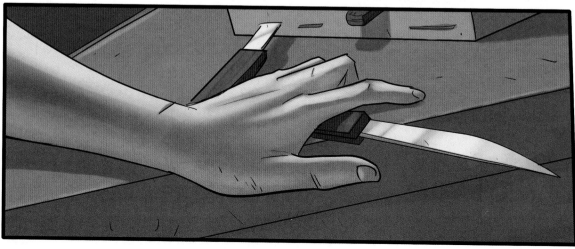

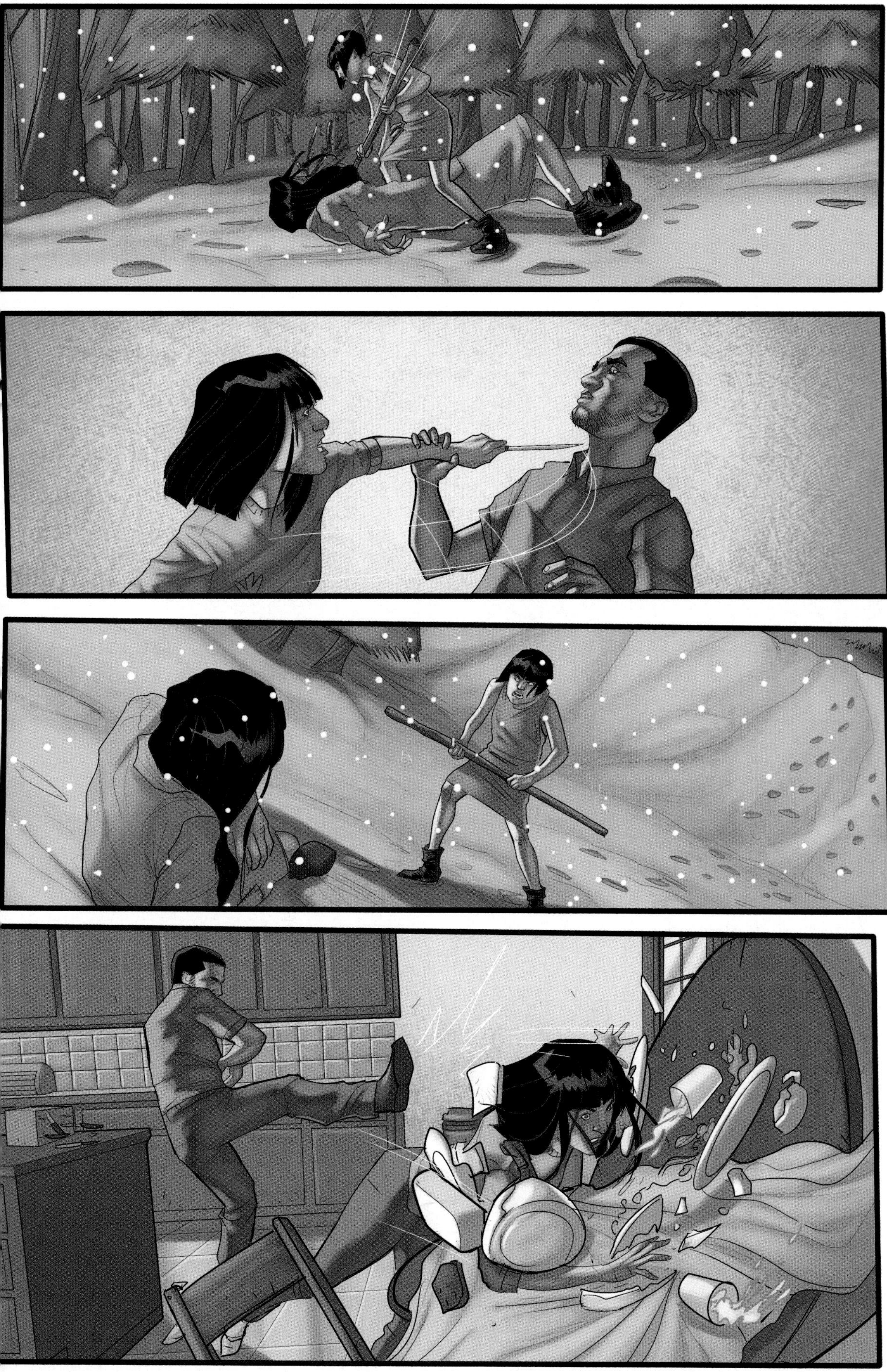

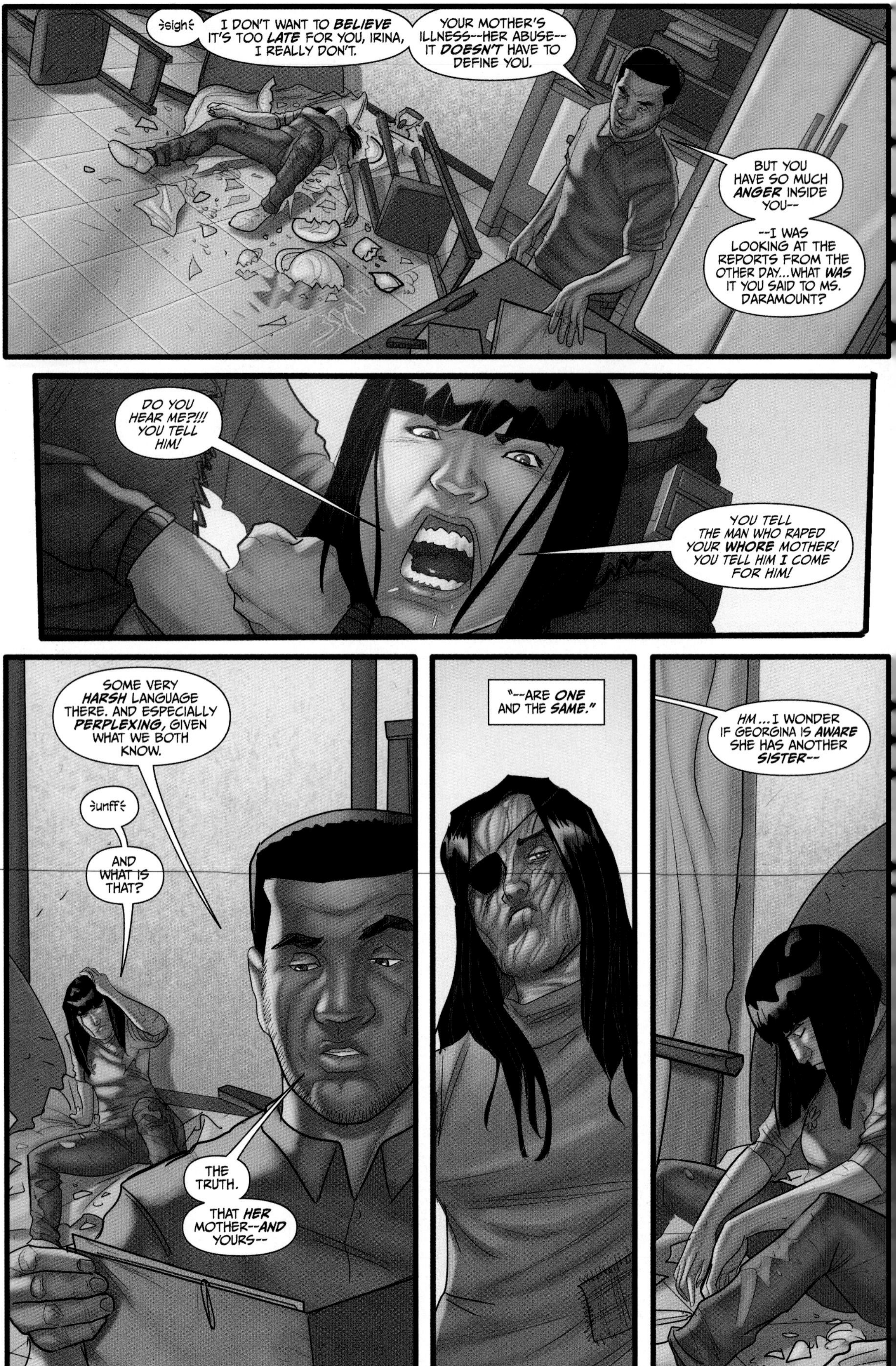

sigh
I DON'T WANT TO BELIEVE IT'S TOO LATE FOR YOU, IRINA, I REALLY DON'T.
YOUR MOTHER'S ILLNESS--HER ABUSE--IT DOESN'T HAVE TO DEFINE YOU.
BUT YOU HAVE SO MUCH ANGER INSIDE YOU--
--I WAS LOOKING AT THE REPORTS FROM THE OTHER DAY...WHAT WAS IT YOU SAID TO MS. DARAMOUNT?
DO YOU HEAR ME?!!! YOU TELL HIM!
YOU TELL THE MAN WHO RAPED YOUR WHORE MOTHER! YOU TELL HIM I COME FOR HIM!
SOME VERY HARSH LANGUAGE THERE. AND ESPECIALLY PERPLEXING, GIVEN WHAT WE BOTH KNOW.
unff
AND WHAT IS THAT?
THE TRUTH.
THAT HER MOTHER--AND YOURS--
"--ARE ONE AND THE SAME."
HM...I WONDER IF GEORGINA IS AWARE SHE HAS ANOTHER SISTER--

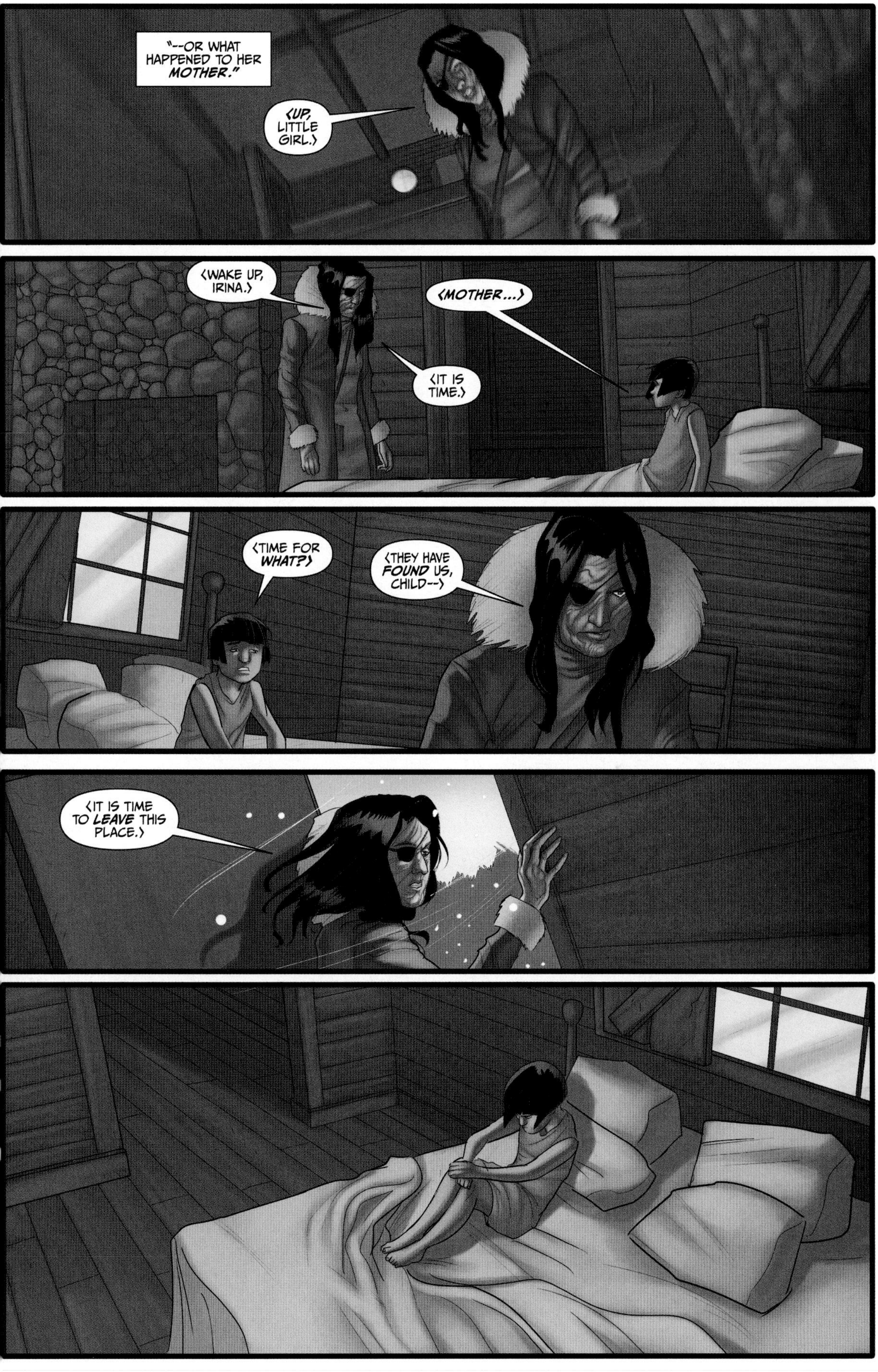
"--OR WHAT HAPPENED TO HER MOTHER."
‹UP, LITTLE GIRL.›
‹WAKE UP, IRINA.›
‹IT IS TIME.›
‹MOTHER...›
‹TIME FOR WHAT?›
‹THEY HAVE FOUND US, CHILD--›
‹IT IS TIME TO LEAVE THIS PLACE.›

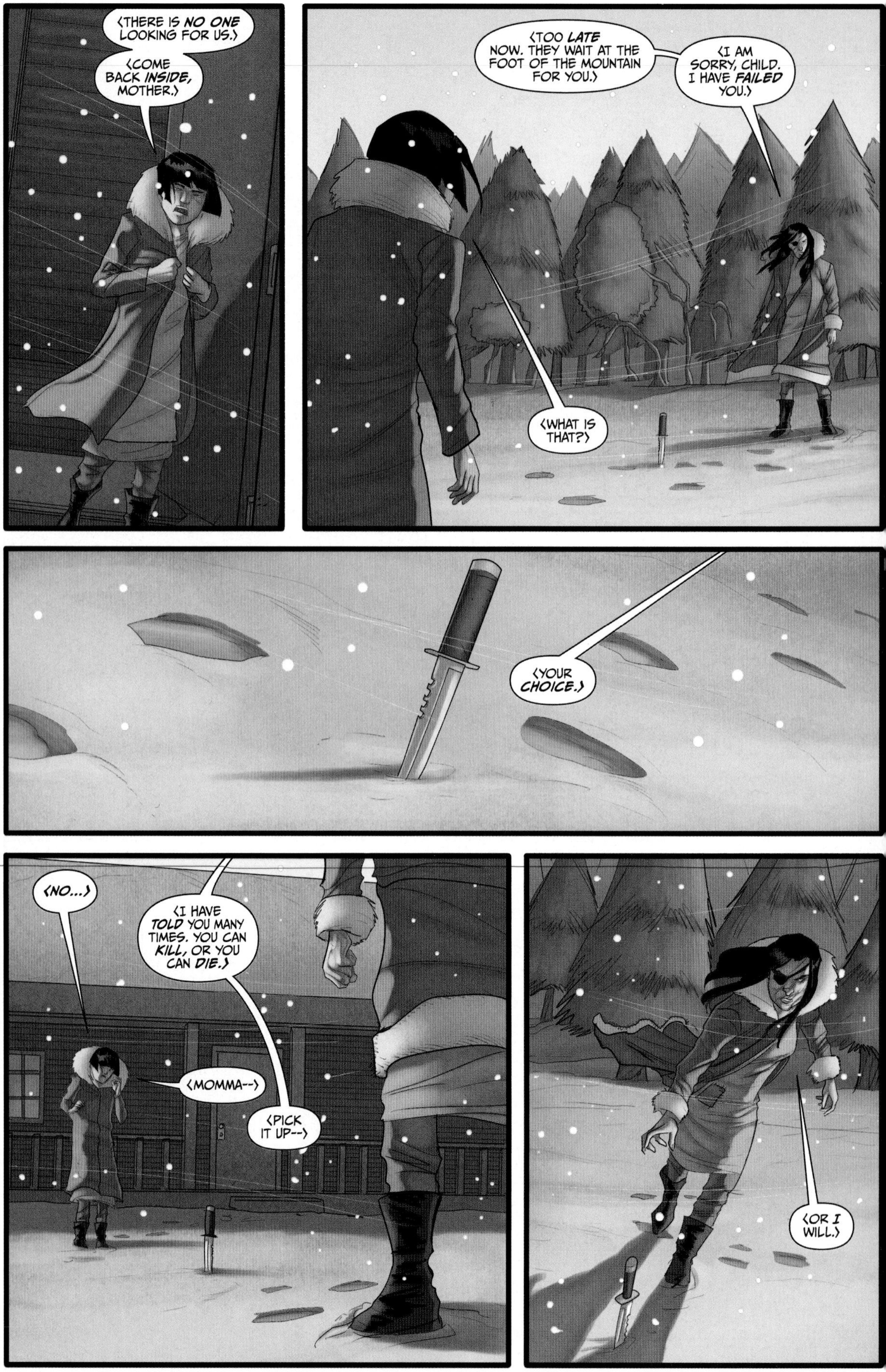

⟨THERE IS *NO ONE* LOOKING FOR US.⟩
⟨COME BACK *INSIDE,* MOTHER.⟩
⟨TOO *LATE* NOW. THEY WAIT AT THE FOOT OF THE MOUNTAIN FOR YOU.⟩
⟨I AM SORRY, CHILD. I HAVE *FAILED* YOU.⟩
⟨WHAT IS THAT?⟩
⟨YOUR *CHOICE.*⟩
⟨*NO...*⟩
⟨I HAVE *TOLD* YOU MANY TIMES. YOU CAN *KILL,* OR YOU CAN *DIE.*⟩
⟨MOMMA--⟩
⟨PICK IT UP--⟩
⟨OR *I* WILL.⟩

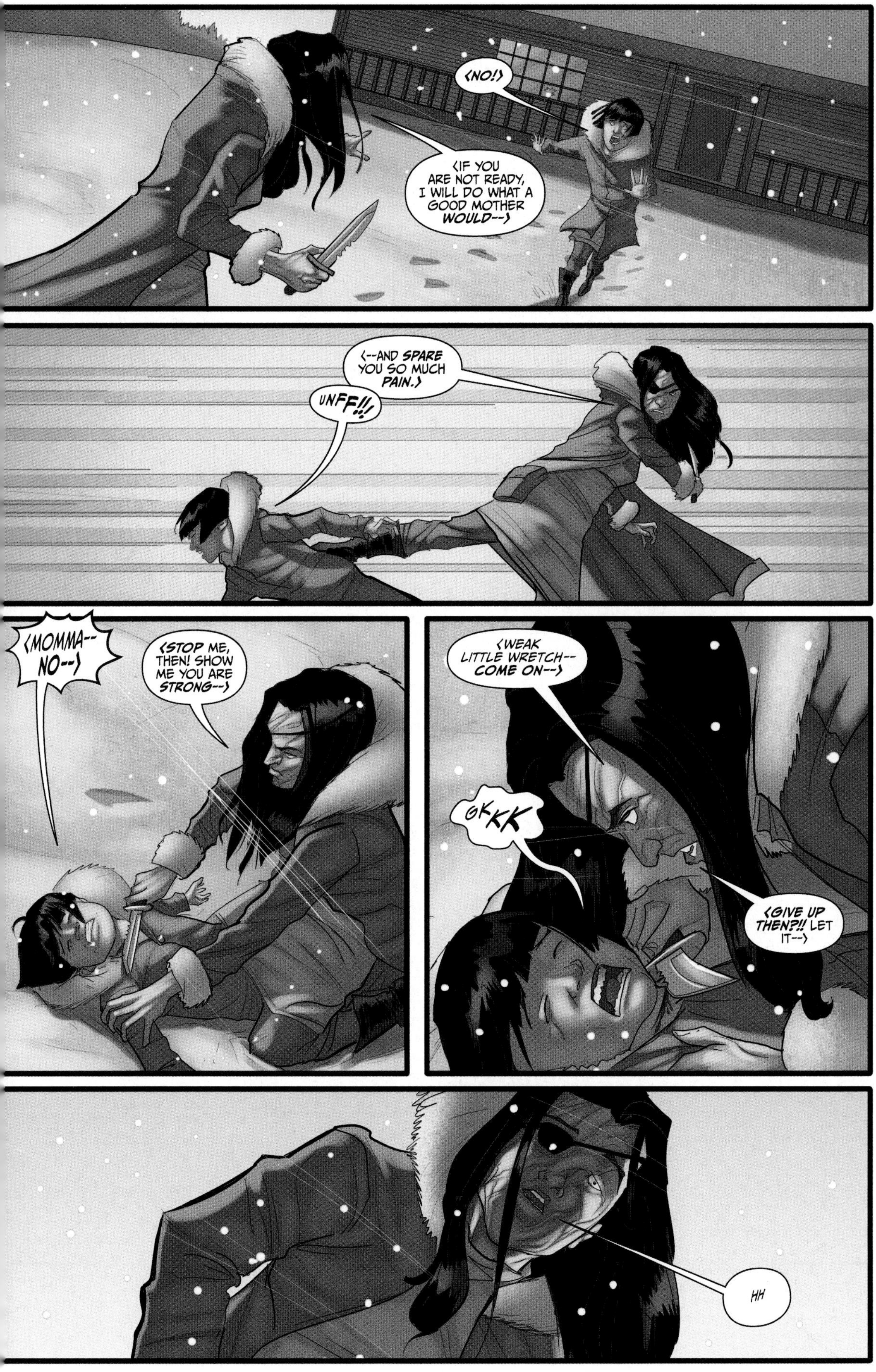

⟨NO!⟩
⟨IF YOU ARE NOT READY, I WILL DO WHAT A GOOD MOTHER WOULD--⟩
⟨--AND SPARE YOU SO MUCH PAIN.⟩
UNFF!!!
⟨MOMMA-- NO--⟩
⟨STOP ME, THEN! SHOW ME YOU ARE STRONG--⟩
⟨WEAK LITTLE WRETCH-- COME ON--⟩
GKKK
⟨GIVE UP THEN?!! LET IT--⟩
HH

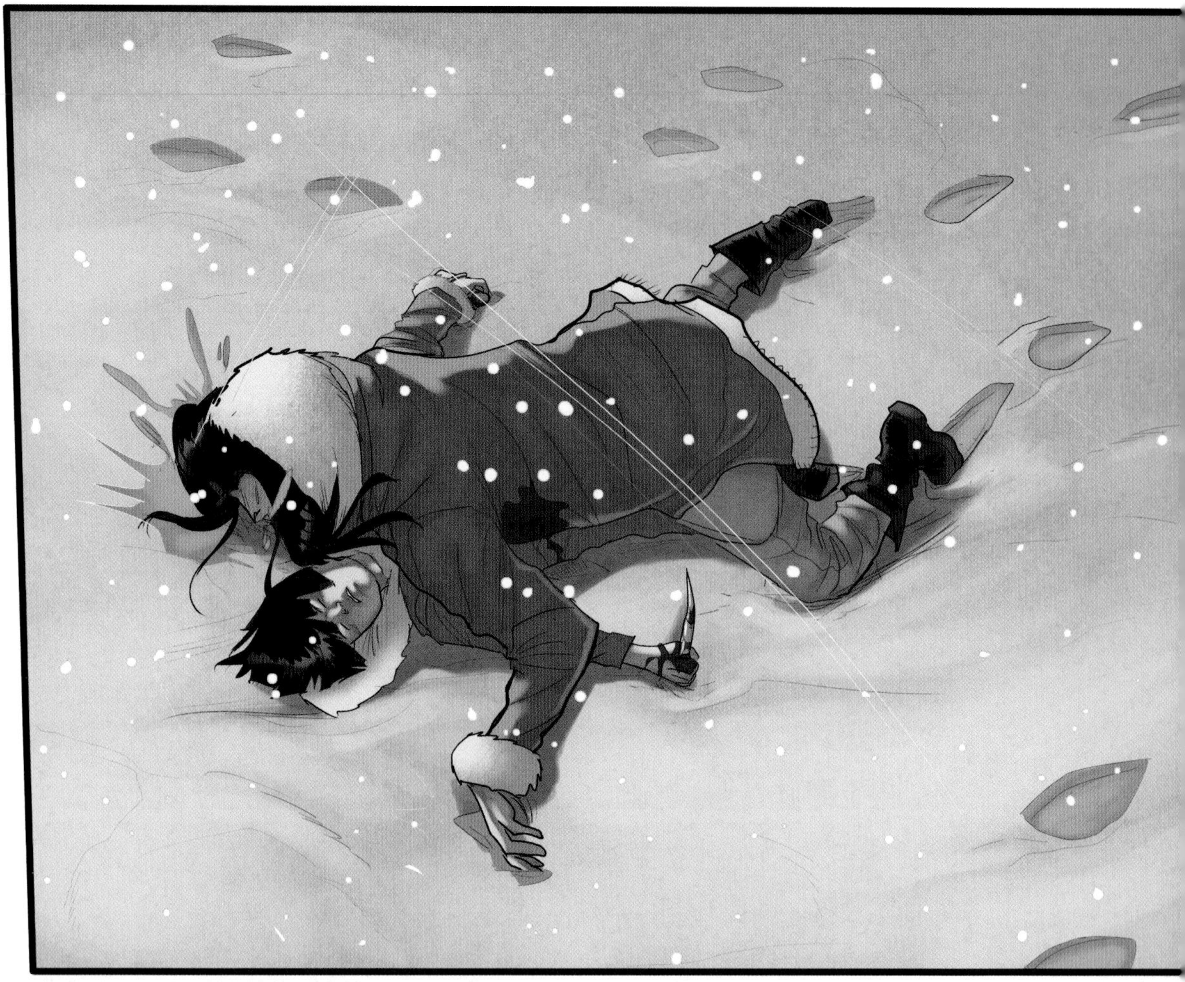

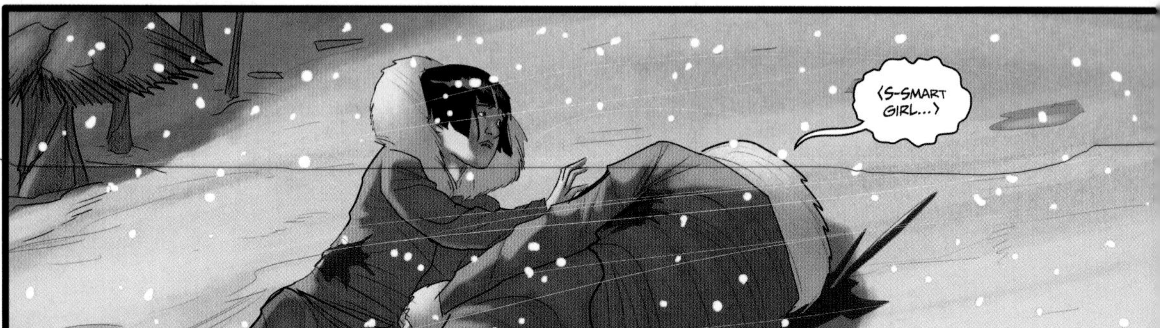
<S-SMART GIRL...>

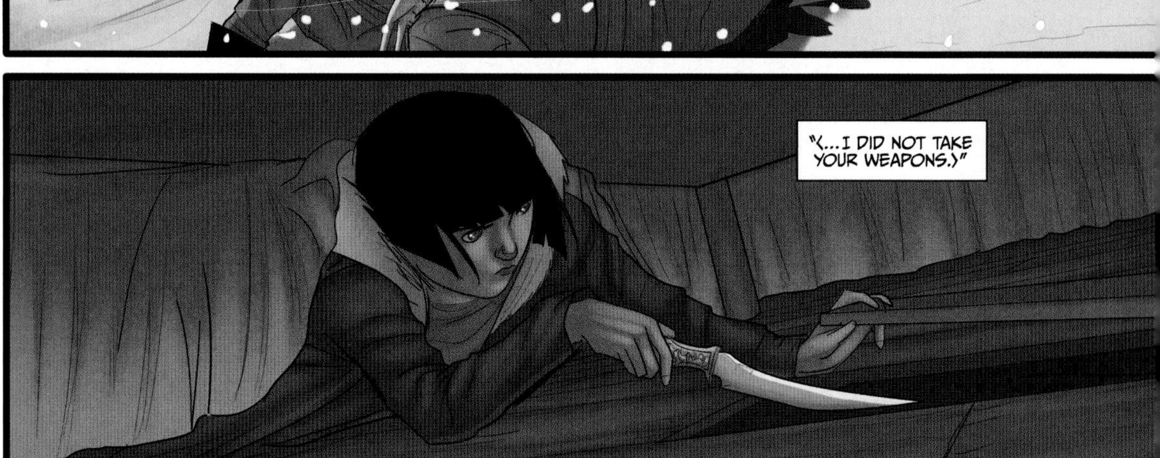
"<...I DID NOT TAKE YOUR WEAPONS.>"

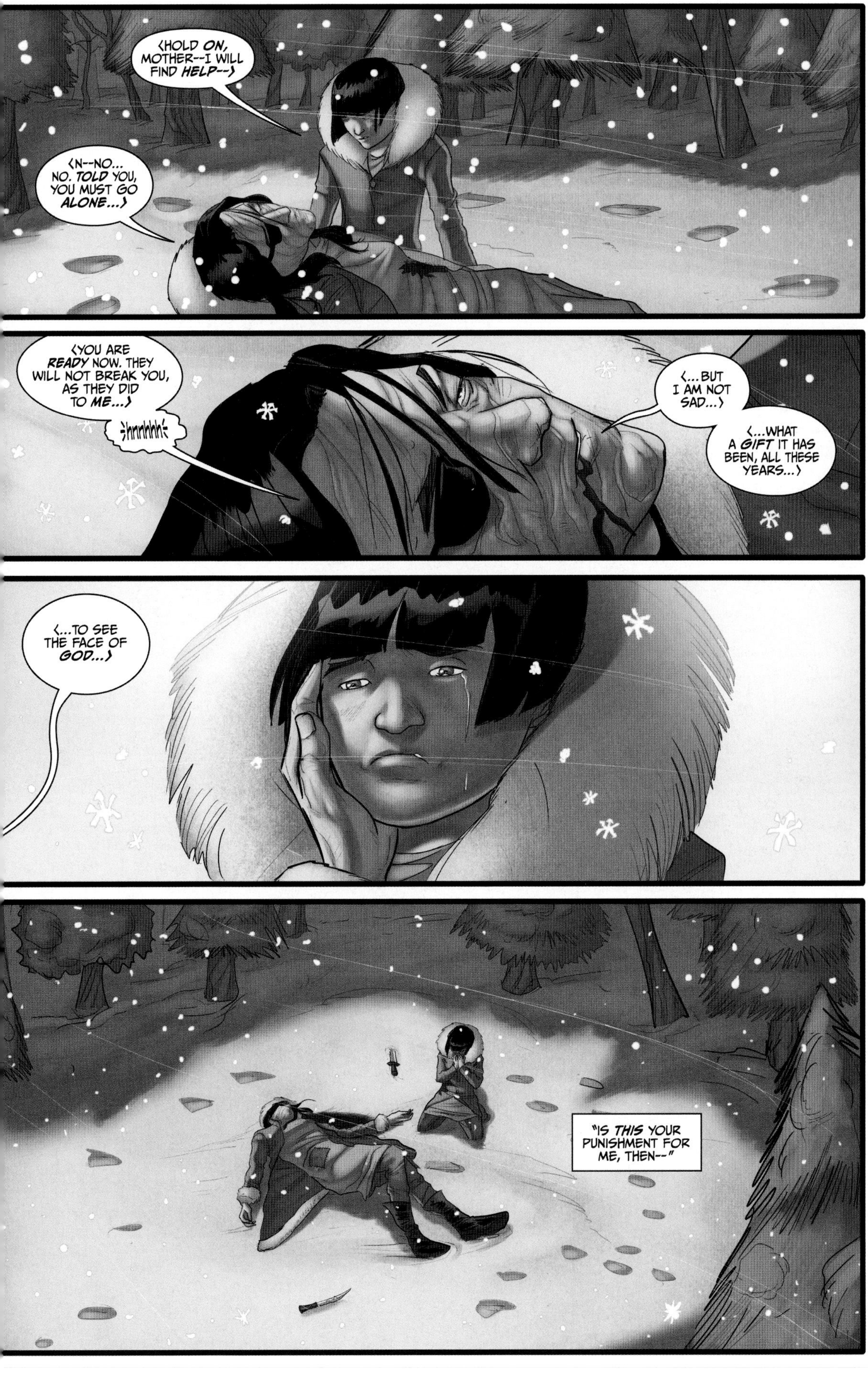
‹HOLD ON, MOTHER--I WILL FIND HELP--›
‹N--NO... NO. TOLD YOU, YOU MUST GO ALONE...›
‹YOU ARE READY NOW. THEY WILL NOT BREAK YOU, AS THEY DID TO ME...›
hhhhhh
‹...BUT I AM NOT SAD...›
‹...WHAT A GIFT IT HAS BEEN, ALL THESE YEARS...›
‹...TO SEE THE FACE OF GOD...›
"IS THIS YOUR PUNISHMENT FOR ME, THEN--"

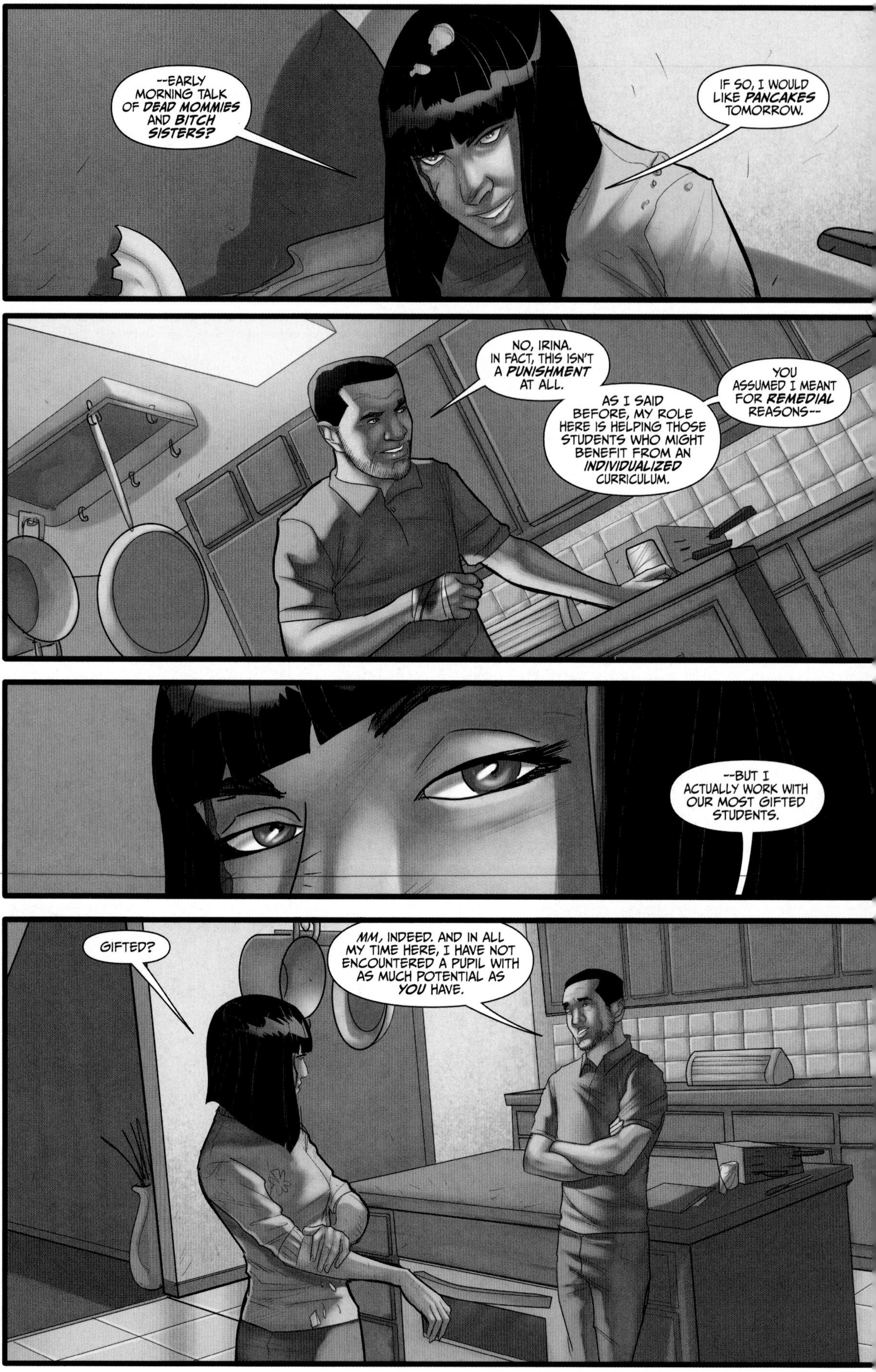
--EARLY MORNING TALK OF DEAD MOMMIES AND BITCH SISTERS?
IF SO, I WOULD LIKE PANCAKES TOMORROW.
NO, IRINA. IN FACT, THIS ISN'T A PUNISHMENT AT ALL.
AS I SAID BEFORE, MY ROLE HERE IS HELPING THOSE STUDENTS WHO MIGHT BENEFIT FROM AN INDIVIDUALIZED CURRICULUM.
YOU ASSUMED I MEANT FOR REMEDIAL REASONS--
--BUT I ACTUALLY WORK WITH OUR MOST GIFTED STUDENTS.
GIFTED?
MM, INDEED. AND IN ALL MY TIME HERE, I HAVE NOT ENCOUNTERED A PUPIL WITH AS MUCH POTENTIAL AS YOU HAVE.

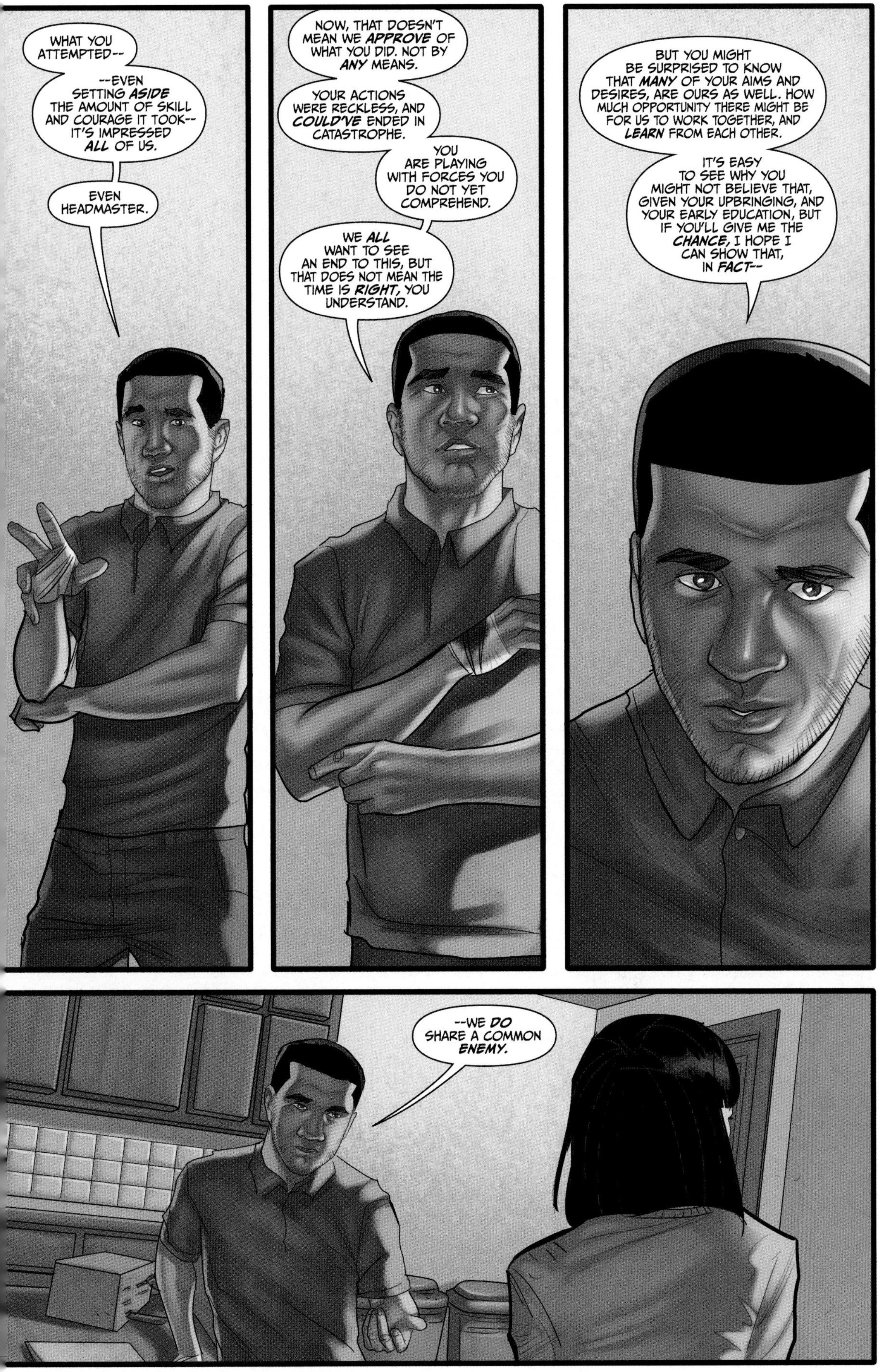
WHAT YOU ATTEMPTED--
--EVEN SETTING ASIDE THE AMOUNT OF SKILL AND COURAGE IT TOOK--IT'S IMPRESSED ALL OF US.
EVEN HEADMASTER.
NOW, THAT DOESN'T MEAN WE APPROVE OF WHAT YOU DID. NOT BY ANY MEANS.
YOUR ACTIONS WERE RECKLESS, AND COULD'VE ENDED IN CATASTROPHE.
YOU ARE PLAYING WITH FORCES YOU DO NOT YET COMPREHEND.
WE ALL WANT TO SEE AN END TO THIS, BUT THAT DOES NOT MEAN THE TIME IS RIGHT, YOU UNDERSTAND.
BUT YOU MIGHT BE SURPRISED TO KNOW THAT MANY OF YOUR AIMS AND DESIRES, ARE OURS AS WELL. HOW MUCH OPPORTUNITY THERE MIGHT BE FOR US TO WORK TOGETHER, AND LEARN FROM EACH OTHER.
IT'S EASY TO SEE WHY YOU MIGHT NOT BELIEVE THAT, GIVEN YOUR UPBRINGING, AND YOUR EARLY EDUCATION, BUT IF YOU'LL GIVE ME THE CHANCE, I HOPE I CAN SHOW THAT, IN FACT--
--WE DO SHARE A COMMON ENEMY.

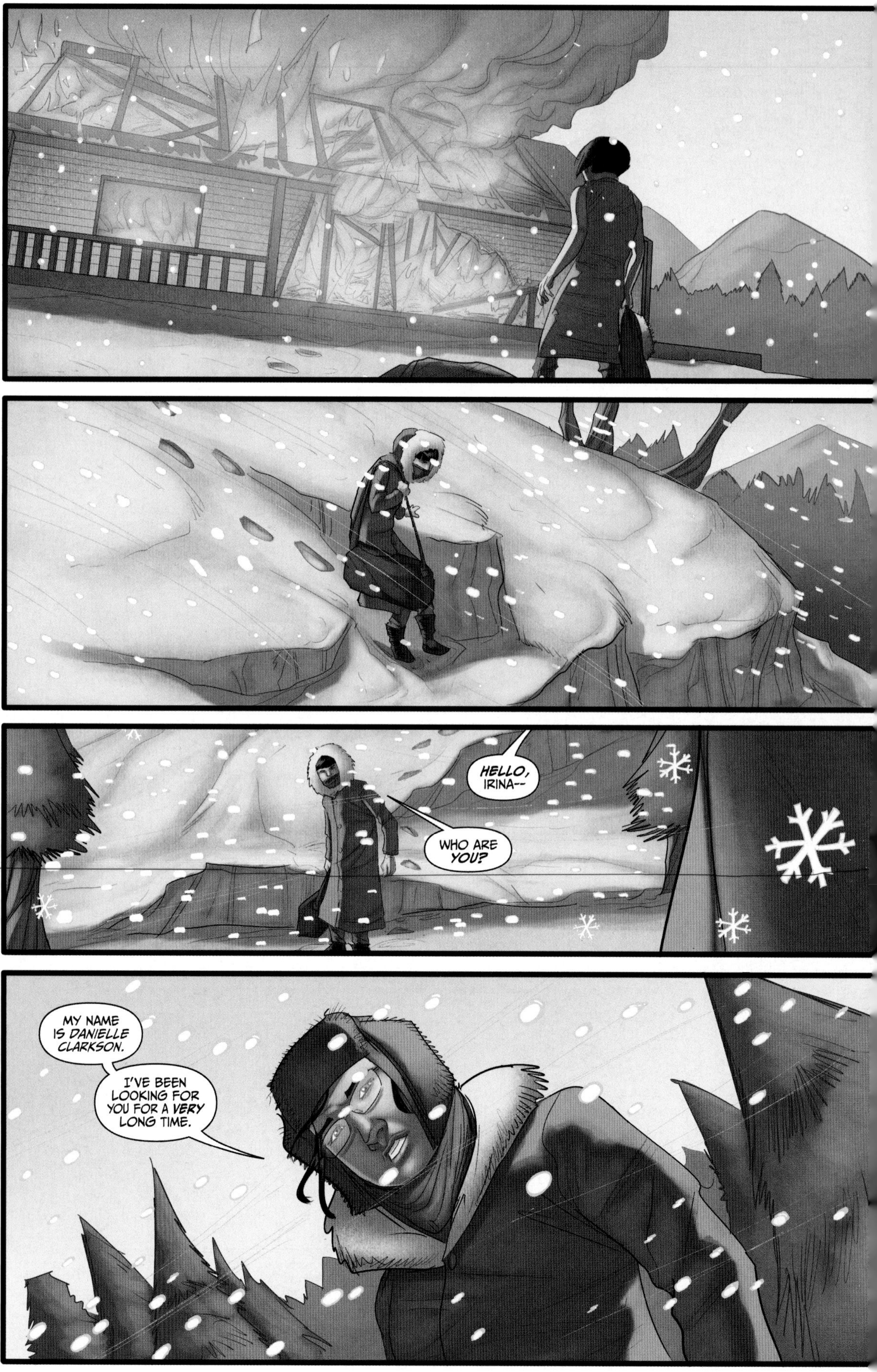
HELLO, IRINA--
WHO ARE YOU?
MY NAME IS DANIELLE CLARKSON.
I'VE BEEN LOOKING FOR YOU FOR A VERY LONG TIME.

thirty**one**

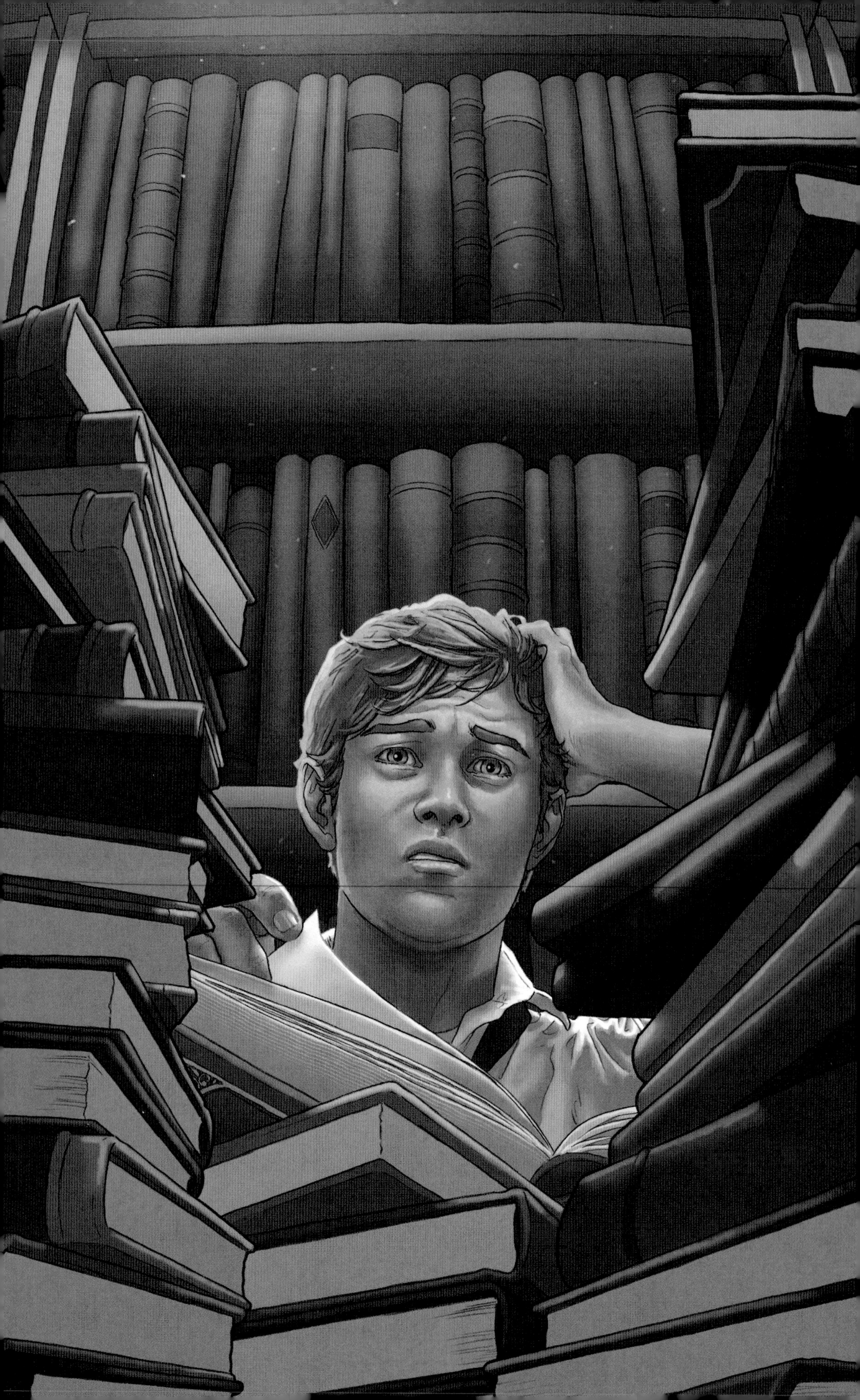

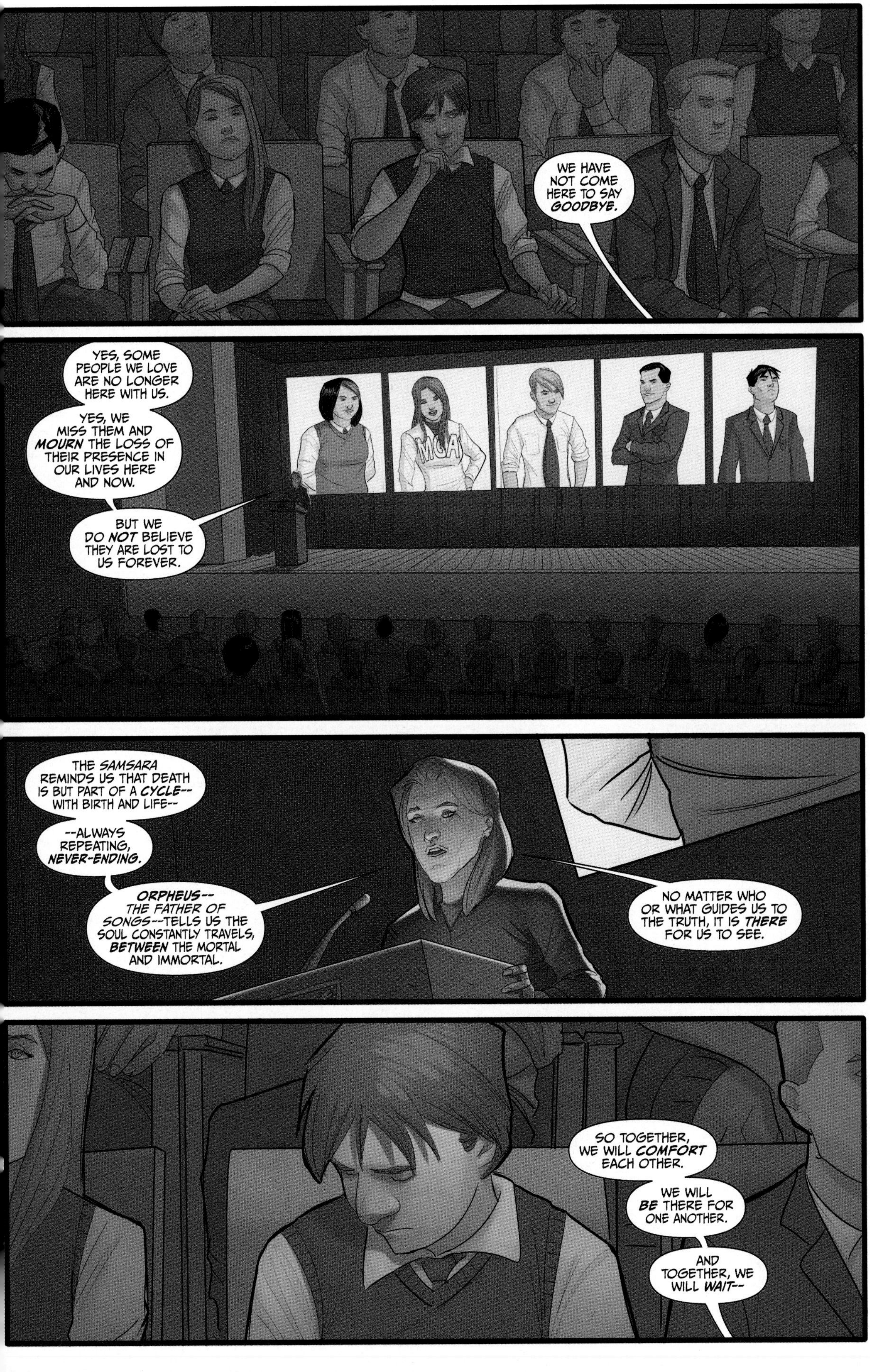
WE HAVE NOT COME HERE TO SAY GOODBYE.
YES, SOME PEOPLE WE LOVE ARE NO LONGER HERE WITH US.
YES, WE MISS THEM AND MOURN THE LOSS OF THEIR PRESENCE IN OUR LIVES HERE AND NOW.
BUT WE DO NOT BELIEVE THEY ARE LOST TO US FOREVER.
MGA
THE SAMSARA REMINDS US THAT DEATH IS BUT PART OF A CYCLE-- WITH BIRTH AND LIFE--
--ALWAYS REPEATING, NEVER-ENDING.
ORPHEUS-- THE FATHER OF SONGS--TELLS US THE SOUL CONSTANTLY TRAVELS, BETWEEN THE MORTAL AND IMMORTAL.
NO MATTER WHO OR WHAT GUIDES US TO THE TRUTH, IT IS THERE FOR US TO SEE.
SO TOGETHER, WE WILL COMFORT EACH OTHER.
WE WILL BE THERE FOR ONE ANOTHER.
AND TOGETHER, WE WILL WAIT--

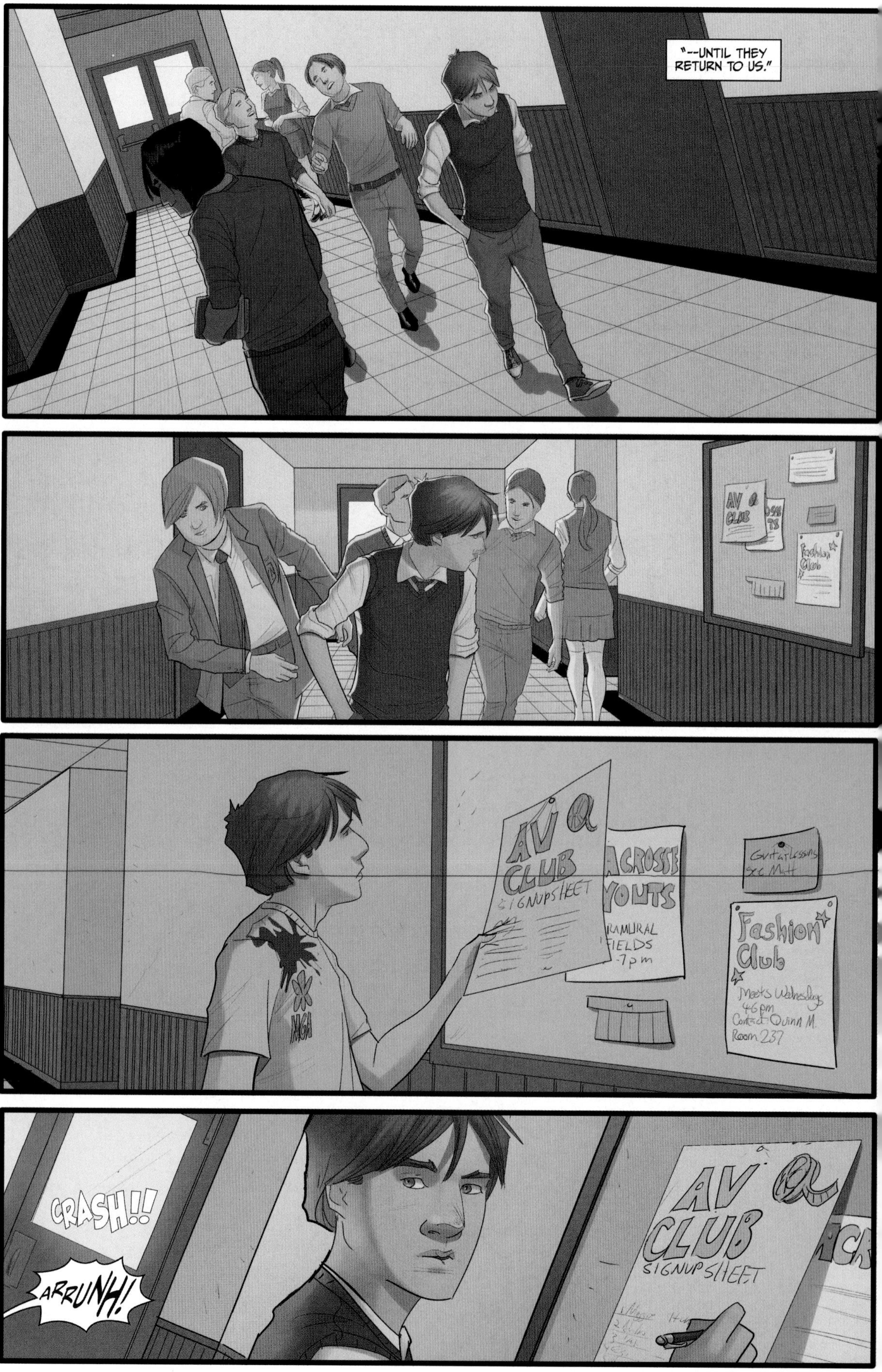
"--UNTIL THEY RETURN TO US."
AV CLUB
SIGNUPSHEET
Fashion Club
Meets Wednesdays
4-6pm
Contact: Quinn M.
Room 237
CRASH!!
ARRUNH!

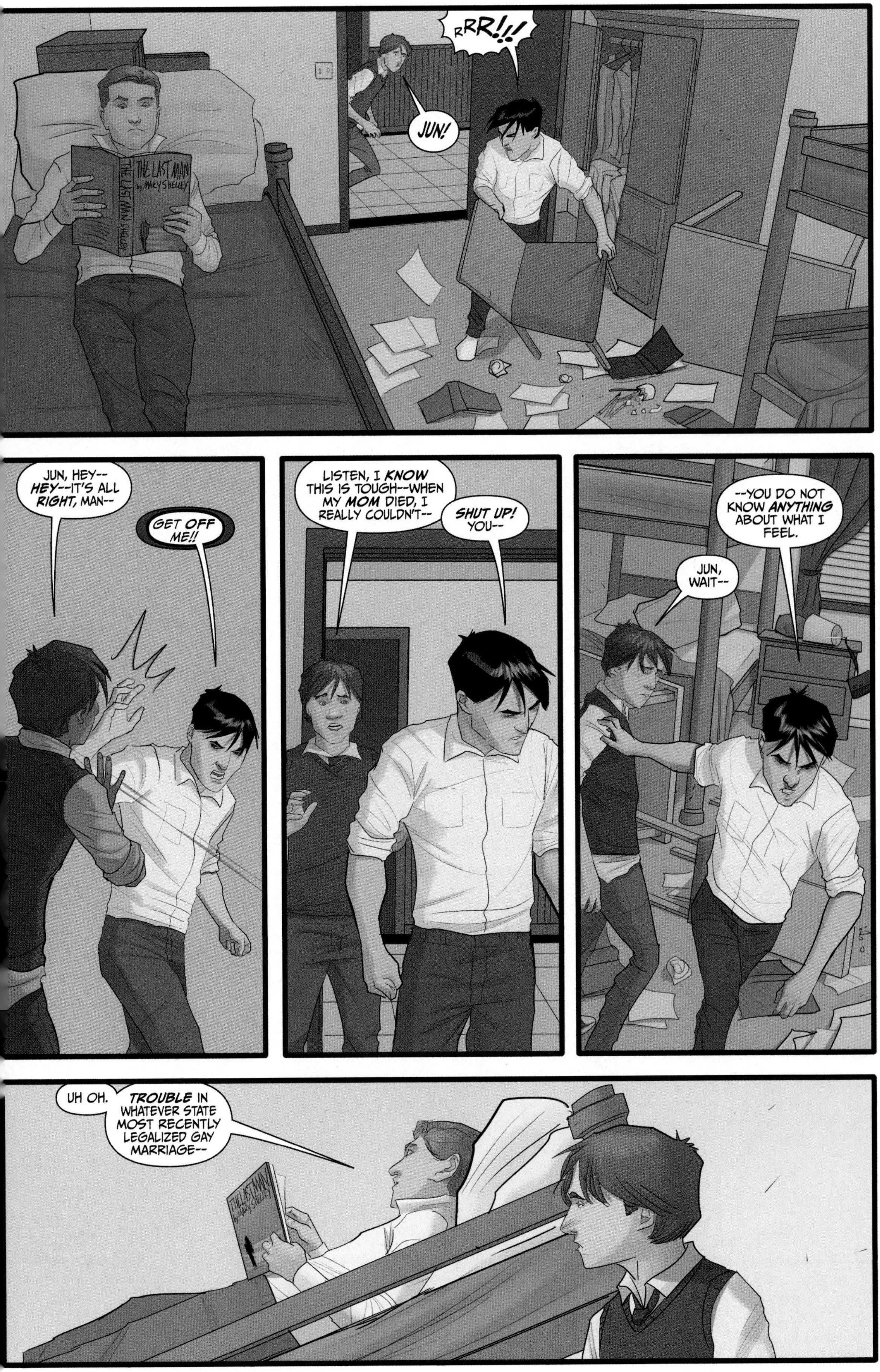

RRR!!!
JUN!
JUN, HEY--
HEY--IT'S ALL RIGHT, MAN--
GET OFF ME!!
LISTEN, I KNOW THIS IS TOUGH--WHEN MY MOM DIED, I REALLY COULDN'T--
SHUT UP! YOU--
--YOU DO NOT KNOW ANYTHING ABOUT WHAT I FEEL.
JUN, WAIT--
UH OH.
TROUBLE IN WHATEVER STATE MOST RECENTLY LEGALIZED GAY MARRIAGE--
THE LAST MAN
by MARY SHELLEY

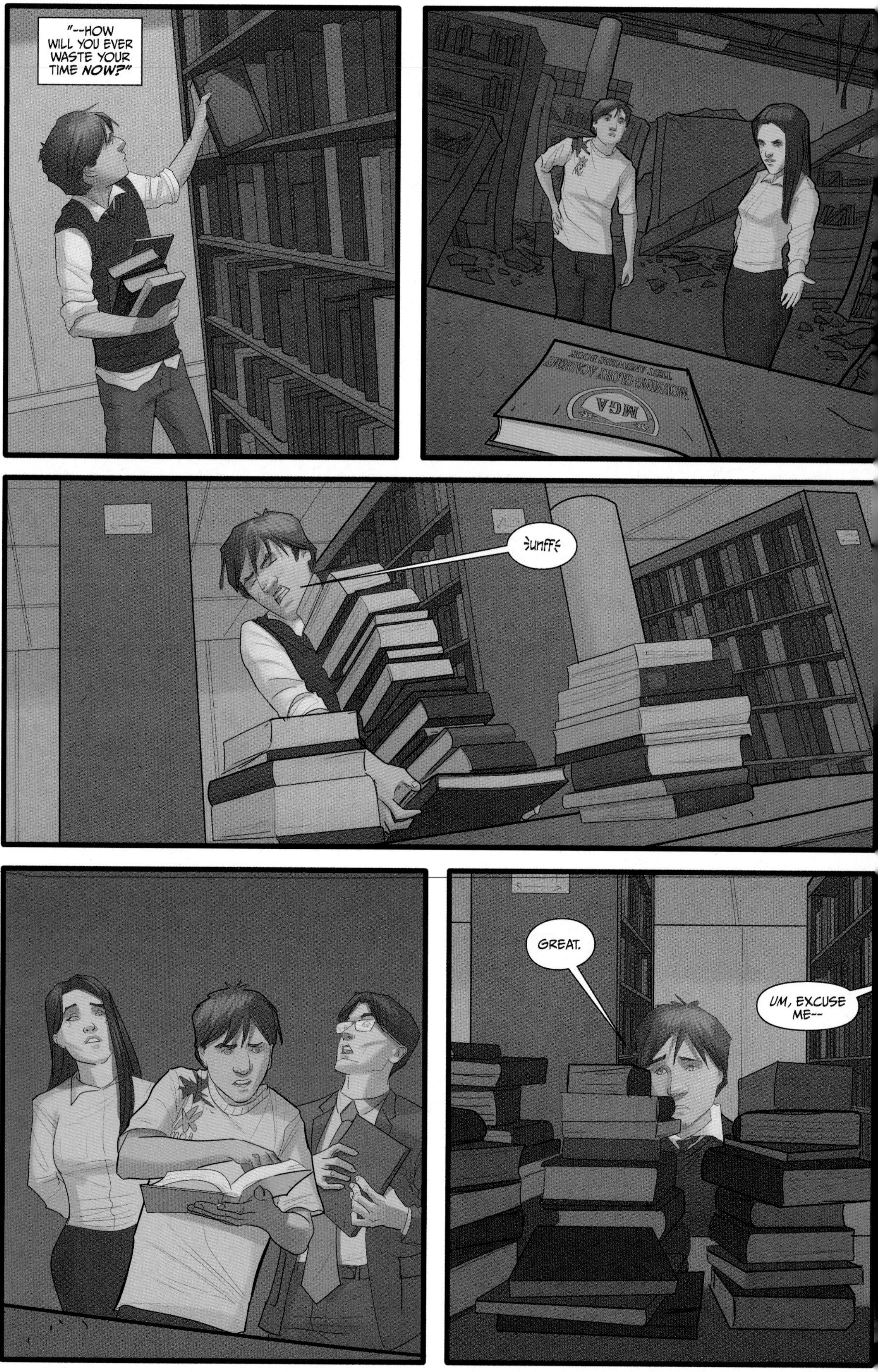
"--HOW WILL YOU EVER WASTE YOUR TIME *NOW?*"
MGA
MORNING GLORY ACADEMY
TEST ANSWERS BOOK
UNFF
GREAT.
UM, EXCUSE ME--

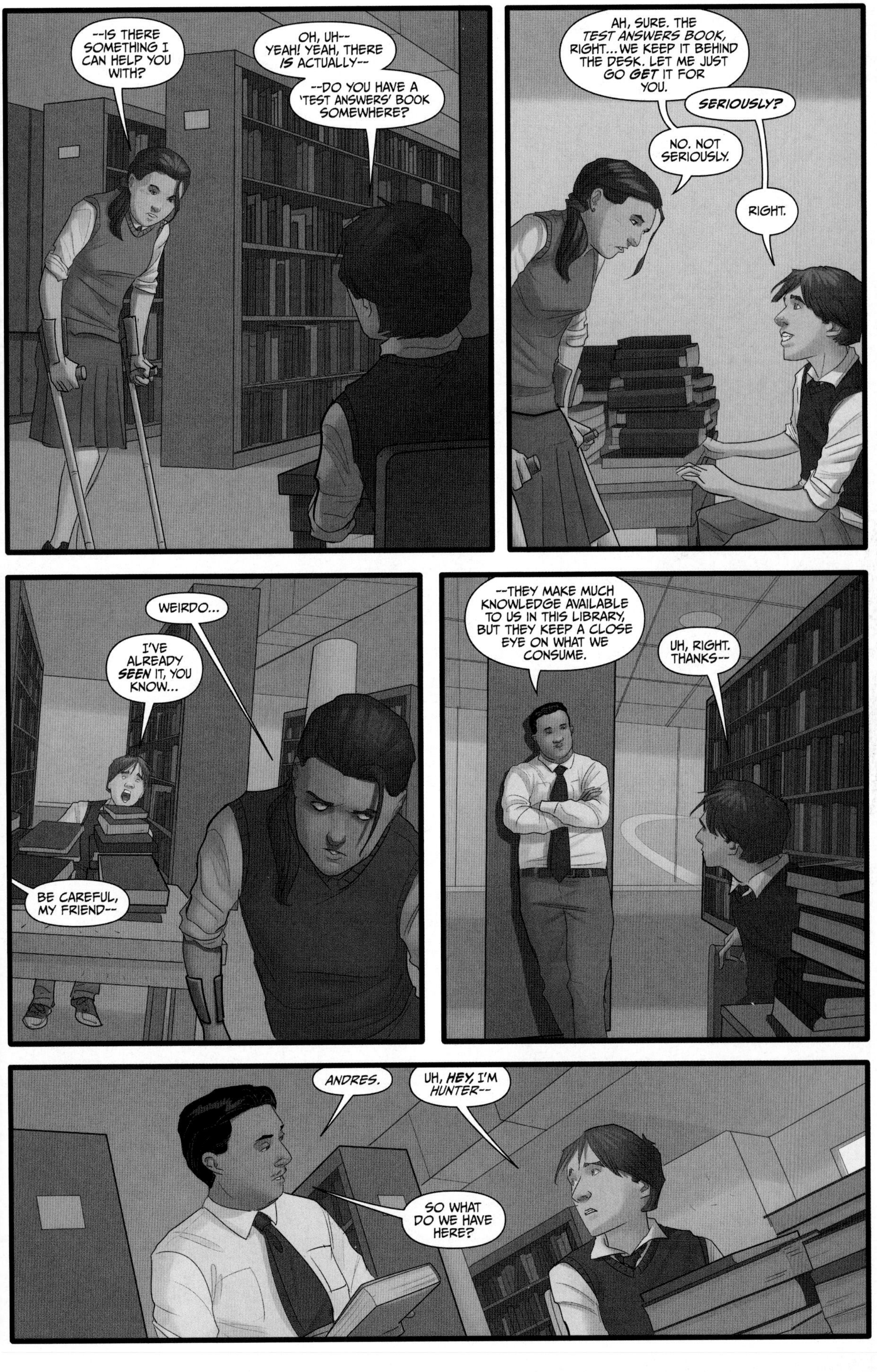
--IS THERE SOMETHING I CAN HELP YOU WITH?
OH, UH-- YEAH! YEAH, THERE IS ACTUALLY--
--DO YOU HAVE A 'TEST ANSWERS' BOOK SOMEWHERE?
AH, SURE. THE TEST ANSWERS BOOK, RIGHT... WE KEEP IT BEHIND THE DESK. LET ME JUST GO GET IT FOR YOU.
SERIOUSLY?
NO. NOT SERIOUSLY.
RIGHT.
WEIRDO...
I'VE ALREADY SEEN IT, YOU KNOW...
BE CAREFUL, MY FRIEND--
--THEY MAKE MUCH KNOWLEDGE AVAILABLE TO US IN THIS LIBRARY, BUT THEY KEEP A CLOSE EYE ON WHAT WE CONSUME.
UH, RIGHT. THANKS--
ANDRES.
UH, HEY, I'M HUNTER--
SO WHAT DO WE HAVE HERE?

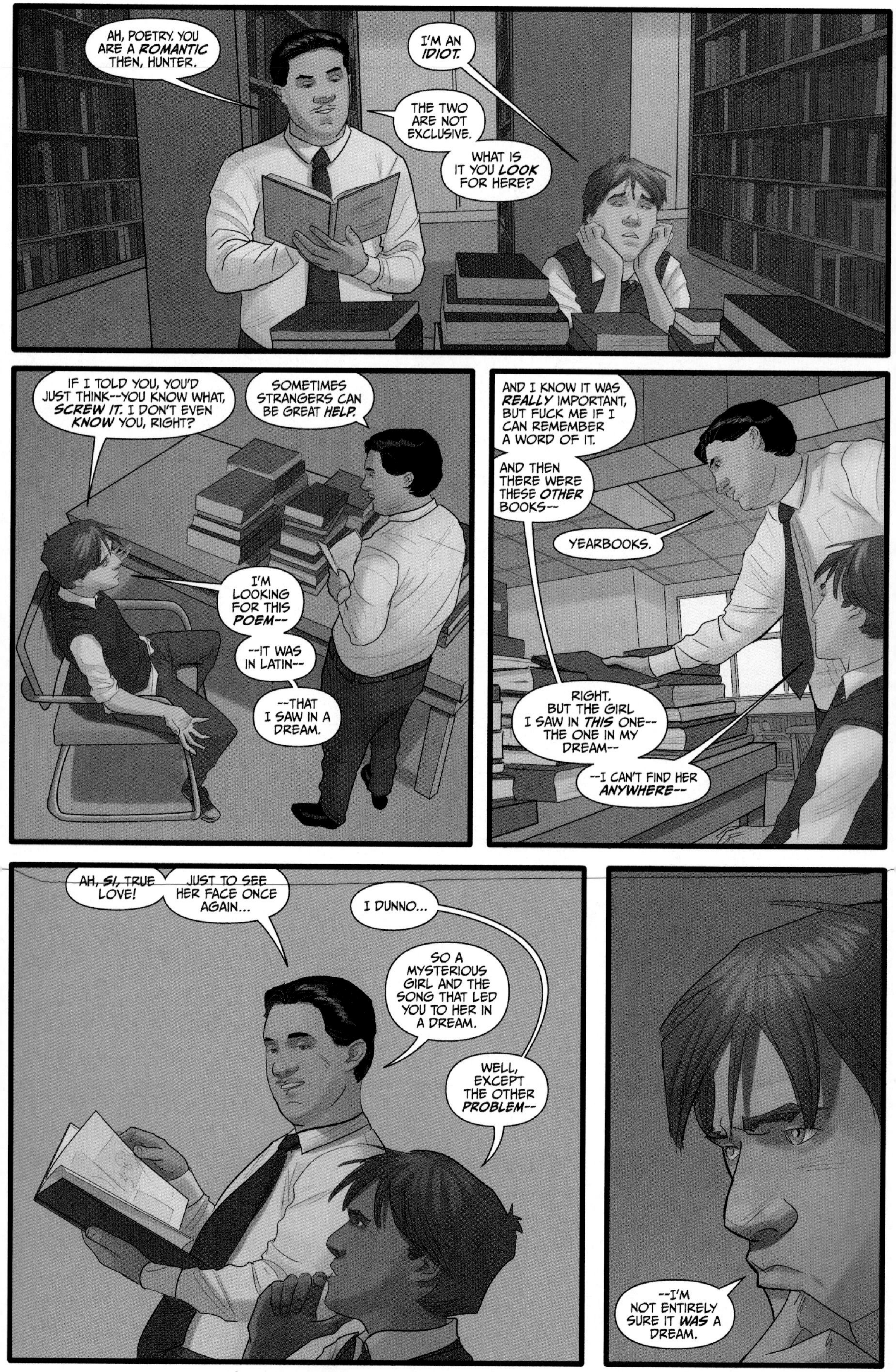

AH, POETRY. YOU ARE A *ROMANTIC* THEN, HUNTER.
I'M AN *IDIOT.*
THE TWO ARE NOT EXCLUSIVE.
WHAT IS IT YOU *LOOK* FOR HERE?
IF I TOLD YOU, YOU'D JUST THINK--YOU KNOW WHAT, *SCREW IT.* I DON'T EVEN *KNOW* YOU, RIGHT?
SOMETIMES STRANGERS CAN BE GREAT *HELP.*
I'M LOOKING FOR THIS *POEM--*
--IT WAS IN LATIN--
--THAT I SAW IN A DREAM.
AND I KNOW IT WAS *REALLY* IMPORTANT, BUT FUCK ME IF I CAN REMEMBER A WORD OF IT.
AND THEN THERE WERE THESE *OTHER* BOOKS--
YEARBOOKS.
RIGHT. BUT THE GIRL I SAW IN *THIS* ONE-- THE ONE IN MY DREAM--
--I CAN'T FIND HER *ANYWHERE--*
AH, *SI,* TRUE LOVE!
JUST TO SEE HER FACE ONCE AGAIN...
I DUNNO...
SO A MYSTERIOUS GIRL AND THE SONG THAT LED YOU TO HER IN A DREAM.
WELL, EXCEPT THE OTHER *PROBLEM--*
--I'M NOT ENTIRELY SURE IT *WAS* A DREAM.

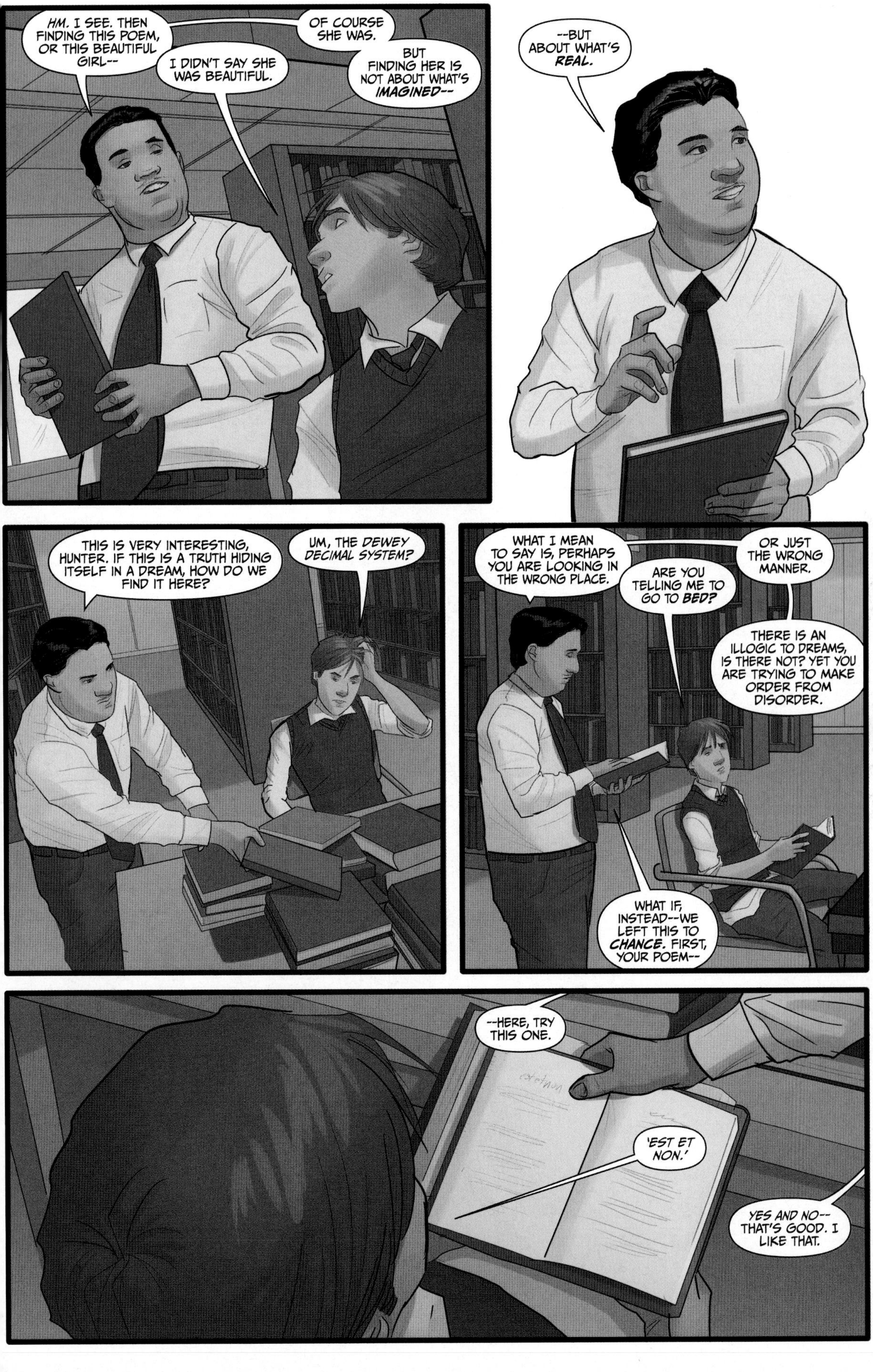

HM. I SEE. THEN FINDING THIS POEM, OR THIS BEAUTIFUL GIRL--
I DIDN'T SAY SHE WAS BEAUTIFUL.
OF COURSE SHE WAS.
BUT FINDING HER IS NOT ABOUT WHAT'S *IMAGINED--*
--BUT ABOUT WHAT'S **REAL.**
THIS IS VERY INTERESTING, HUNTER. IF THIS IS A TRUTH HIDING ITSELF IN A DREAM, HOW DO WE FIND IT HERE?
UM, THE *DEWEY DECIMAL SYSTEM?*
WHAT I MEAN TO SAY IS, PERHAPS YOU ARE LOOKING IN THE WRONG PLACE.
ARE YOU TELLING ME TO GO TO *BED?*
OR JUST THE WRONG MANNER.
THERE IS AN ILLOGIC TO DREAMS, IS THERE NOT? YET YOU ARE TRYING TO MAKE ORDER FROM DISORDER.
WHAT IF, INSTEAD--WE LEFT THIS TO ***CHANCE.*** FIRST, YOUR POEM--
--HERE, TRY THIS ONE.
'EST ET NON.'
YES AND NO-- THAT'S GOOD. I LIKE THAT.

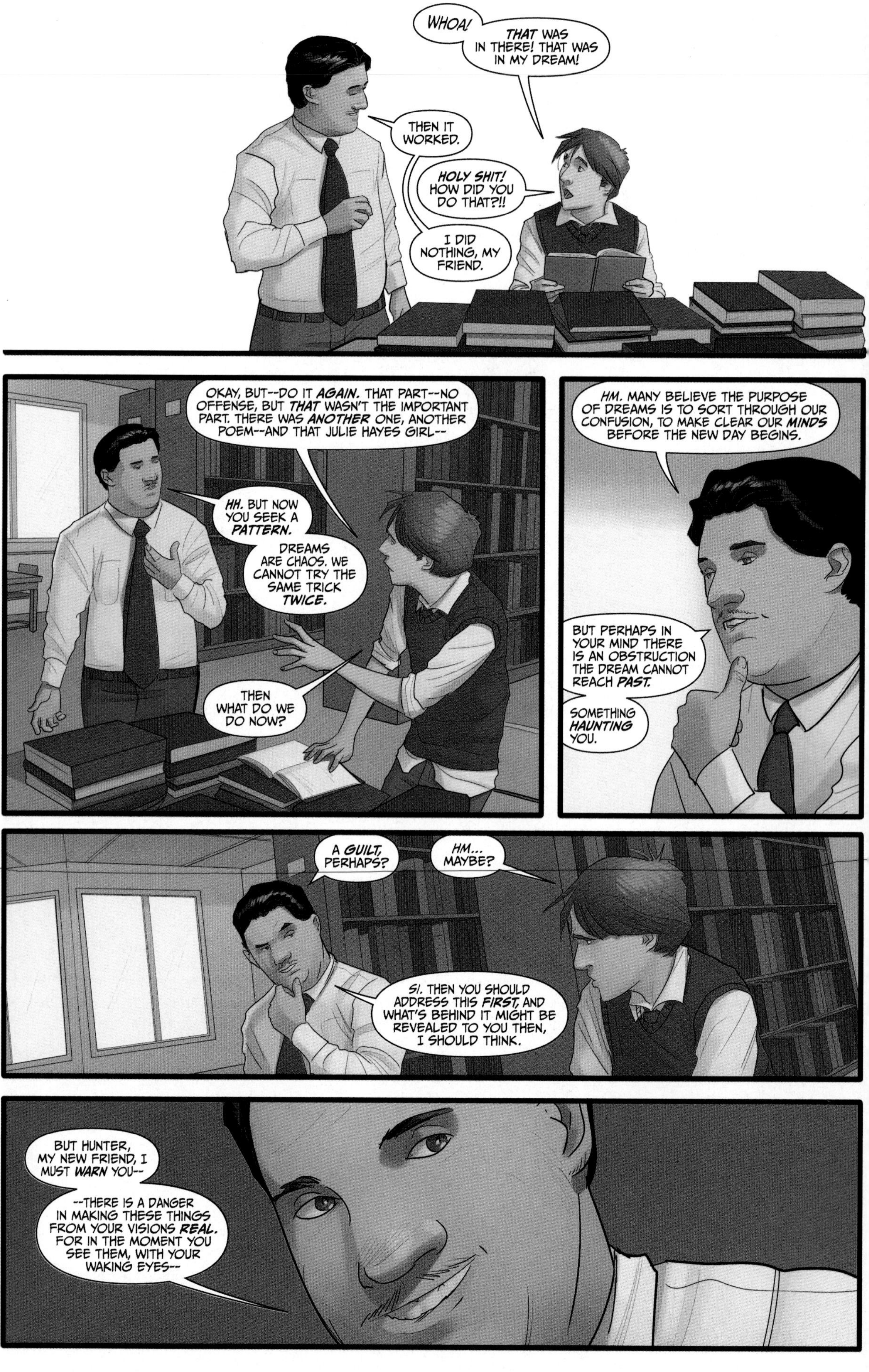
WHOA!
THAT WAS IN THERE! THAT WAS IN MY DREAM!
THEN IT WORKED.
HOLY SHIT! HOW DID YOU DO THAT?!!
I DID NOTHING, MY FRIEND.
OKAY, BUT--DO IT AGAIN. THAT PART--NO OFFENSE, BUT THAT WASN'T THE IMPORTANT PART. THERE WAS ANOTHER ONE, ANOTHER POEM--AND THAT JULIE HAYES GIRL--
HH. BUT NOW YOU SEEK A PATTERN.
DREAMS ARE CHAOS. WE CANNOT TRY THE SAME TRICK TWICE.
THEN WHAT DO WE DO NOW?
HM. MANY BELIEVE THE PURPOSE OF DREAMS IS TO SORT THROUGH OUR CONFUSION, TO MAKE CLEAR OUR MINDS BEFORE THE NEW DAY BEGINS.
BUT PERHAPS IN YOUR MIND THERE IS AN OBSTRUCTION THE DREAM CANNOT REACH PAST.
SOMETHING HAUNTING YOU.
A GUILT, PERHAPS?
HM... MAYBE?
SI. THEN YOU SHOULD ADDRESS THIS FIRST, AND WHAT'S BEHIND IT MIGHT BE REVEALED TO YOU THEN, I SHOULD THINK.
BUT HUNTER, MY NEW FRIEND, I MUST WARN YOU--
--THERE IS A DANGER IN MAKING THESE THINGS FROM YOUR VISIONS REAL. FOR IN THE MOMENT YOU SEE THEM, WITH YOUR WAKING EYES--

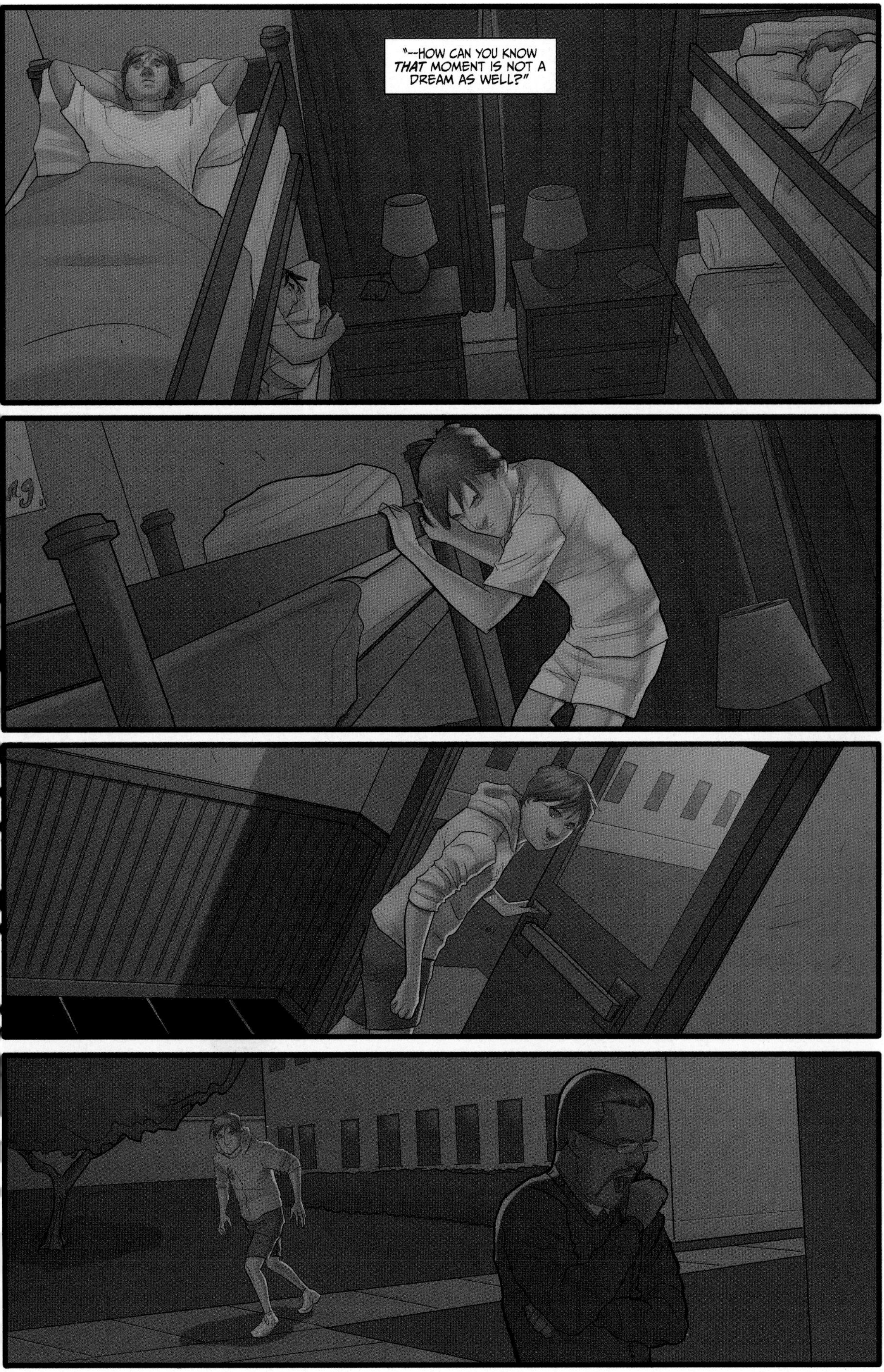
"--HOW CAN YOU KNOW *THAT* MOMENT IS NOT A DREAM AS WELL?"

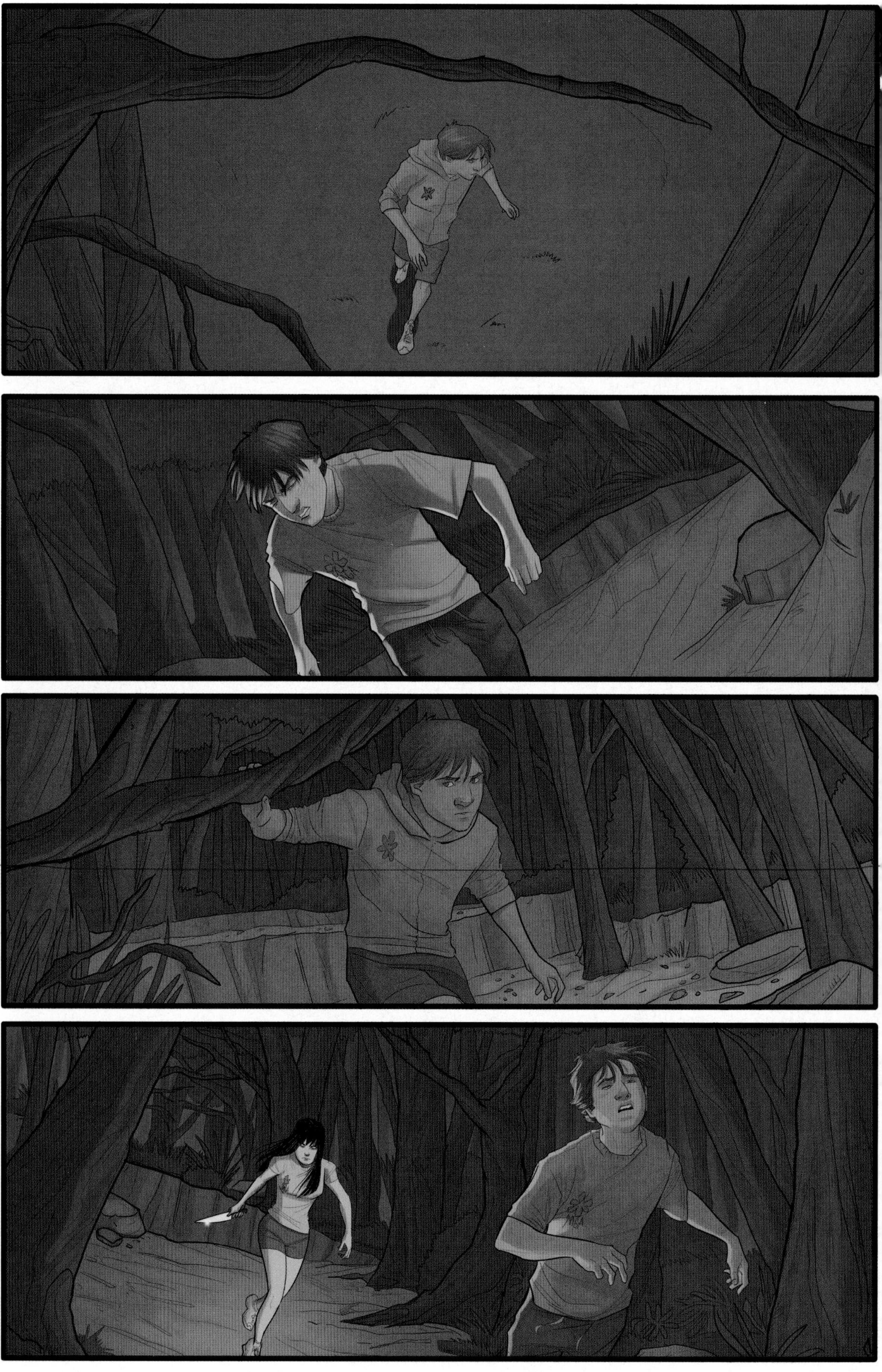

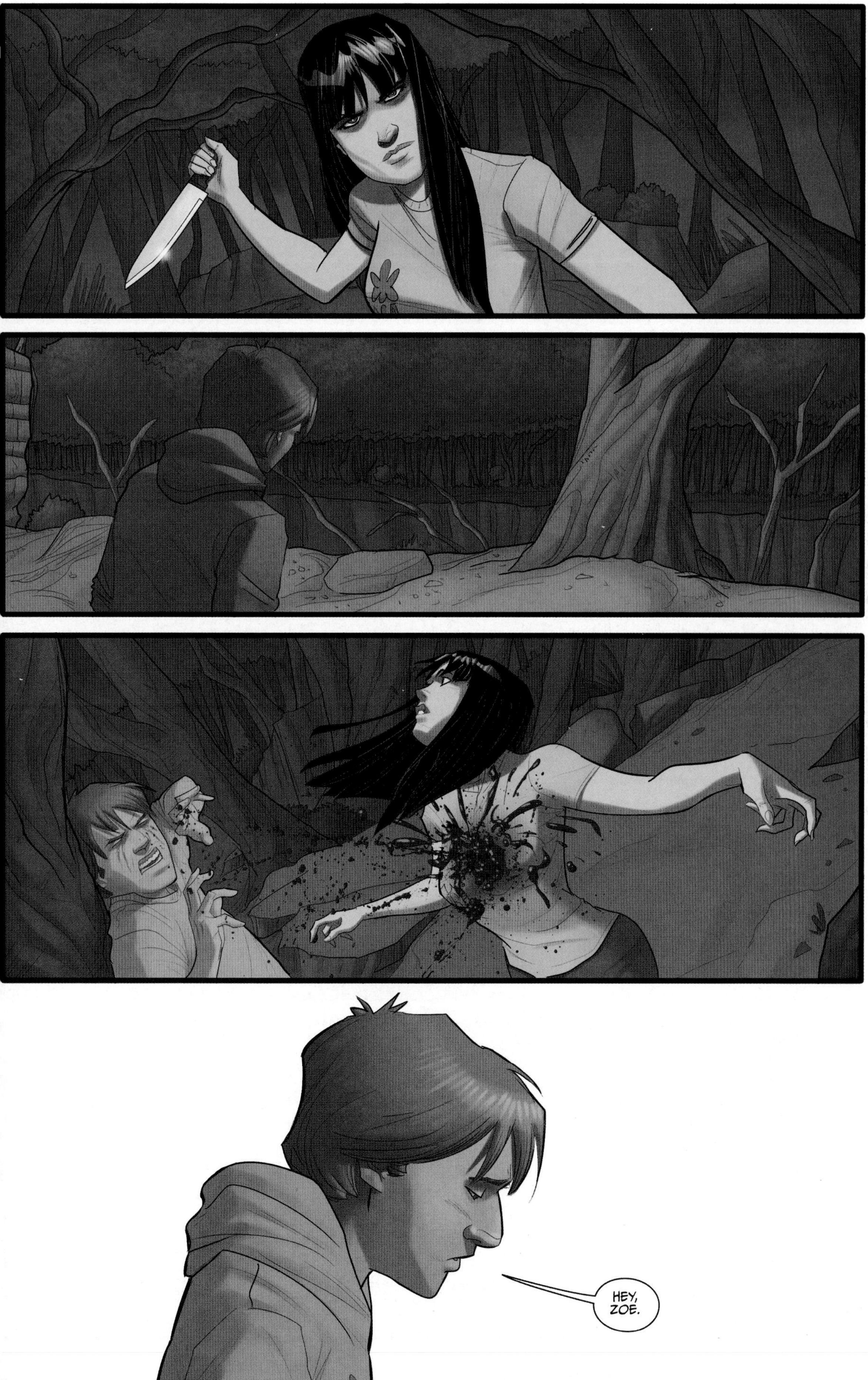
HEY, ZOE.

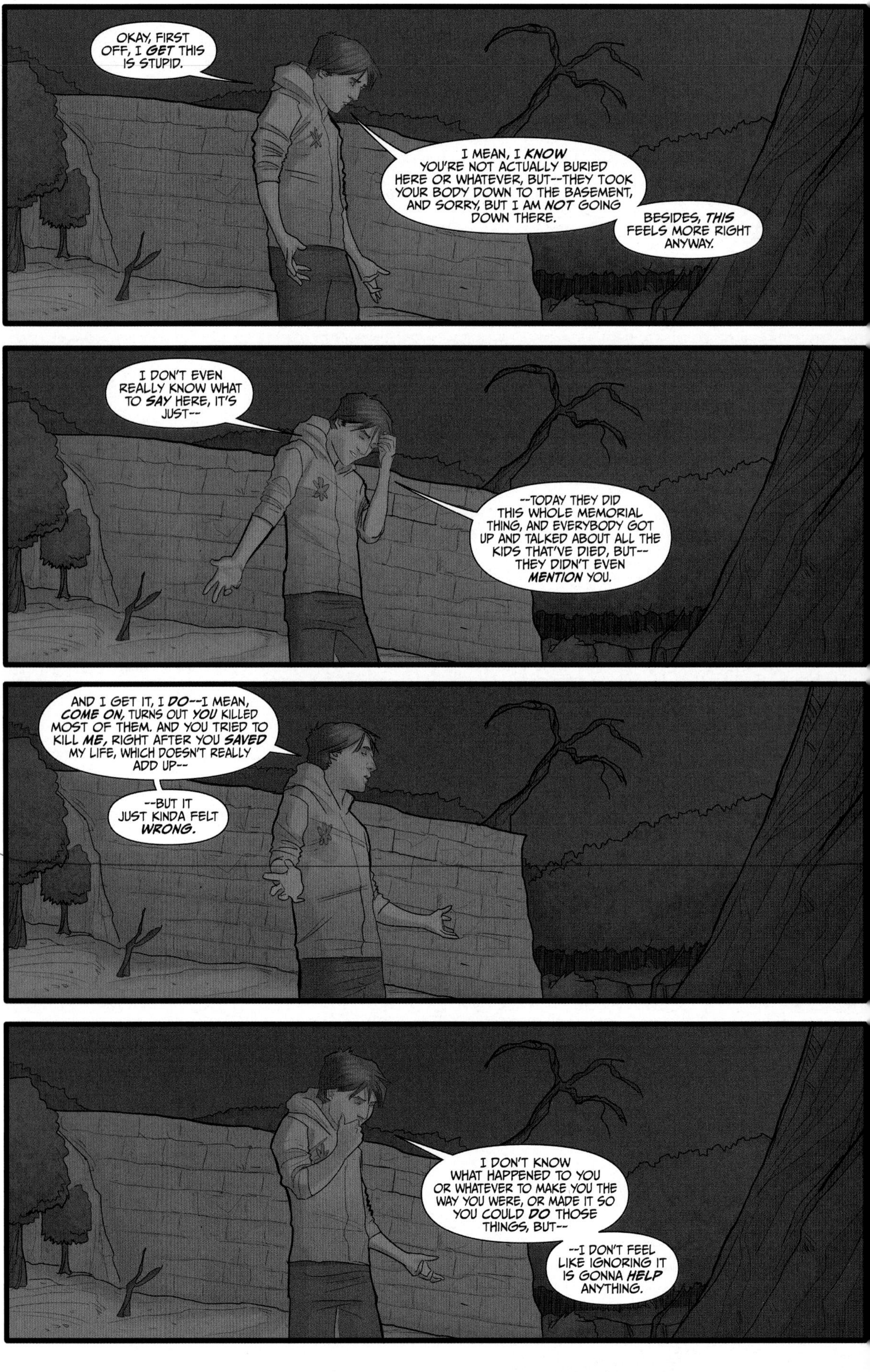
OKAY, FIRST OFF, I GET THIS IS STUPID.
I MEAN, I KNOW YOU'RE NOT ACTUALLY BURIED HERE OR WHATEVER, BUT--THEY TOOK YOUR BODY DOWN TO THE BASEMENT, AND SORRY, BUT I AM NOT GOING DOWN THERE.
BESIDES, THIS FEELS MORE RIGHT ANYWAY.
I DON'T EVEN REALLY KNOW WHAT TO SAY HERE, IT'S JUST--
--TODAY THEY DID THIS WHOLE MEMORIAL THING, AND EVERYBODY GOT UP AND TALKED ABOUT ALL THE KIDS THAT'VE DIED, BUT-- THEY DIDN'T EVEN MENTION YOU.
AND I GET IT, I DO--I MEAN, COME ON, TURNS OUT YOU KILLED MOST OF THEM. AND YOU TRIED TO KILL ME, RIGHT AFTER YOU SAVED MY LIFE, WHICH DOESN'T REALLY ADD UP--
--BUT IT JUST KINDA FELT WRONG.
I DON'T KNOW WHAT HAPPENED TO YOU OR WHATEVER TO MAKE YOU THE WAY YOU WERE, OR MADE IT SO YOU COULD DO THOSE THINGS, BUT--
--I DON'T FEEL LIKE IGNORING IT IS GONNA HELP ANYTHING.

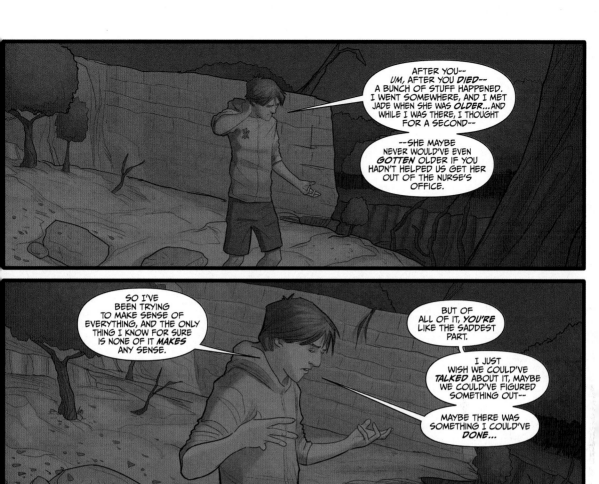

AFTER YOU--
UM, AFTER YOU *DIED*--
A BUNCH OF STUFF HAPPENED.
I WENT SOMEWHERE, AND I MET
JADE WHEN SHE WAS *OLDER...*AND
WHILE I WAS THERE, I THOUGHT
FOR A SECOND--

--SHE MAYBE
NEVER WOULD'VE EVEN
GOTTEN OLDER IF YOU
HADN'T HELPED US GET HER
OUT OF THE NURSE'S
OFFICE.

SO I'VE
BEEN TRYING
TO MAKE SENSE OF
EVERYTHING, AND THE ONLY
THING I KNOW FOR SURE
IS NONE OF IT *MAKES*
ANY SENSE.

BUT OF
ALL OF IT, *YOU'RE*
LIKE THE SADDEST
PART.

I JUST
WISH WE COULD'VE
TALKED ABOUT IT, MAYBE
WE COULD'VE FIGURED
SOMETHING OUT--

MAYBE THERE WAS
SOMETHING I COULD'VE
DONE...

...AND
I'M SORRY I
CALLED YOU
A SLUT.

SNAP!

ZOE?

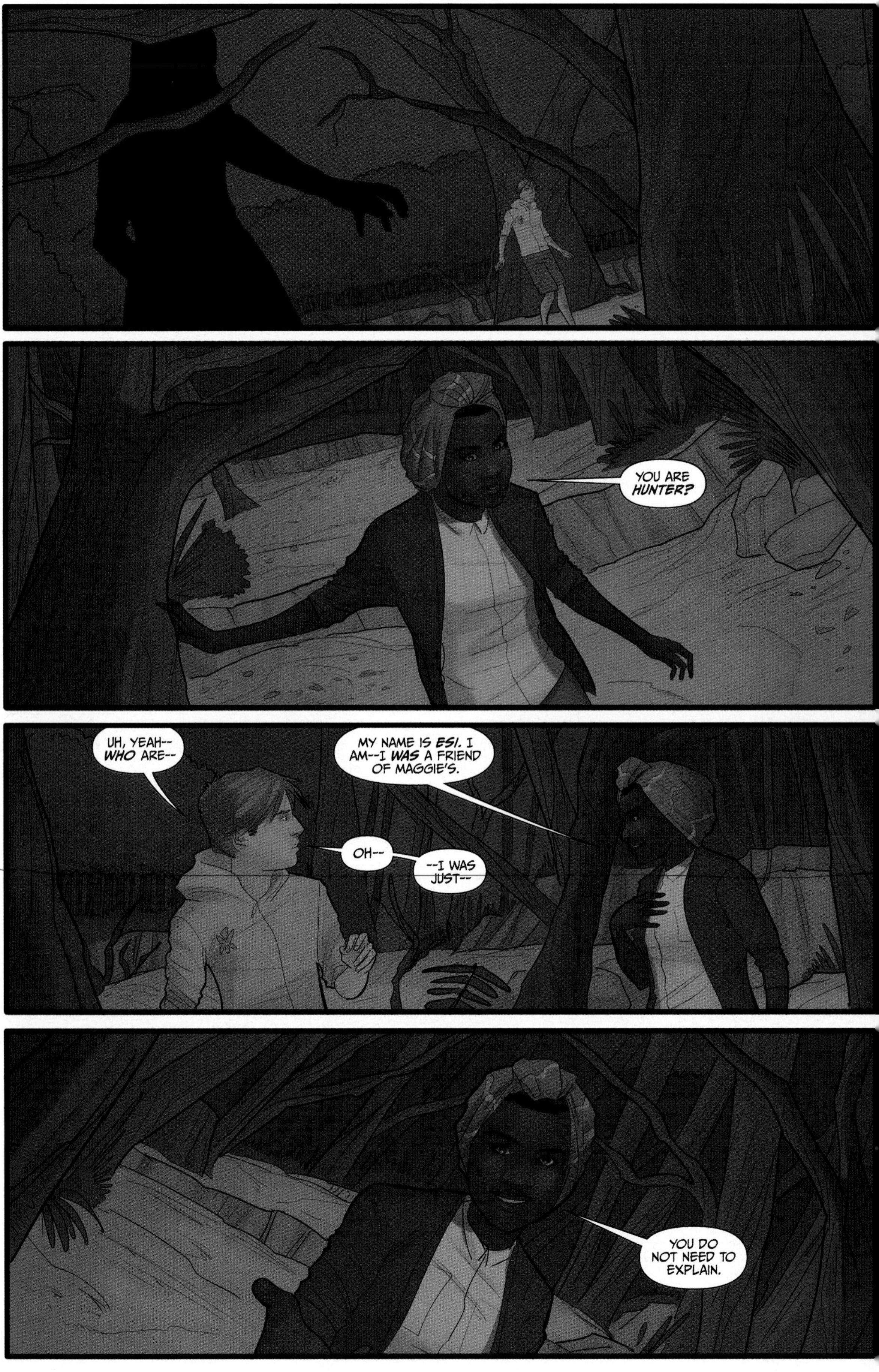
YOU ARE *HUNTER?*
UH, YEAH-- *WHO* ARE--
MY NAME IS *ESI.* I AM--I *WAS* A FRIEND OF MAGGIE'S.
OH--
--I WAS JUST--
YOU DO NOT NEED TO EXPLAIN.

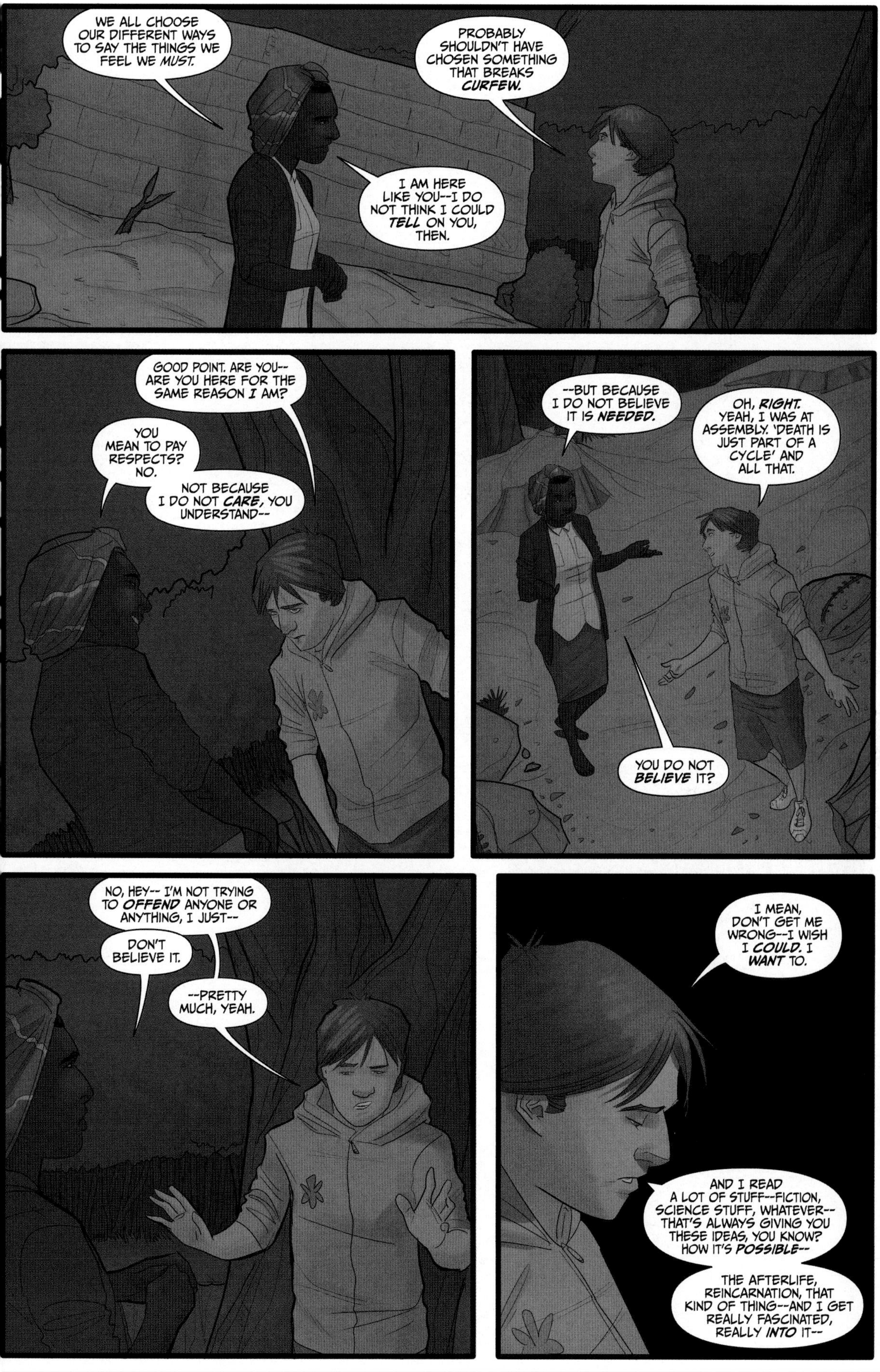
WE ALL CHOOSE OUR DIFFERENT WAYS TO SAY THE THINGS WE FEEL WE MUST.
PROBABLY SHOULDN'T HAVE CHOSEN SOMETHING THAT BREAKS CURFEW.
I AM HERE LIKE YOU--I DO NOT THINK I COULD TELL ON YOU, THEN.
GOOD POINT. ARE YOU--ARE YOU HERE FOR THE SAME REASON I AM?
YOU MEAN TO PAY RESPECTS? NO.
NOT BECAUSE I DO NOT CARE, YOU UNDERSTAND--
--BUT BECAUSE I DO NOT BELIEVE IT IS NEEDED.
OH, RIGHT. YEAH, I WAS AT ASSEMBLY. 'DEATH IS JUST PART OF A CYCLE' AND ALL THAT.
YOU DO NOT BELIEVE IT?
NO, HEY-- I'M NOT TRYING TO OFFEND ANYONE OR ANYTHING, I JUST--
DON'T BELIEVE IT.
--PRETTY MUCH, YEAH.
I MEAN, DON'T GET ME WRONG--I WISH I COULD. I WANT TO.
AND I READ A LOT OF STUFF--FICTION, SCIENCE STUFF, WHATEVER--THAT'S ALWAYS GIVING YOU THESE IDEAS, YOU KNOW? HOW IT'S POSSIBLE--
THE AFTERLIFE, REINCARNATION, THAT KIND OF THING--AND I GET REALLY FASCINATED, REALLY INTO IT--

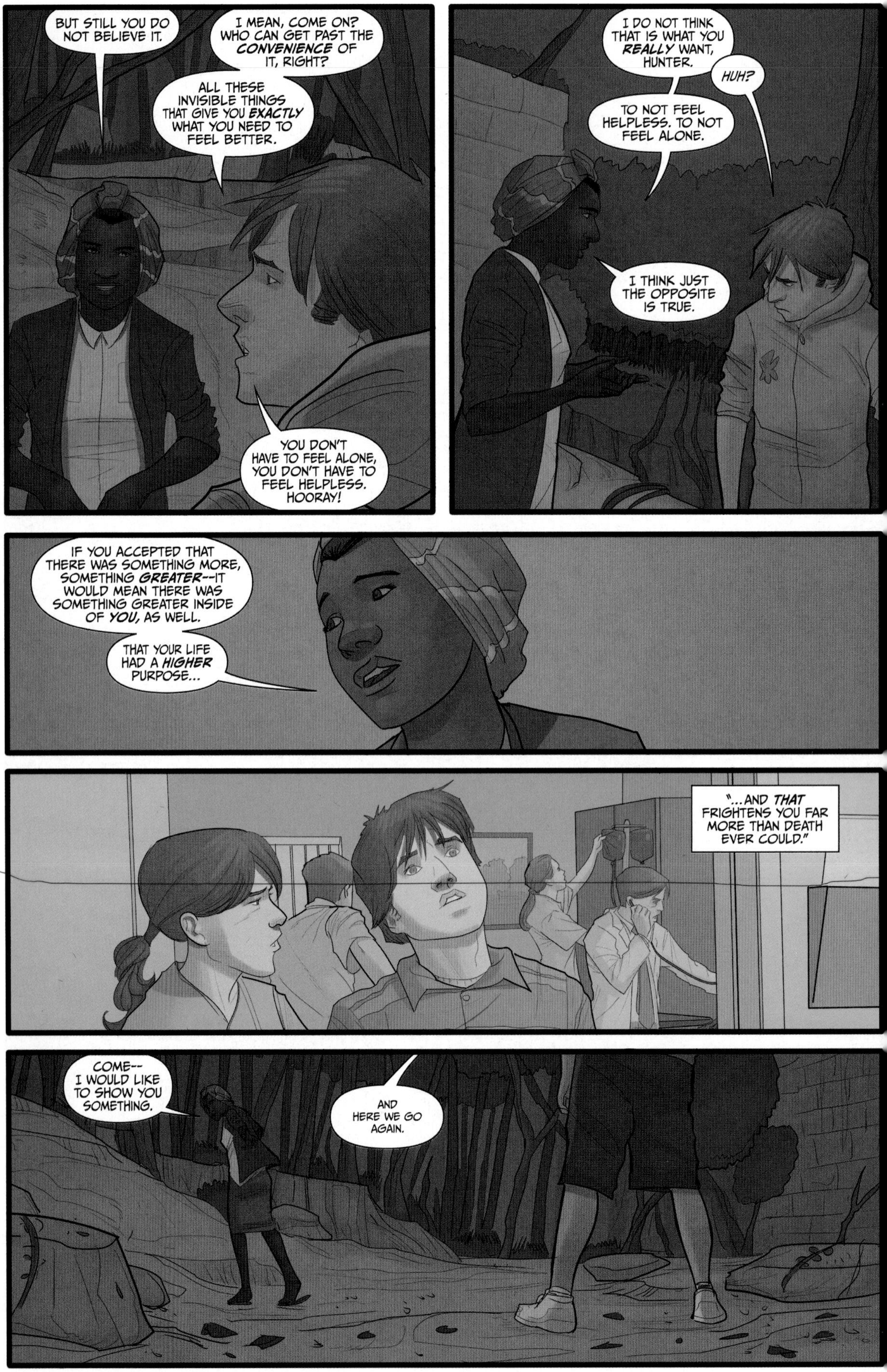
BUT STILL YOU DO NOT BELIEVE IT.
I MEAN, COME ON? WHO CAN GET PAST THE CONVENIENCE OF IT, RIGHT?
ALL THESE INVISIBLE THINGS THAT GIVE YOU EXACTLY WHAT YOU NEED TO FEEL BETTER.
YOU DON'T HAVE TO FEEL ALONE, YOU DON'T HAVE TO FEEL HELPLESS. HOORAY!
I DO NOT THINK THAT IS WHAT YOU REALLY WANT, HUNTER.
HUH?
TO NOT FEEL HELPLESS. TO NOT FEEL ALONE.
I THINK JUST THE OPPOSITE IS TRUE.
IF YOU ACCEPTED THAT THERE WAS SOMETHING MORE, SOMETHING GREATER--IT WOULD MEAN THERE WAS SOMETHING GREATER INSIDE OF YOU, AS WELL.
THAT YOUR LIFE HAD A HIGHER PURPOSE...
"...AND THAT FRIGHTENS YOU FAR MORE THAN DEATH EVER COULD."
COME-- I WOULD LIKE TO SHOW YOU SOMETHING.
AND HERE WE GO AGAIN.

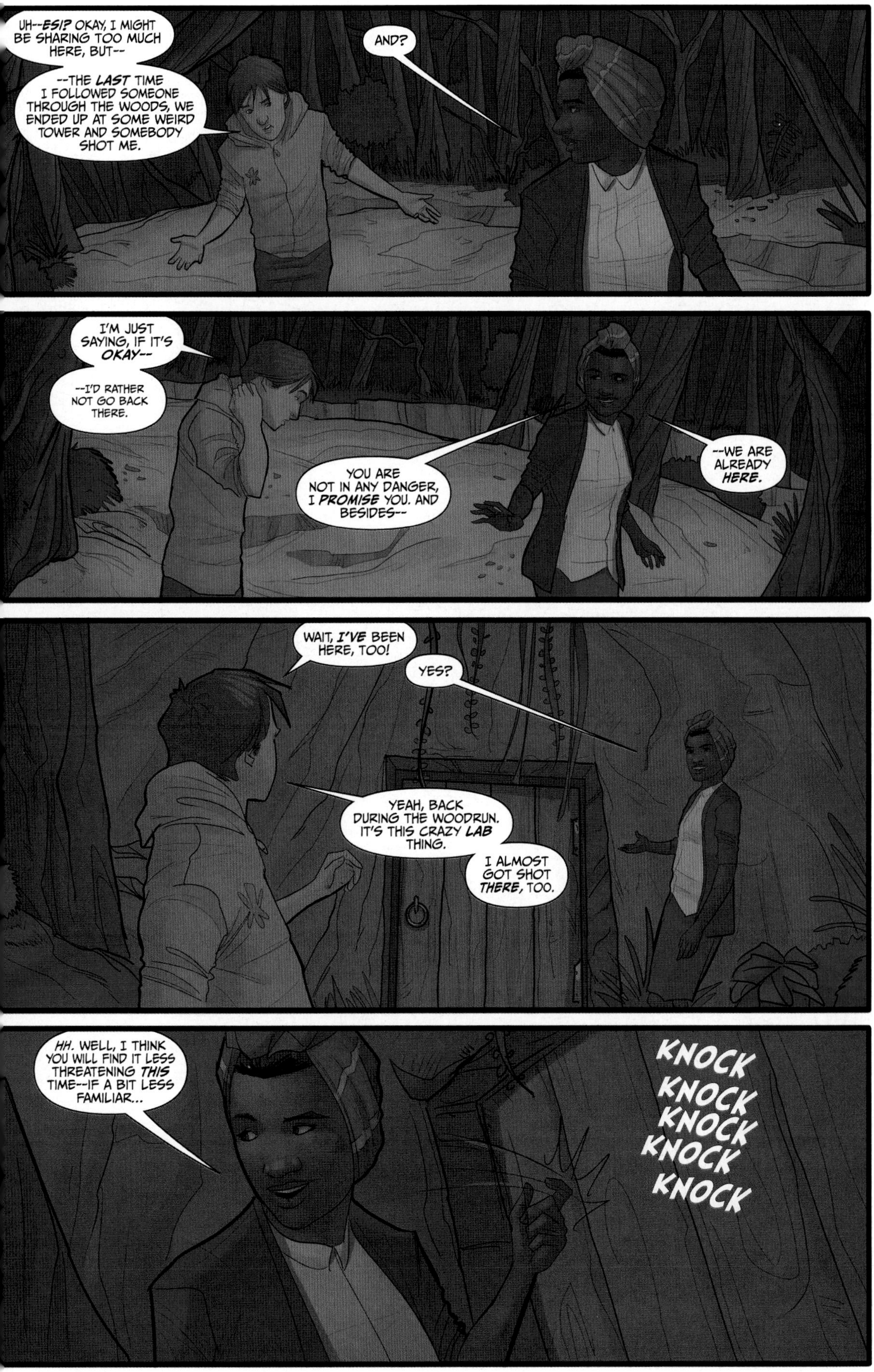
UH--ESI? OKAY, I MIGHT BE SHARING TOO MUCH HERE, BUT--
--THE LAST TIME I FOLLOWED SOMEONE THROUGH THE WOODS, WE ENDED UP AT SOME WEIRD TOWER AND SOMEBODY SHOT ME.
AND?
I'M JUST SAYING, IF IT'S OKAY--
--I'D RATHER NOT GO BACK THERE.
YOU ARE NOT IN ANY DANGER, I PROMISE YOU. AND BESIDES--
--WE ARE ALREADY HERE.
WAIT, I'VE BEEN HERE, TOO!
YES?
YEAH, BACK DURING THE WOODRUN. IT'S THIS CRAZY LAB THING.
I ALMOST GOT SHOT THERE, TOO.
HH. WELL, I THINK YOU WILL FIND IT LESS THREATENING THIS TIME--IF A BIT LESS FAMILIAR...
KNOCK
KNOCK
KNOCK
KNOCK
KNOCK

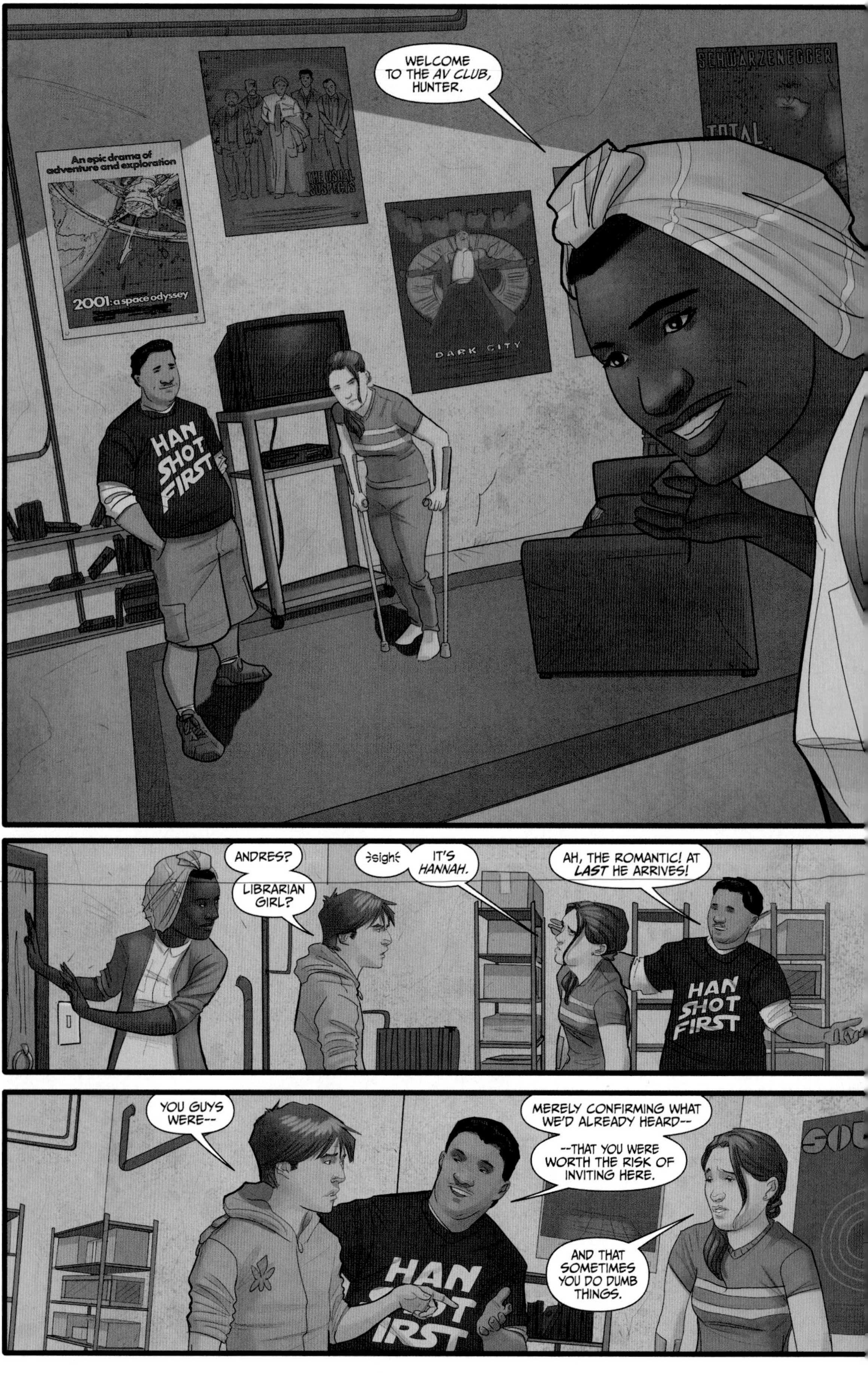

An epic drama of adventure and exploration
2001: a space odyssey
THE USUAL SUSPECTS
DARK CITY
SCHWARZENEGGER
TOTAL
WELCOME TO THE *AV CLUB*, HUNTER.
HAN SHOT FIRST
ANDRES?
LIBRARIAN GIRL?
sigh
IT'S *HANNAH.*
AH, THE ROMANTIC! AT *LAST* HE ARRIVES!
HAN SHOT FIRST
YOU GUYS WERE--
MERELY CONFIRMING WHAT WE'D ALREADY HEARD--
--THAT YOU WERE WORTH THE RISK OF INVITING HERE.
AND THAT SOMETIMES YOU DO DUMB THINGS.

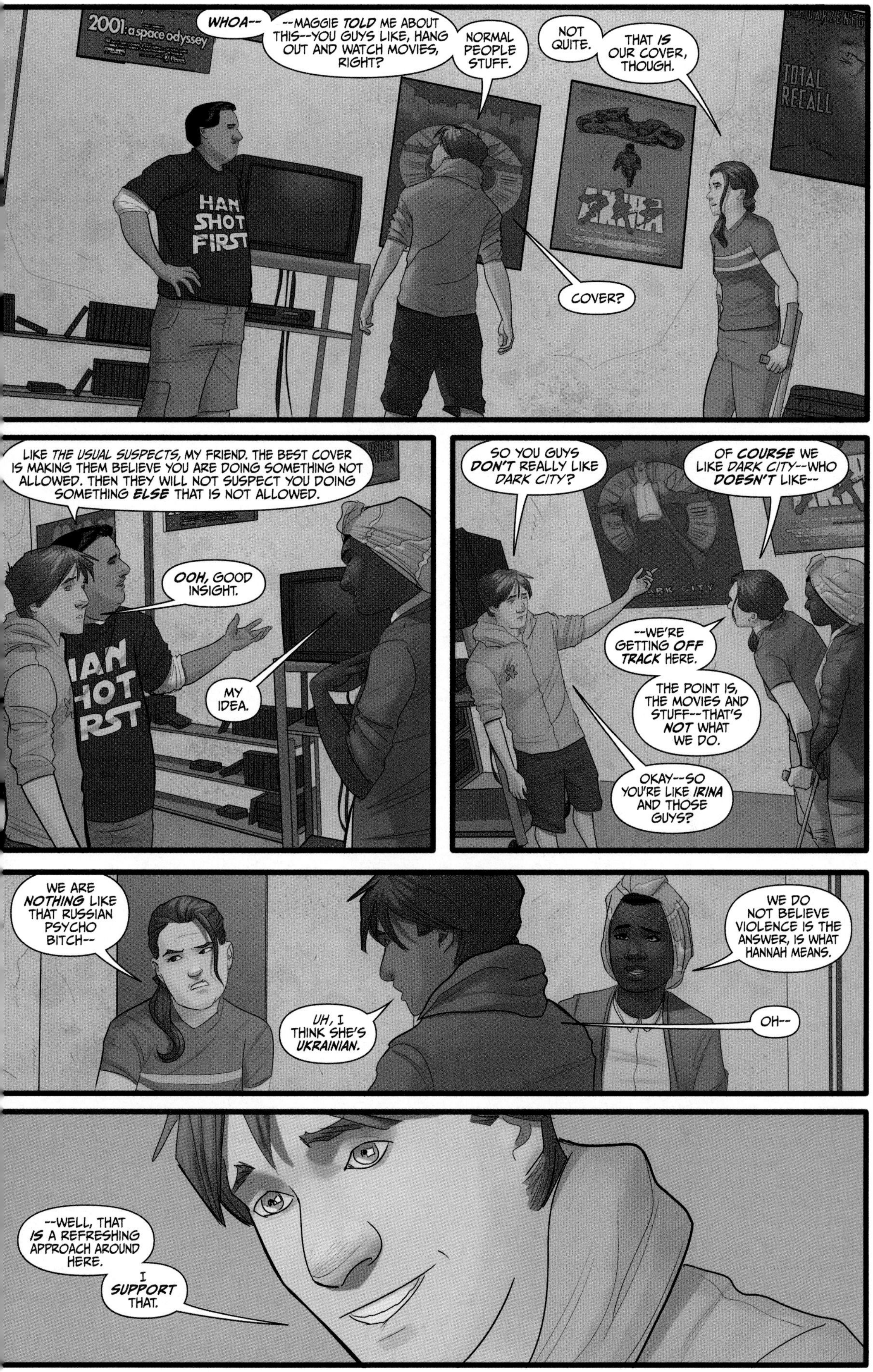
WHOA--
--MAGGIE TOLD ME ABOUT THIS--YOU GUYS LIKE, HANG OUT AND WATCH MOVIES, RIGHT?
NORMAL PEOPLE STUFF.
NOT QUITE.
THAT IS OUR COVER, THOUGH.
COVER?
LIKE THE USUAL SUSPECTS, MY FRIEND. THE BEST COVER IS MAKING THEM BELIEVE YOU ARE DOING SOMETHING NOT ALLOWED. THEN THEY WILL NOT SUSPECT YOU DOING SOMETHING ELSE THAT IS NOT ALLOWED.
OOH, GOOD INSIGHT.
MY IDEA.
SO YOU GUYS DON'T REALLY LIKE DARK CITY?
OF COURSE WE LIKE DARK CITY--WHO DOESN'T LIKE--
--WE'RE GETTING OFF TRACK HERE.
THE POINT IS, THE MOVIES AND STUFF--THAT'S NOT WHAT WE DO.
OKAY--SO YOU'RE LIKE IRINA AND THOSE GUYS?
WE ARE NOTHING LIKE THAT RUSSIAN PSYCHO BITCH--
UH, I THINK SHE'S UKRAINIAN.
WE DO NOT BELIEVE VIOLENCE IS THE ANSWER, IS WHAT HANNAH MEANS.
OH--
--WELL, THAT IS A REFRESHING APPROACH AROUND HERE.
I SUPPORT THAT.

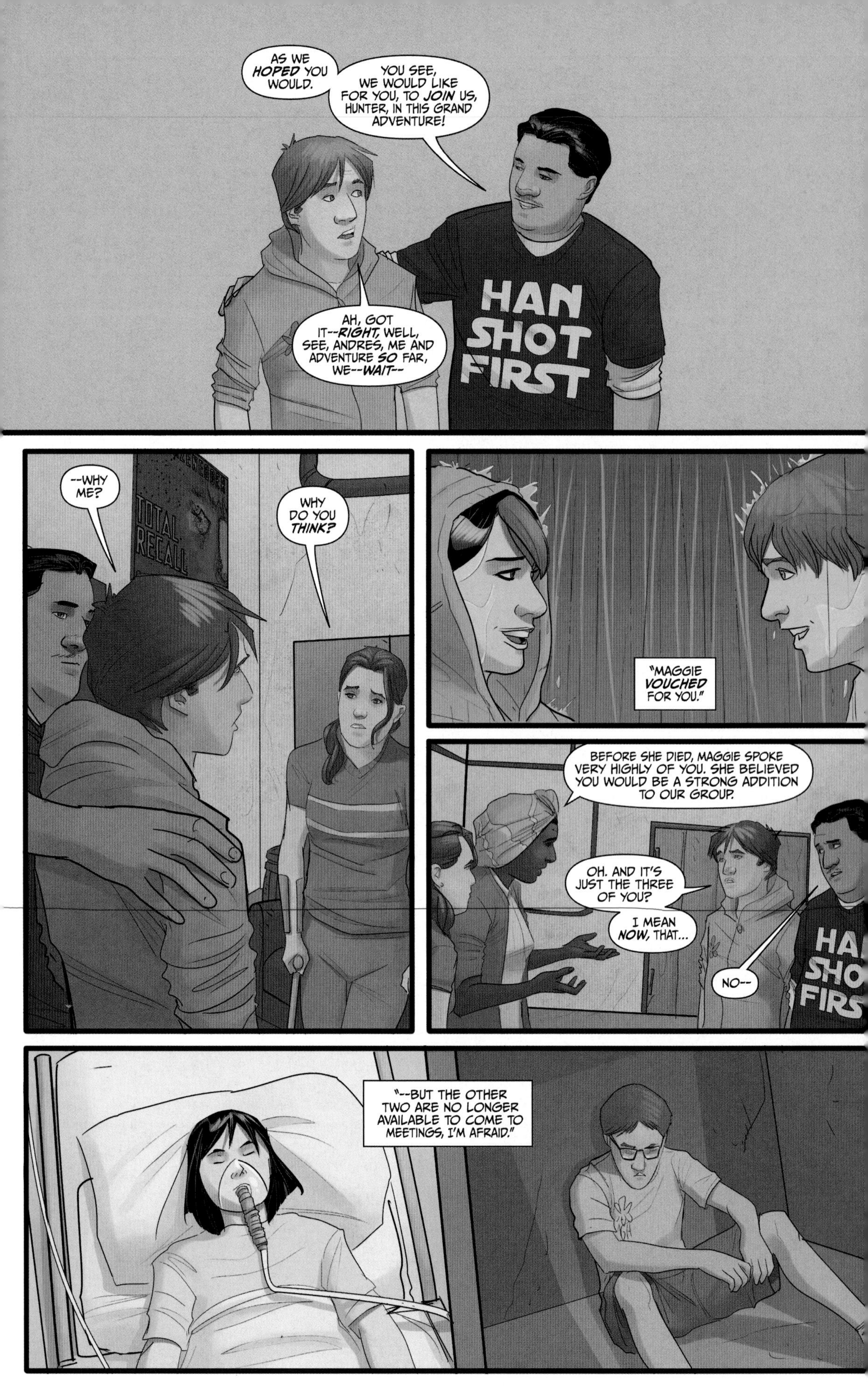
AS WE HOPED YOU WOULD.
YOU SEE, WE WOULD LIKE FOR YOU, TO JOIN US, HUNTER, IN THIS GRAND ADVENTURE!
HAN SHOT FIRST
AH, GOT IT--RIGHT, WELL, SEE, ANDRES, ME AND ADVENTURE SO FAR, WE--WAIT--
--WHY ME?
TOTAL RECALL
WHY DO YOU THINK?
"MAGGIE VOUCHED FOR YOU."
BEFORE SHE DIED, MAGGIE SPOKE VERY HIGHLY OF YOU. SHE BELIEVED YOU WOULD BE A STRONG ADDITION TO OUR GROUP.
OH. AND IT'S JUST THE THREE OF YOU?
I MEAN NOW, THAT...
NO--
"--BUT THE OTHER TWO ARE NO LONGER AVAILABLE TO COME TO MEETINGS, I'M AFRAID."

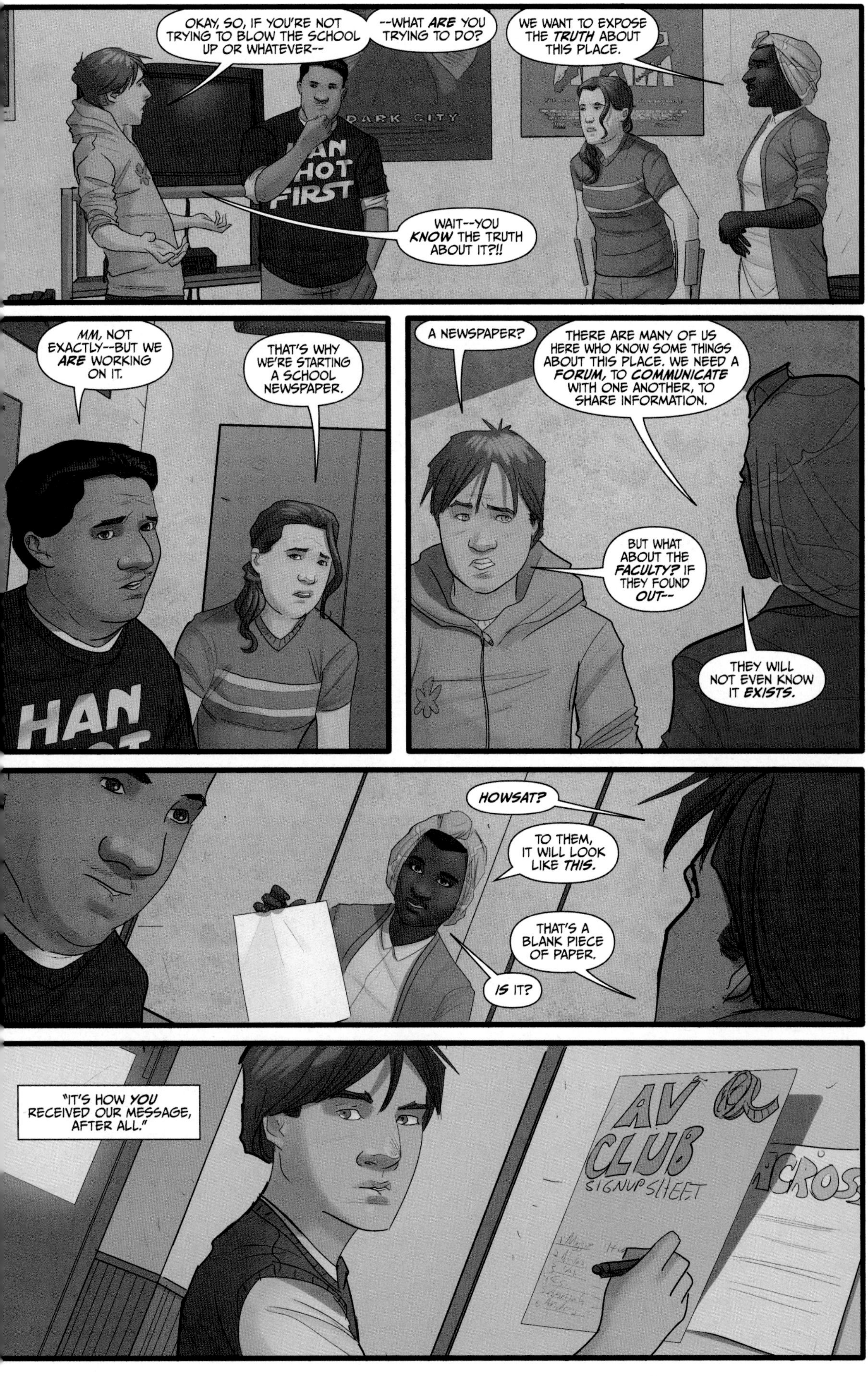
OKAY, SO, IF YOU'RE NOT TRYING TO BLOW THE SCHOOL UP OR WHATEVER--
--WHAT ARE YOU TRYING TO DO?
WE WANT TO EXPOSE THE TRUTH ABOUT THIS PLACE.
WAIT--YOU KNOW THE TRUTH ABOUT IT?!!
DARK CITY
HAN SHOT FIRST
MM, NOT EXACTLY--BUT WE ARE WORKING ON IT.
THAT'S WHY WE'RE STARTING A SCHOOL NEWSPAPER.
A NEWSPAPER?
THERE ARE MANY OF US HERE WHO KNOW SOME THINGS ABOUT THIS PLACE. WE NEED A FORUM, TO COMMUNICATE WITH ONE ANOTHER, TO SHARE INFORMATION.
BUT WHAT ABOUT THE FACULTY? IF THEY FOUND OUT--
THEY WILL NOT EVEN KNOW IT EXISTS.
HOWSAT?
TO THEM, IT WILL LOOK LIKE THIS.
THAT'S A BLANK PIECE OF PAPER.
IS IT?
"IT'S HOW YOU RECEIVED OUR MESSAGE, AFTER ALL."
AV CLUB
SIGNUP SHEET

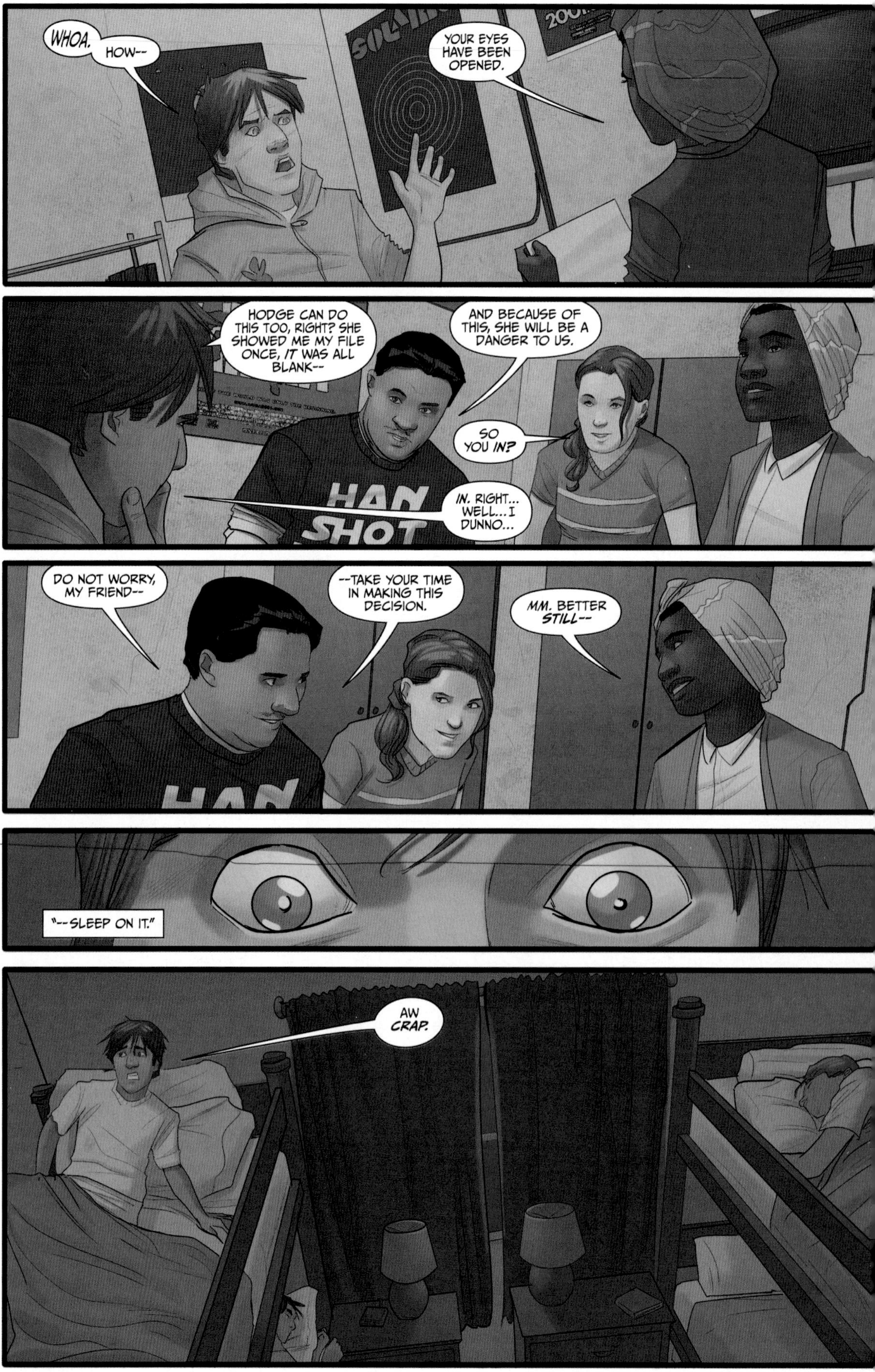
WHOA.
HOW--
YOUR EYES HAVE BEEN OPENED.
HODGE CAN DO THIS TOO, RIGHT? SHE SHOWED ME MY FILE ONCE, IT WAS ALL BLANK--
AND BECAUSE OF THIS, SHE WILL BE A DANGER TO US.
SO YOU IN?
IN. RIGHT... WELL... I DUNNO...
HAN SHOT
DO NOT WORRY, MY FRIEND--
--TAKE YOUR TIME IN MAKING THIS DECISION.
MM. BETTER STILL--
"--SLEEP ON IT."
AW CRAP.

thirty**two**

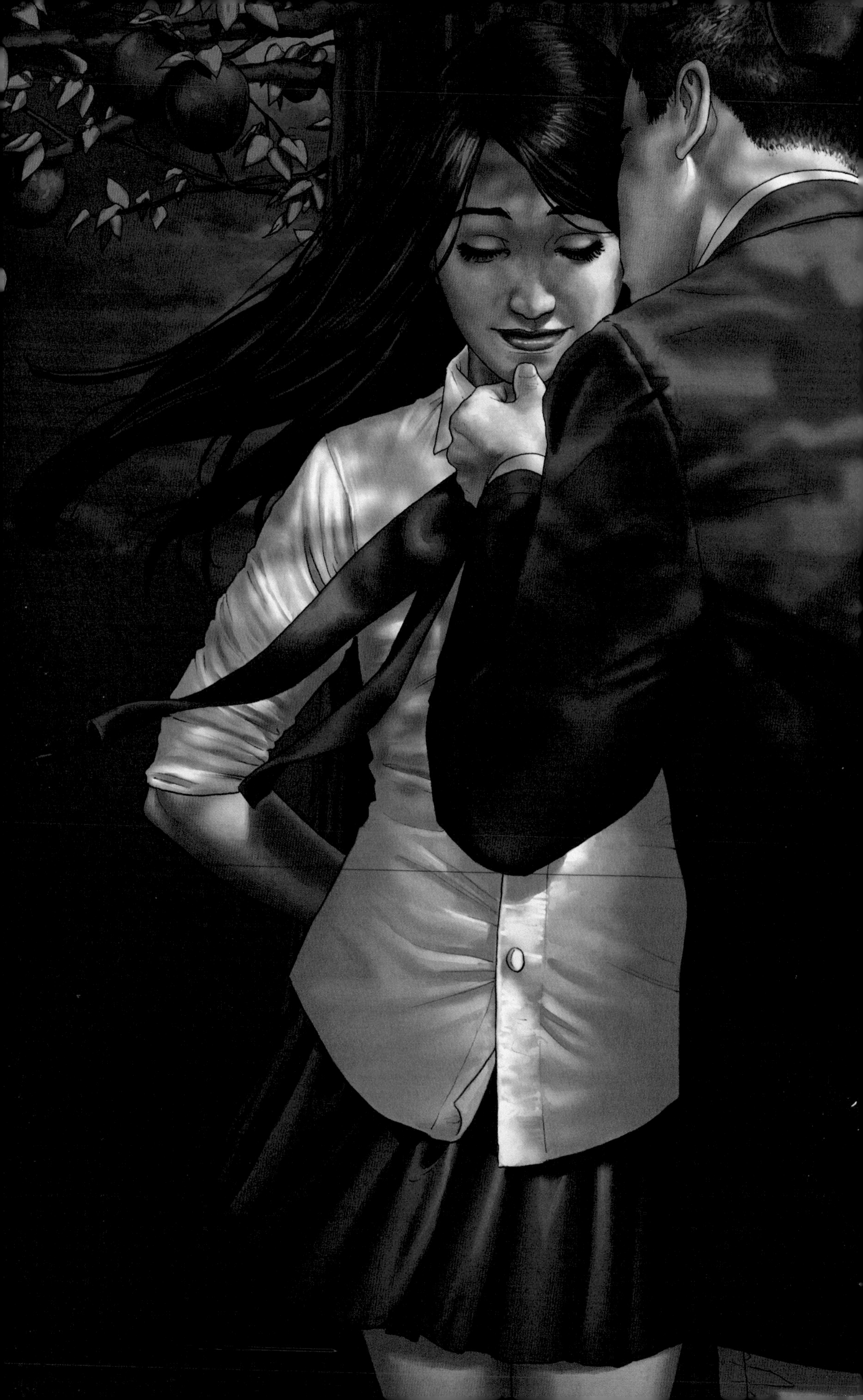

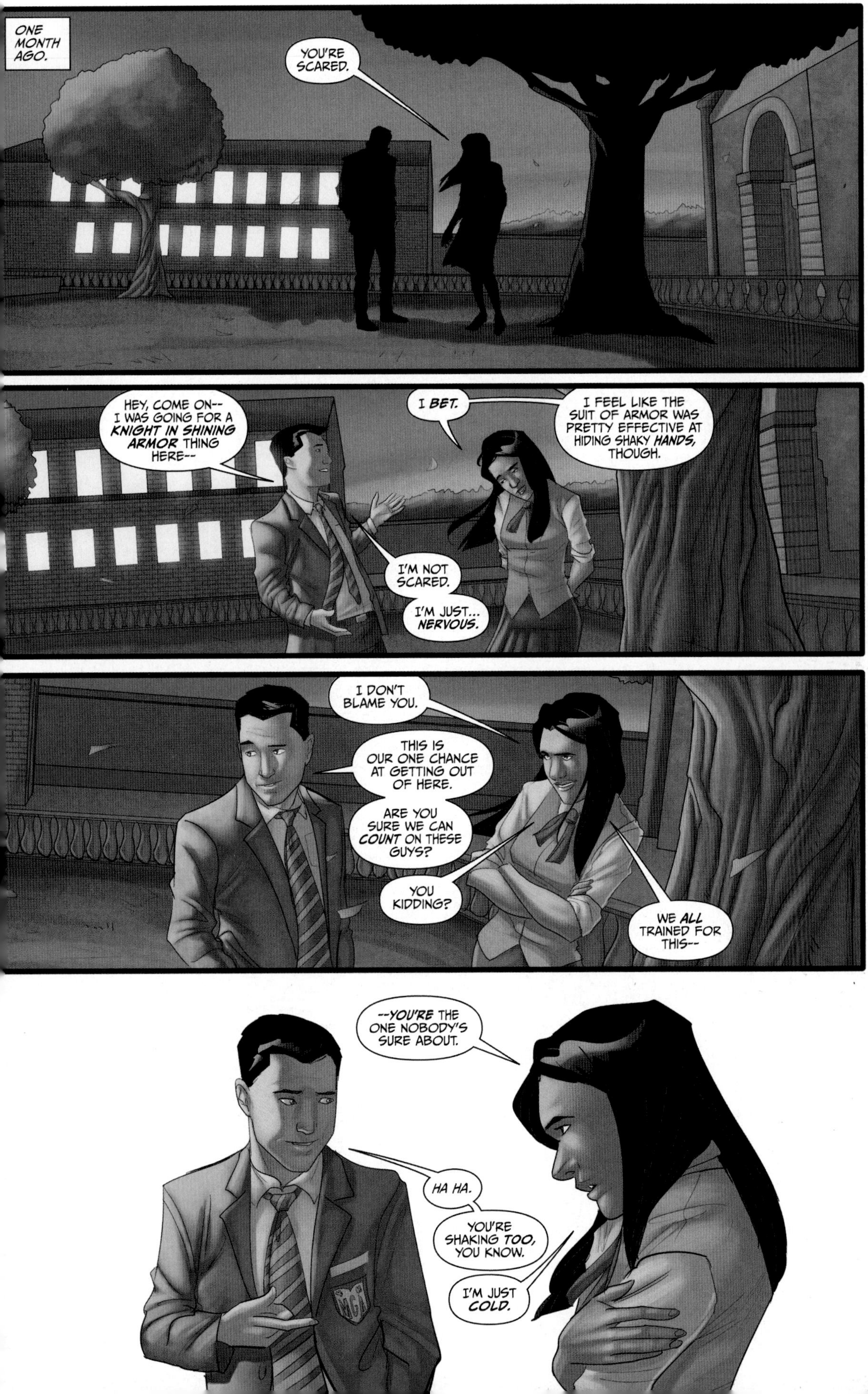
ONE MONTH AGO.
YOU'RE SCARED.
HEY, COME ON-- I WAS GOING FOR A KNIGHT IN SHINING ARMOR THING HERE--
I BET.
I FEEL LIKE THE SUIT OF ARMOR WAS PRETTY EFFECTIVE AT HIDING SHAKY HANDS, THOUGH.
I'M NOT SCARED.
I'M JUST... NERVOUS.
I DON'T BLAME YOU.
THIS IS OUR ONE CHANCE AT GETTING OUT OF HERE.
ARE YOU SURE WE CAN COUNT ON THESE GUYS?
YOU KIDDING?
WE ALL TRAINED FOR THIS--
--YOU'RE THE ONE NOBODY'S SURE ABOUT.
HA HA.
YOU'RE SHAKING TOO, YOU KNOW.
I'M JUST COLD.

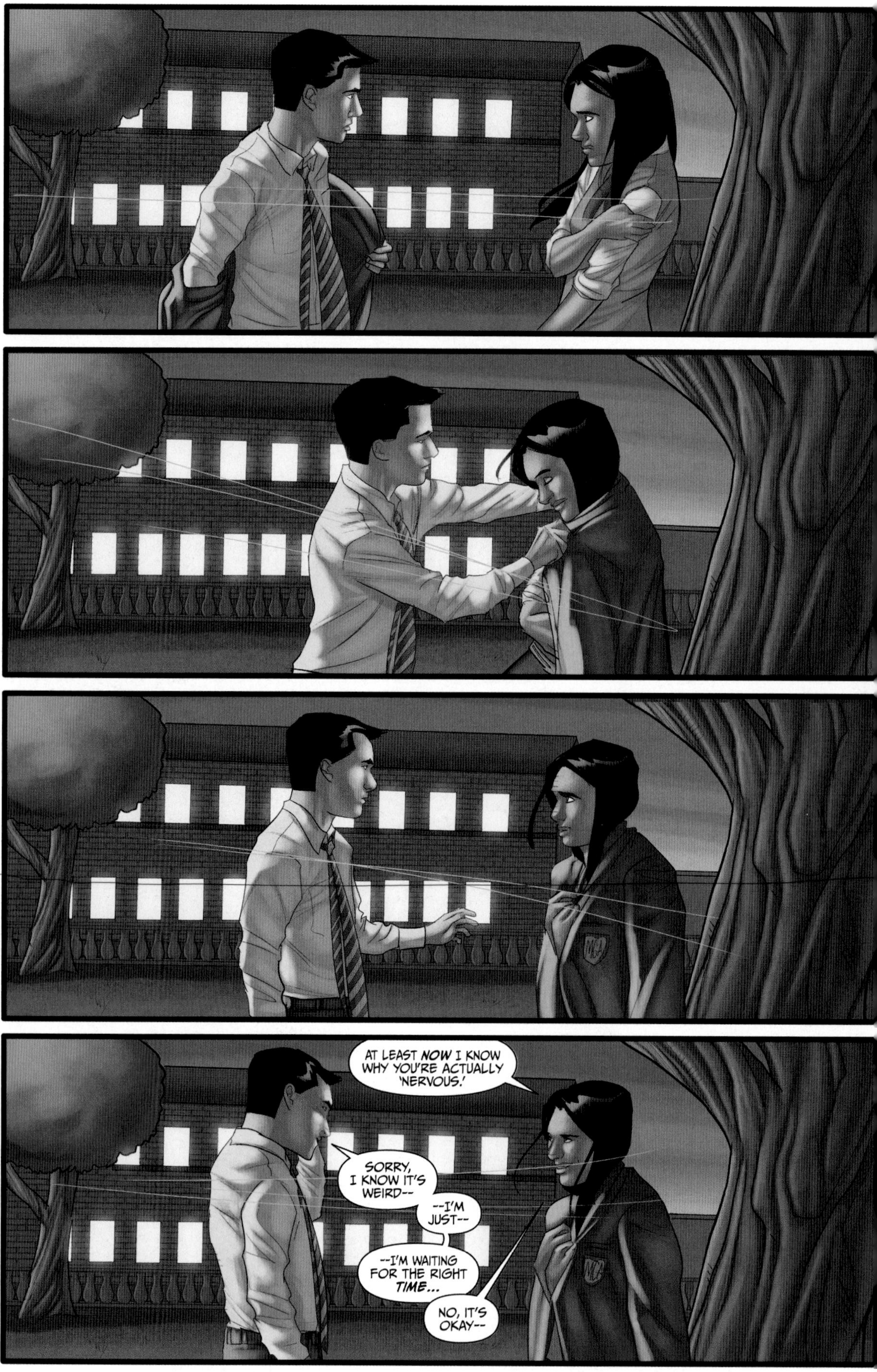
AT LEAST *NOW* I KNOW WHY YOU'RE ACTUALLY 'NERVOUS.'
SORRY, I KNOW IT'S WEIRD--
--I'M JUST--
--I'M WAITING FOR THE RIGHT *TIME*...
NO, IT'S OKAY--

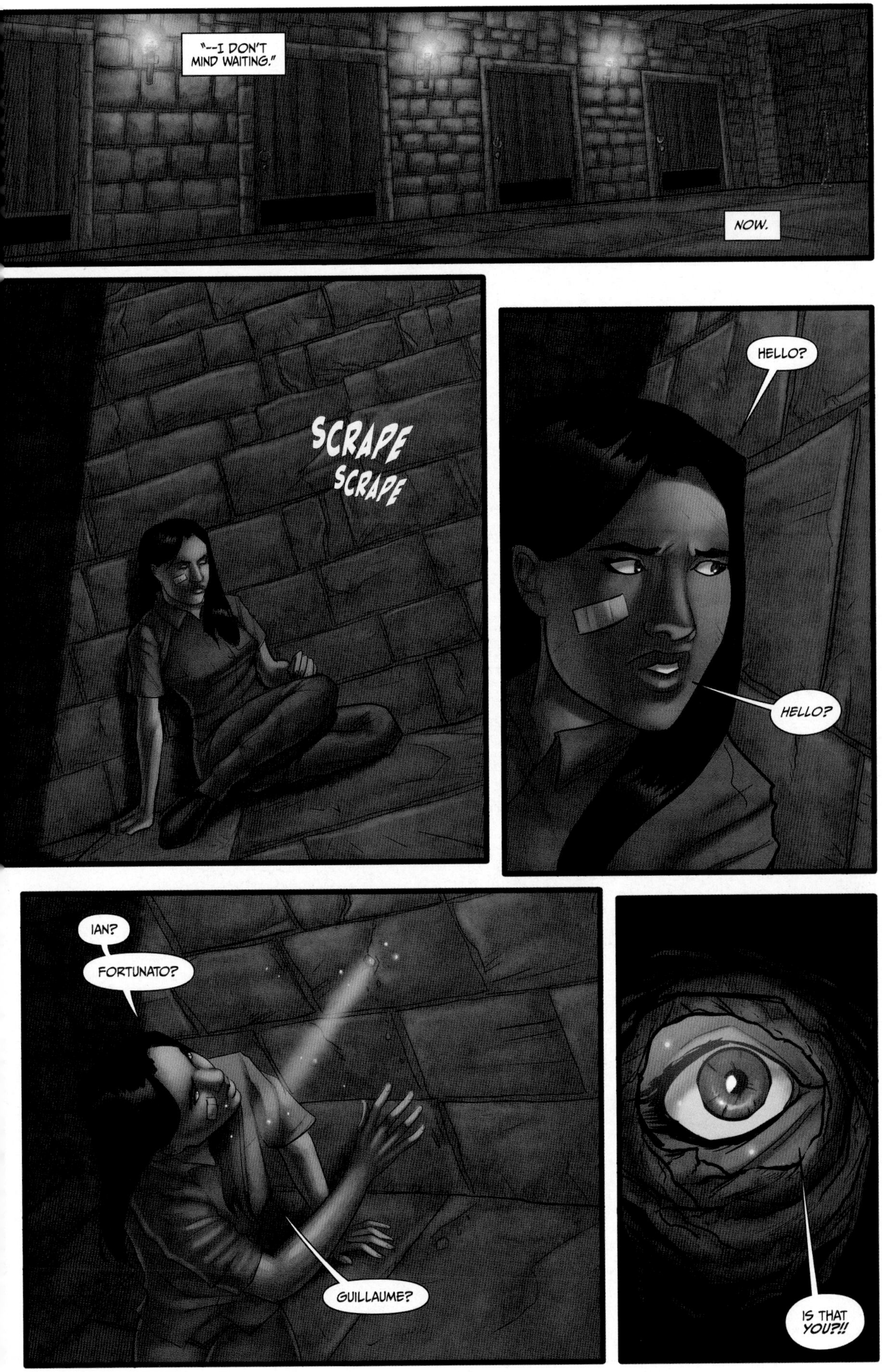
"--I DON'T MIND WAITING."
NOW.
SCRAPE
SCRAPE
HELLO?
HELLO?
IAN?
FORTUNATO?
GUILLAUME?
IS THAT YOU?!!

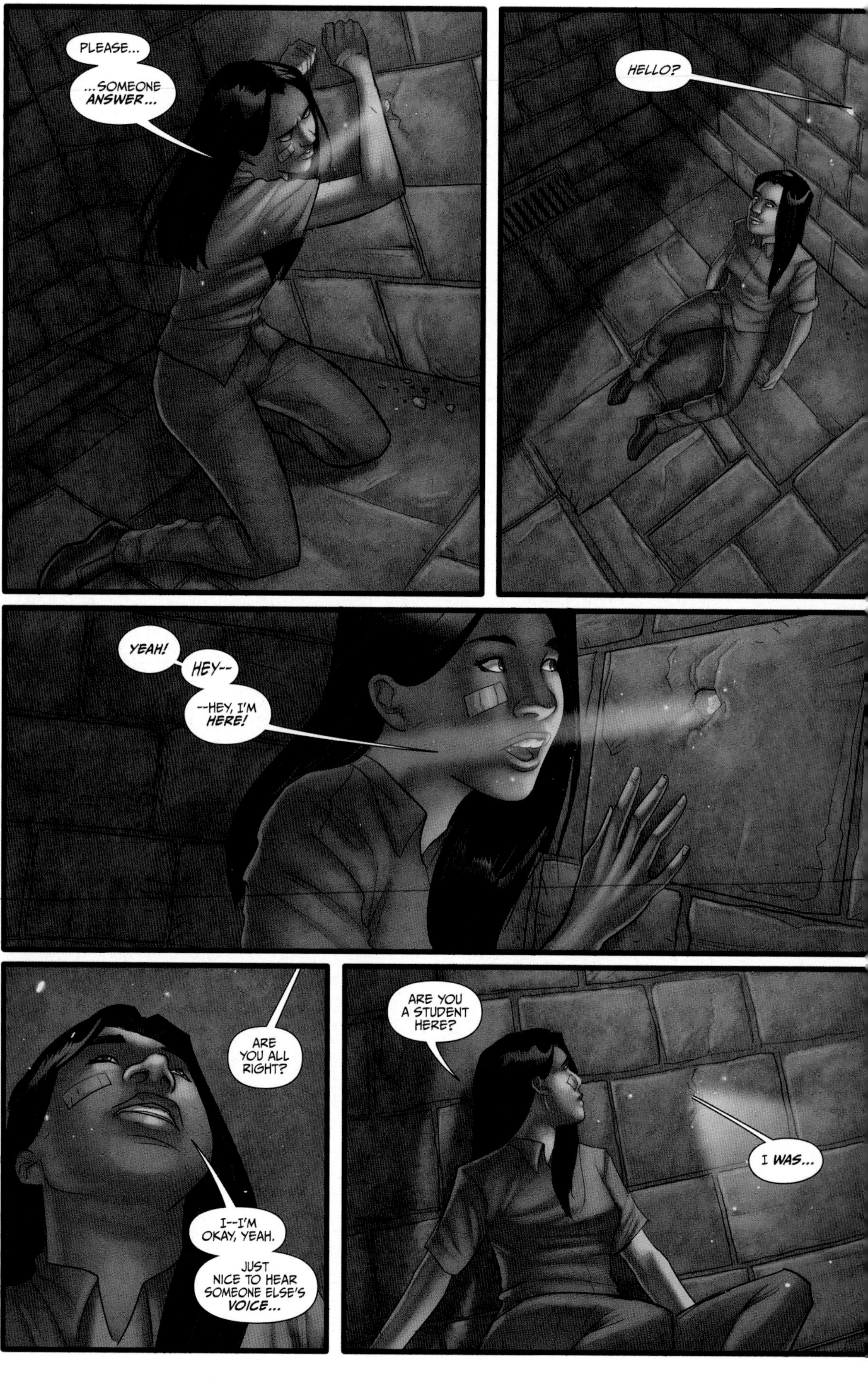
PLEASE...
...SOMEONE ANSWER...
HELLO?
YEAH!
HEY--
--HEY, I'M HERE!
ARE YOU ALL RIGHT?
I--I'M OKAY, YEAH.
JUST NICE TO HEAR SOMEONE ELSE'S VOICE...
ARE YOU A STUDENT HERE?
I WAS...

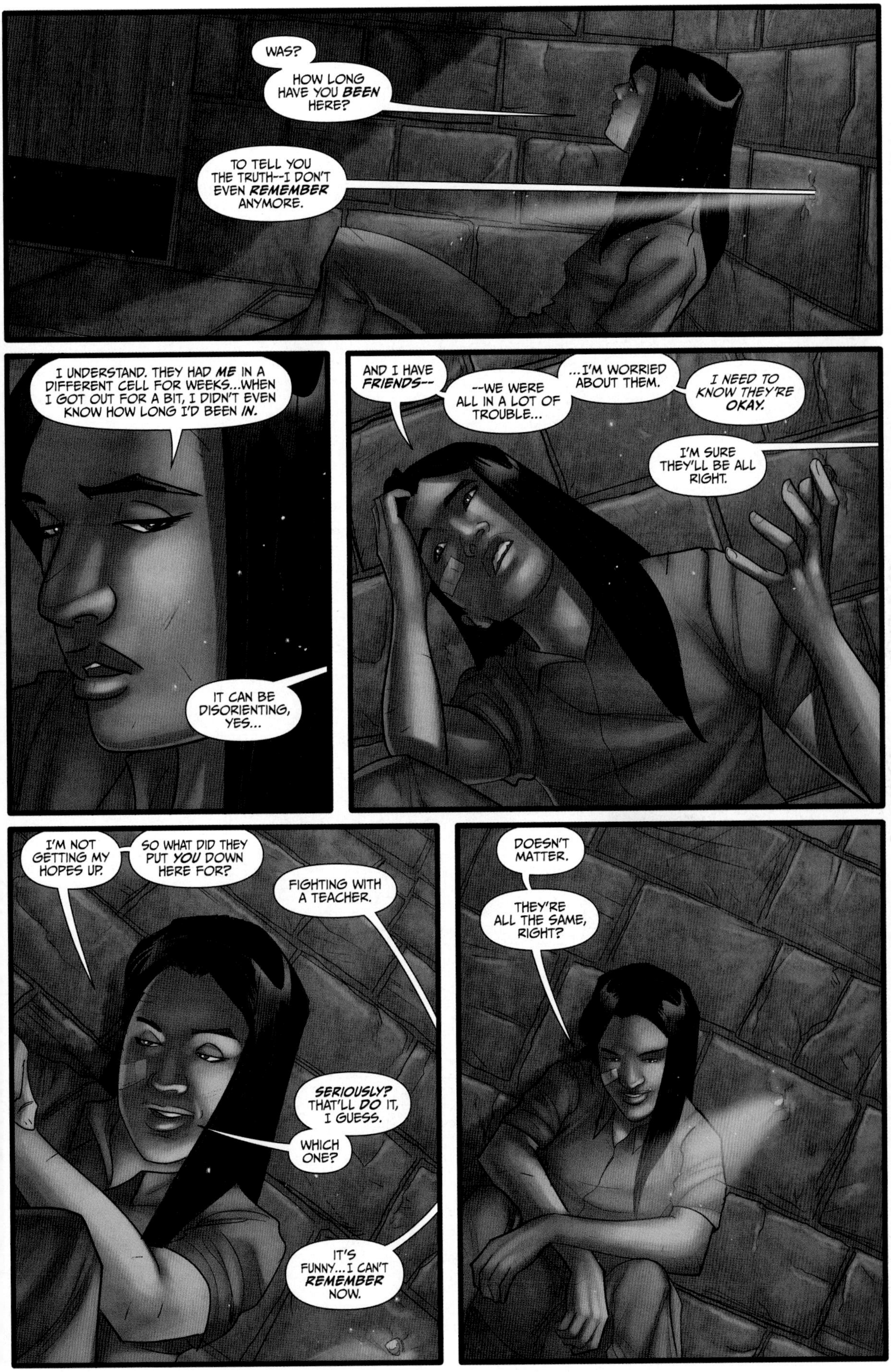
WAS?
HOW LONG HAVE YOU BEEN HERE?
TO TELL YOU THE TRUTH--I DON'T EVEN REMEMBER ANYMORE.
I UNDERSTAND. THEY HAD ME IN A DIFFERENT CELL FOR WEEKS...WHEN I GOT OUT FOR A BIT, I DIDN'T EVEN KNOW HOW LONG I'D BEEN IN.
IT CAN BE DISORIENTING, YES...
AND I HAVE FRIENDS--
--WE WERE ALL IN A LOT OF TROUBLE...
...I'M WORRIED ABOUT THEM.
I NEED TO KNOW THEY'RE OKAY.
I'M SURE THEY'LL BE ALL RIGHT.
I'M NOT GETTING MY HOPES UP.
SO WHAT DID THEY PUT YOU DOWN HERE FOR?
FIGHTING WITH A TEACHER.
SERIOUSLY? THAT'LL DO IT, I GUESS.
WHICH ONE?
IT'S FUNNY...I CAN'T REMEMBER NOW.
DOESN'T MATTER.
THEY'RE ALL THE SAME, RIGHT?

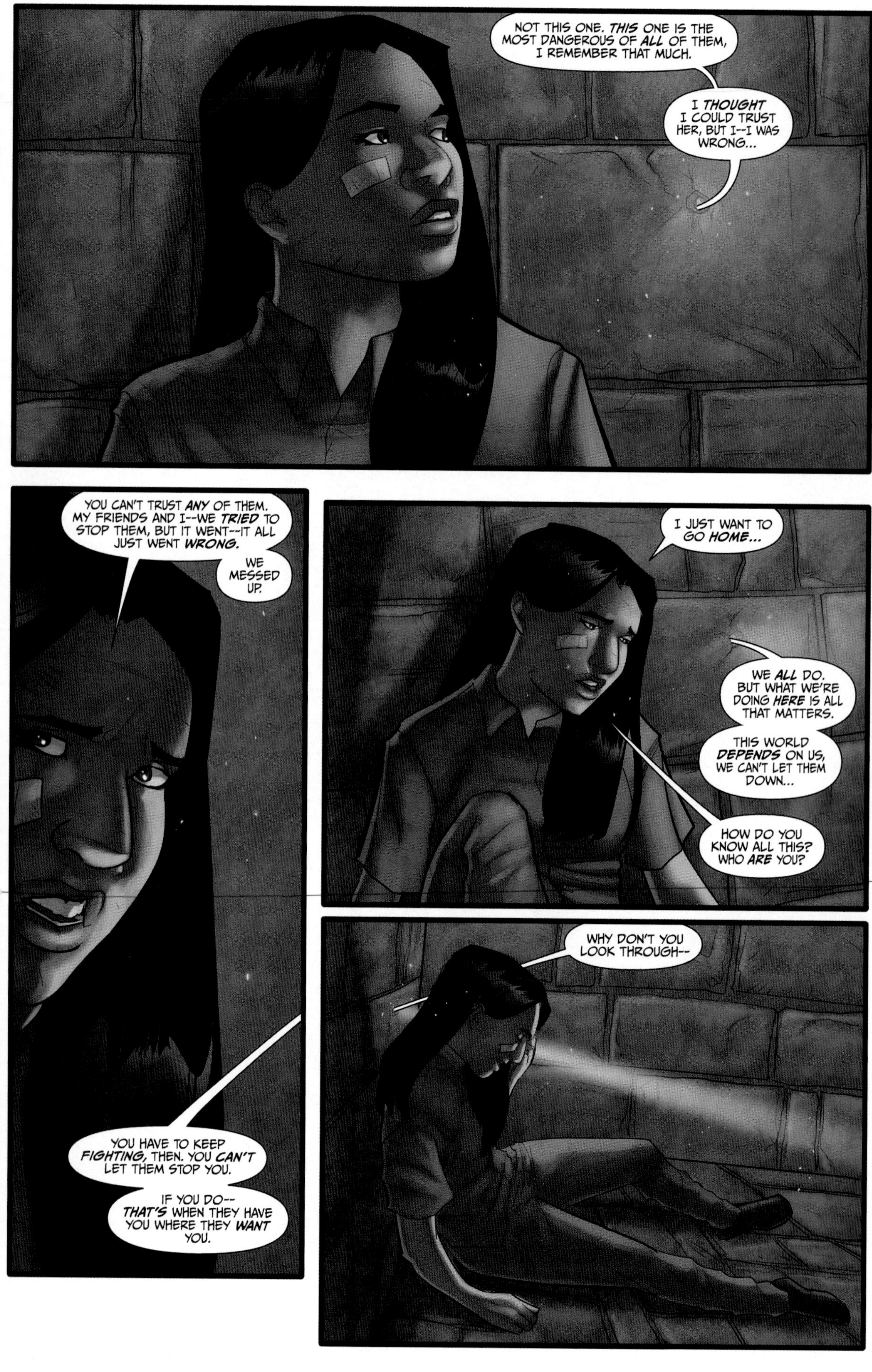
NOT THIS ONE. THIS ONE IS THE MOST DANGEROUS OF ALL OF THEM, I REMEMBER THAT MUCH.
I THOUGHT I COULD TRUST HER, BUT I--I WAS WRONG...
YOU CAN'T TRUST ANY OF THEM. MY FRIENDS AND I--WE TRIED TO STOP THEM, BUT IT WENT--IT ALL JUST WENT WRONG.
WE MESSED UP.
I JUST WANT TO GO HOME...
WE ALL DO. BUT WHAT WE'RE DOING HERE IS ALL THAT MATTERS.
THIS WORLD DEPENDS ON US, WE CAN'T LET THEM DOWN...
HOW DO YOU KNOW ALL THIS? WHO ARE YOU?
YOU HAVE TO KEEP FIGHTING, THEN. YOU CAN'T LET THEM STOP YOU.
IF YOU DO-- THAT'S WHEN THEY HAVE YOU WHERE THEY WANT YOU.
WHY DON'T YOU LOOK THROUGH--

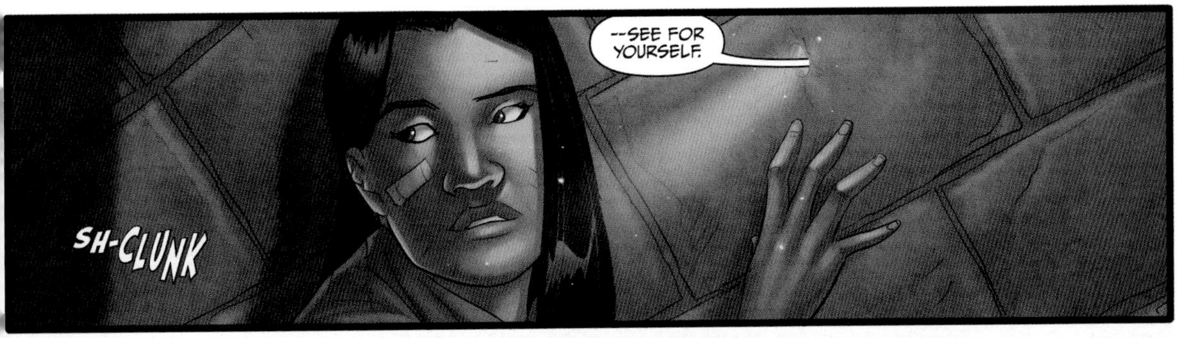
--SEE FOR YOURSELF.
SH-CLUNK

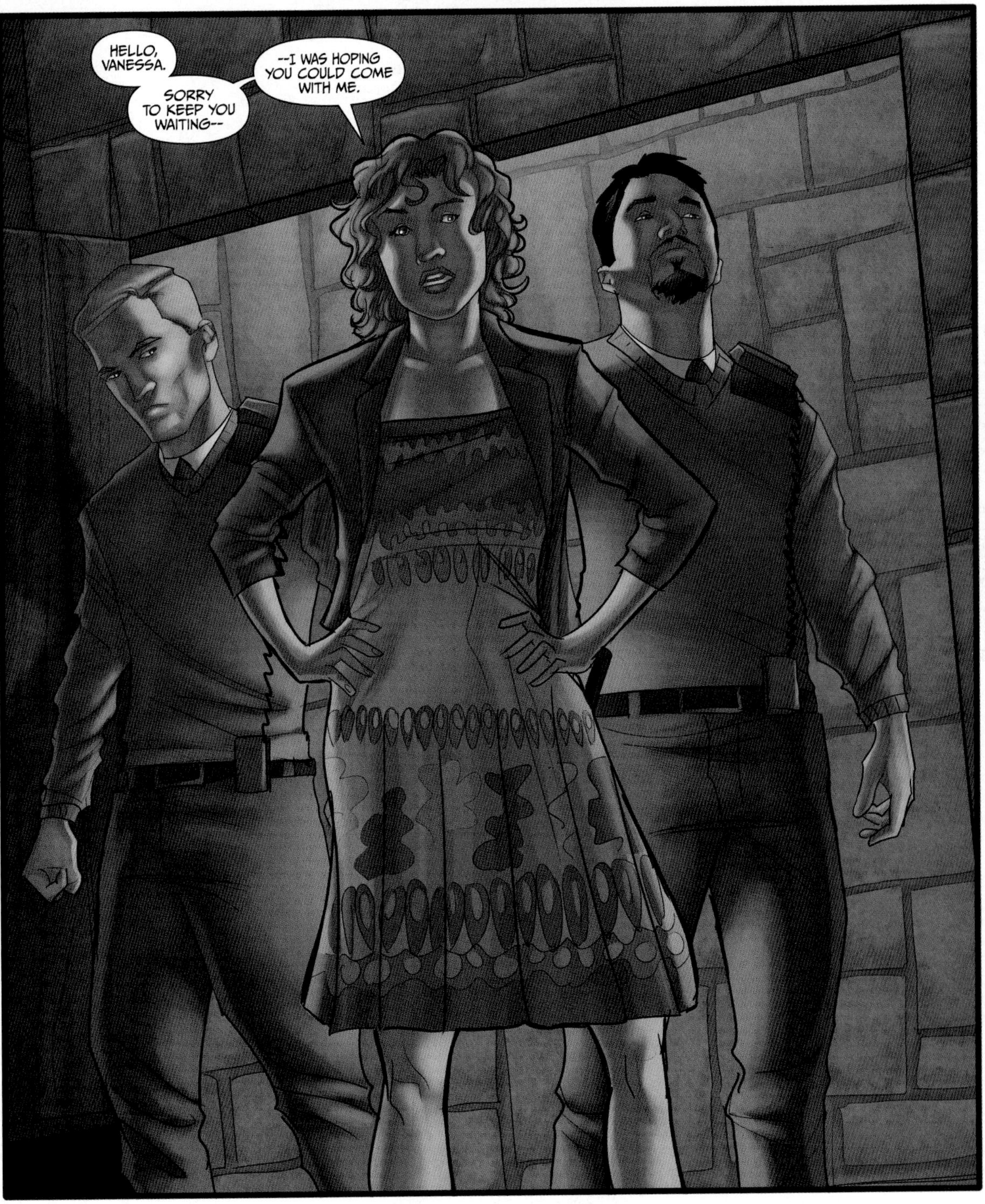
HELLO, VANESSA.
SORRY TO KEEP YOU WAITING--
--I WAS HOPING YOU COULD COME WITH ME.

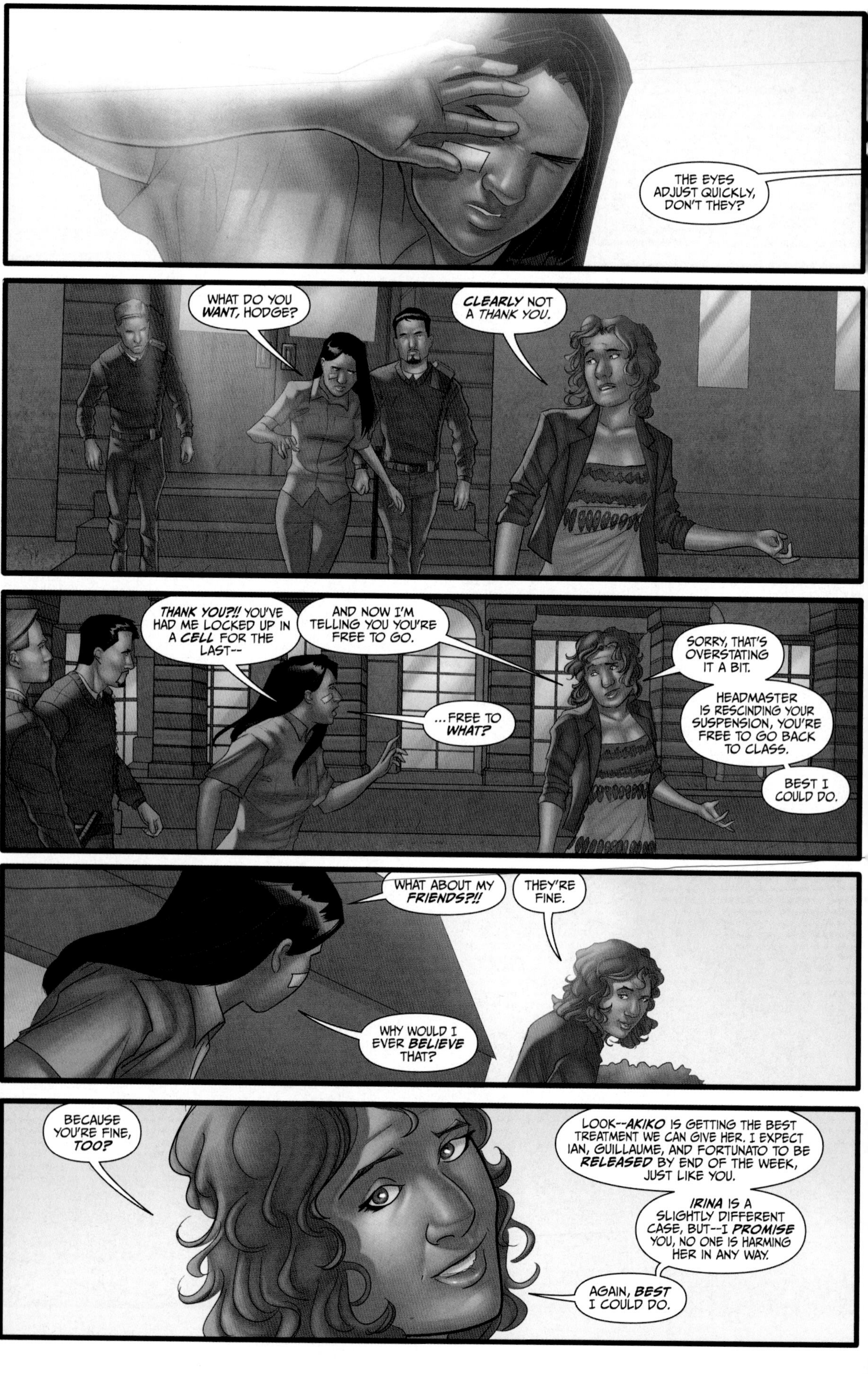
THE EYES ADJUST QUICKLY, DON'T THEY?
WHAT DO YOU WANT, HODGE?
CLEARLY NOT A THANK YOU.
THANK YOU?!! YOU'VE HAD ME LOCKED UP IN A CELL FOR THE LAST--
AND NOW I'M TELLING YOU YOU'RE FREE TO GO.
...FREE TO WHAT?
SORRY, THAT'S OVERSTATING IT A BIT.
HEADMASTER IS RESCINDING YOUR SUSPENSION, YOU'RE FREE TO GO BACK TO CLASS.
BEST I COULD DO.
WHAT ABOUT MY FRIENDS?!!
THEY'RE FINE.
WHY WOULD I EVER BELIEVE THAT?
BECAUSE YOU'RE FINE, TOO?
LOOK--AKIKO IS GETTING THE BEST TREATMENT WE CAN GIVE HER. I EXPECT IAN, GUILLAUME, AND FORTUNATO TO BE RELEASED BY END OF THE WEEK, JUST LIKE YOU.
IRINA IS A SLIGHTLY DIFFERENT CASE, BUT--I PROMISE YOU, NO ONE IS HARMING HER IN ANY WAY.
AGAIN, BEST I COULD DO.

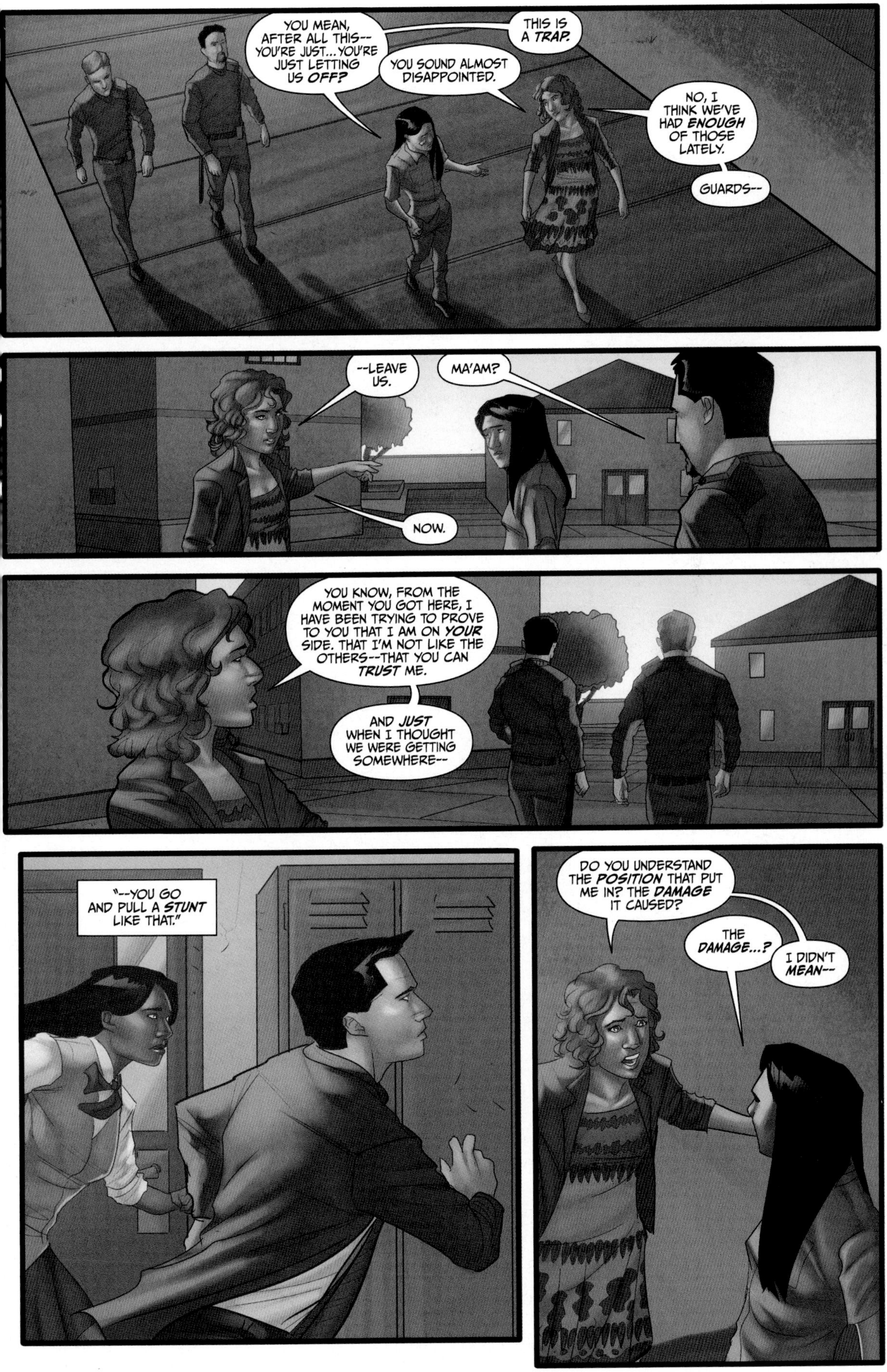
YOU MEAN, AFTER ALL THIS-- YOU'RE JUST...YOU'RE JUST LETTING US *OFF?*
THIS IS A *TRAP.*
YOU SOUND ALMOST DISAPPOINTED.
NO, I THINK WE'VE HAD *ENOUGH* OF THOSE LATELY.
GUARDS--
--LEAVE US.
MA'AM?
NOW.
YOU KNOW, FROM THE MOMENT YOU GOT HERE, I HAVE BEEN TRYING TO PROVE TO YOU THAT I AM ON *YOUR* SIDE. THAT I'M NOT LIKE THE OTHERS--THAT YOU CAN *TRUST* ME.
AND *JUST* WHEN I THOUGHT WE WERE GETTING SOMEWHERE--
"--YOU GO AND PULL A *STUNT* LIKE THAT."
DO YOU UNDERSTAND THE *POSITION* THAT PUT ME IN? THE *DAMAGE* IT CAUSED?
THE *DAMAGE...?*
I DIDN'T *MEAN*--

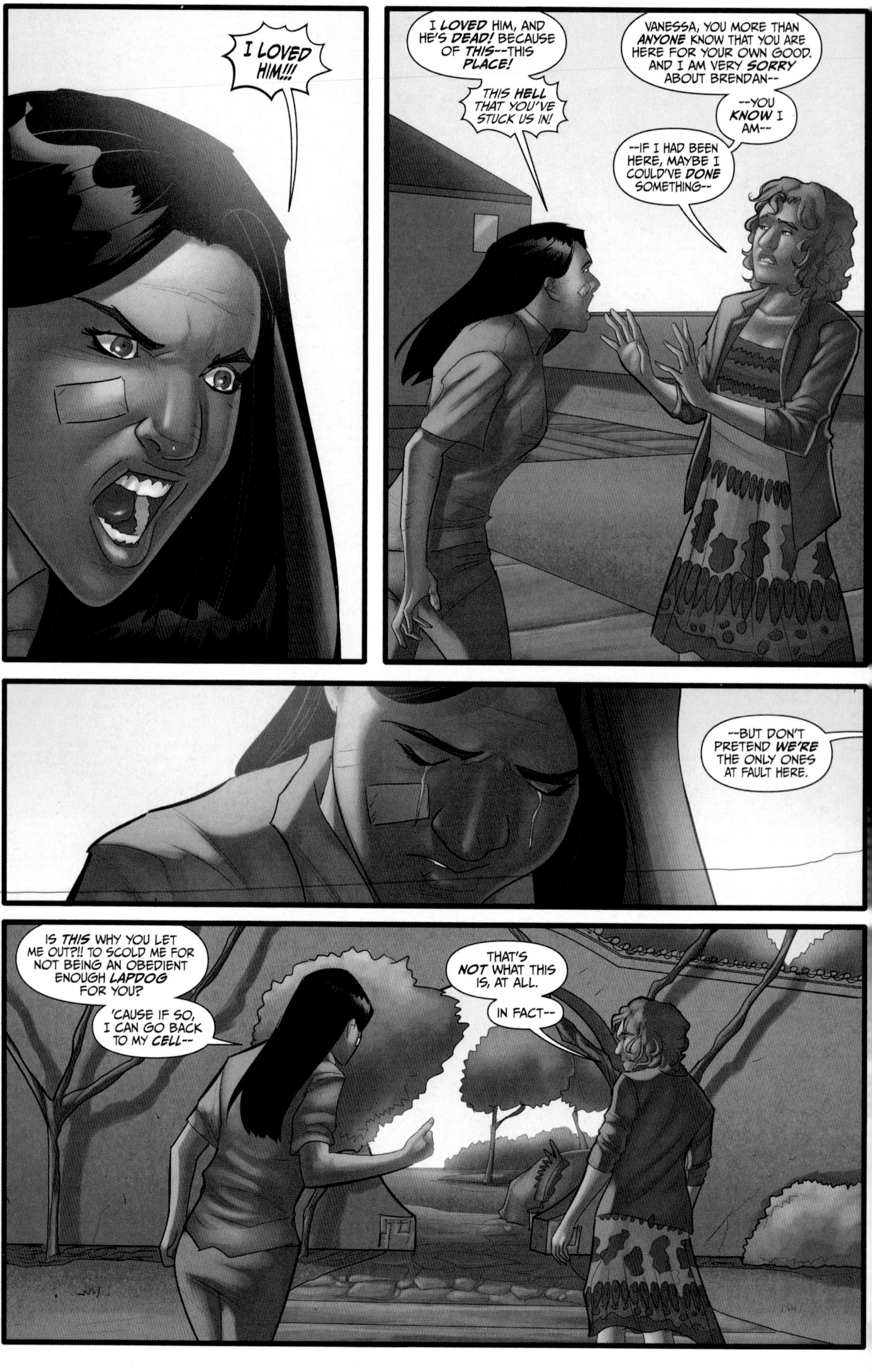
I LOVED HIM!!!
I LOVED HIM, AND HE'S DEAD! BECAUSE OF THIS--THIS PLACE!
THIS HELL THAT YOU'VE STUCK US IN!
VANESSA, YOU MORE THAN ANYONE KNOW THAT YOU ARE HERE FOR YOUR OWN GOOD. AND I AM VERY SORRY ABOUT BRENDAN--
--YOU KNOW I AM--
--IF I HAD BEEN HERE, MAYBE I COULD'VE DONE SOMETHING--
--BUT DON'T PRETEND WE'RE THE ONLY ONES AT FAULT HERE.
IS THIS WHY YOU LET ME OUT?!! TO SCOLD ME FOR NOT BEING AN OBEDIENT ENOUGH LAPDOG FOR YOU?
'CAUSE IF SO, I CAN GO BACK TO MY CELL--
THAT'S NOT WHAT THIS IS, AT ALL.
IN FACT--

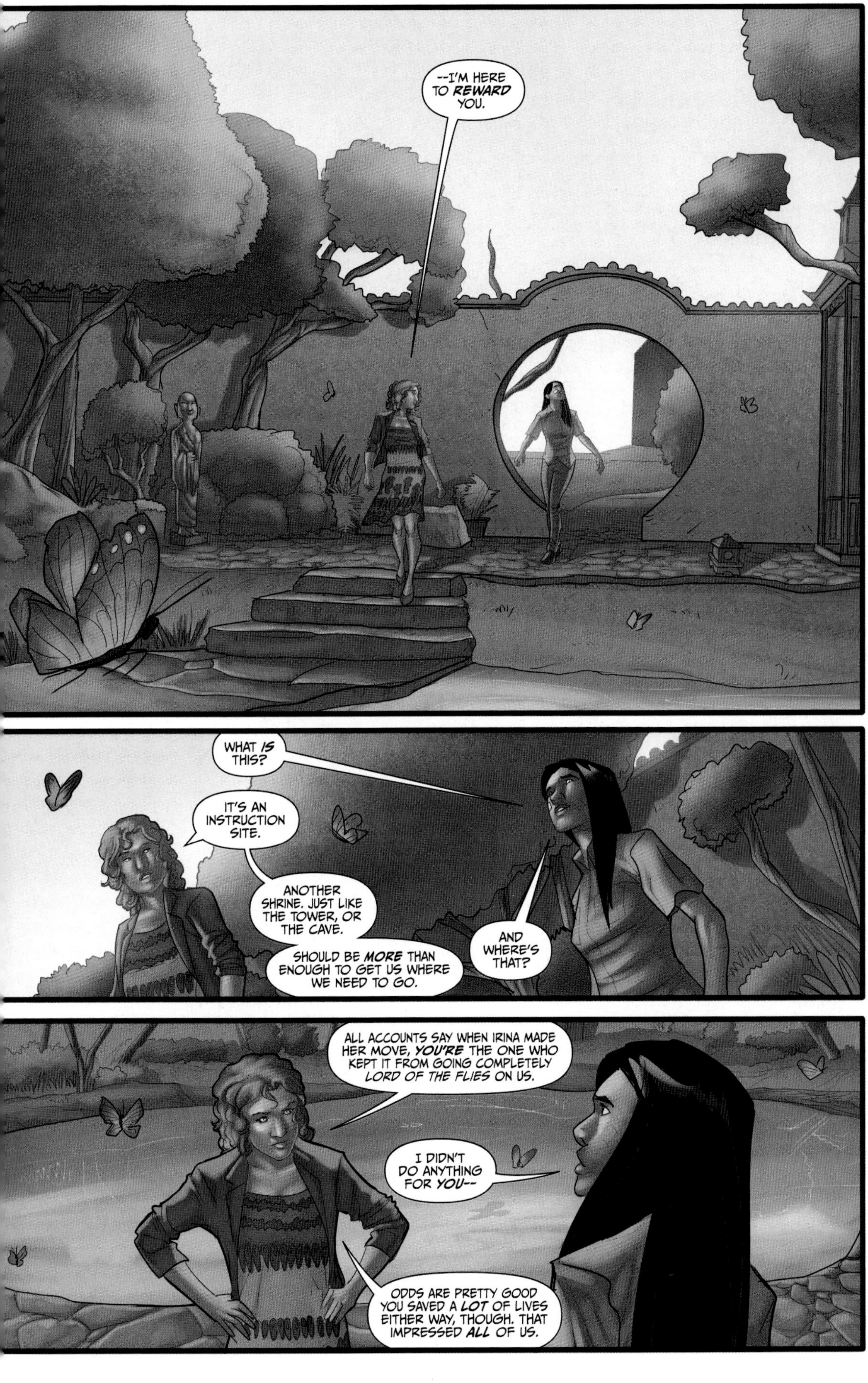
--I'M HERE TO REWARD YOU.
WHAT IS THIS?
IT'S AN INSTRUCTION SITE.
ANOTHER SHRINE. JUST LIKE THE TOWER, OR THE CAVE.
SHOULD BE MORE THAN ENOUGH TO GET US WHERE WE NEED TO GO.
AND WHERE'S THAT?
ALL ACCOUNTS SAY WHEN IRINA MADE HER MOVE, YOU'RE THE ONE WHO KEPT IT FROM GOING COMPLETELY LORD OF THE FLIES ON US.
I DIDN'T DO ANYTHING FOR YOU--
ODDS ARE PRETTY GOOD YOU SAVED A LOT OF LIVES EITHER WAY, THOUGH. THAT IMPRESSED ALL OF US.

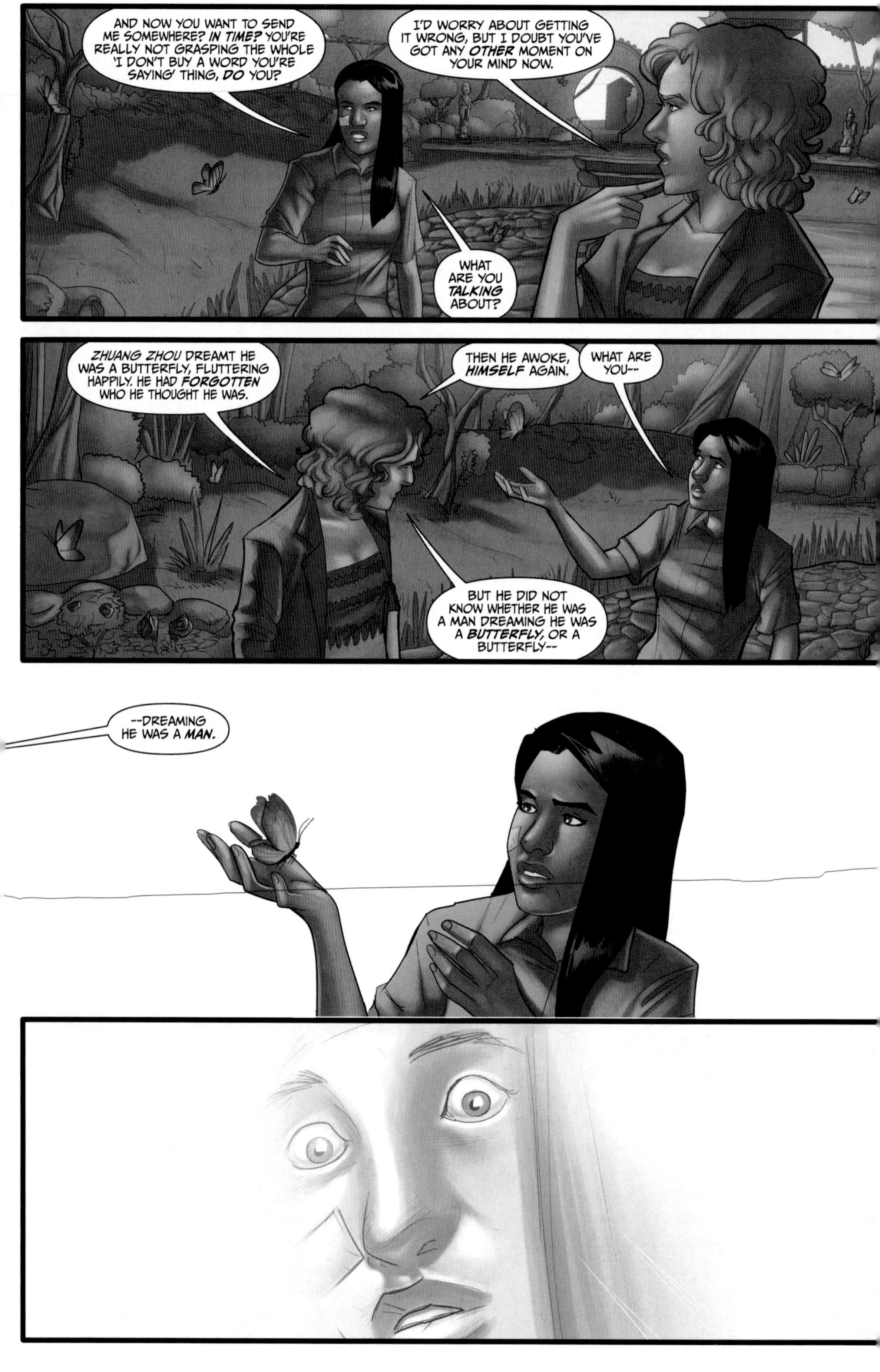
AND NOW YOU WANT TO SEND ME SOMEWHERE? *IN TIME?* YOU'RE REALLY NOT GRASPING THE WHOLE 'I DON'T BUY A WORD YOU'RE SAYING' THING, *DO* YOU?
I'D WORRY ABOUT GETTING IT WRONG, BUT I DOUBT YOU'VE GOT ANY *OTHER* MOMENT ON YOUR MIND NOW.
WHAT ARE YOU *TALKING* ABOUT?
ZHUANG ZHOU DREAMT HE WAS A BUTTERFLY, FLUTTERING HAPPILY. HE HAD *FORGOTTEN* WHO HE THOUGHT HE WAS.
THEN HE AWOKE, *HIMSELF* AGAIN.
WHAT ARE YOU--
BUT HE DID NOT KNOW WHETHER HE WAS A MAN DREAMING HE WAS A *BUTTERFLY*, OR A BUTTERFLY--
--DREAMING HE WAS A *MAN.*

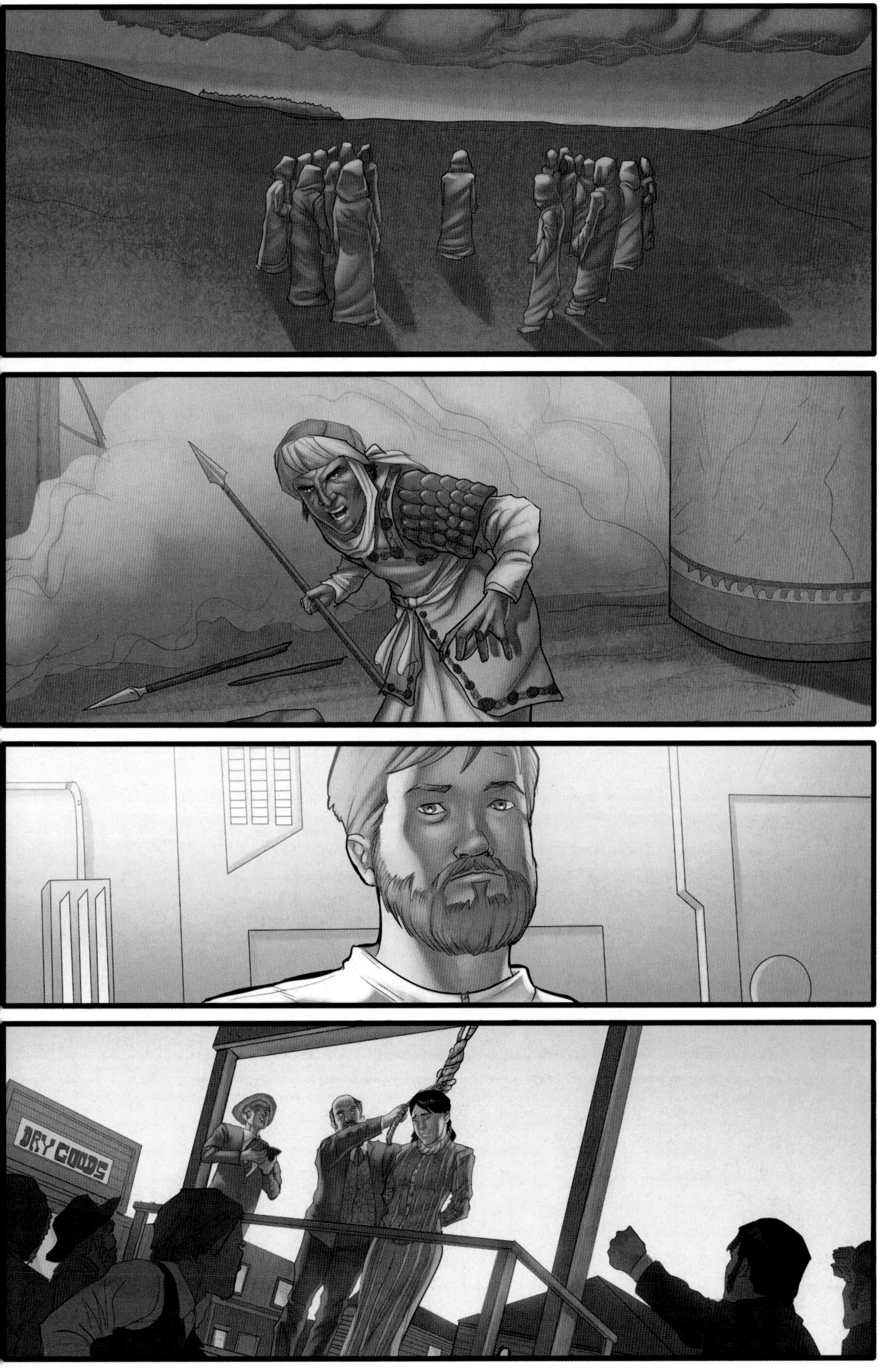
DRY GOODS

EASY--

ʒuhnnʒ

--JUST TAKE IT SLOW--

I'M ALL RIGHT--

ʒhnnʒ

--I'M *FINE.* WHERE *ARE* WE, ANY--

OH.

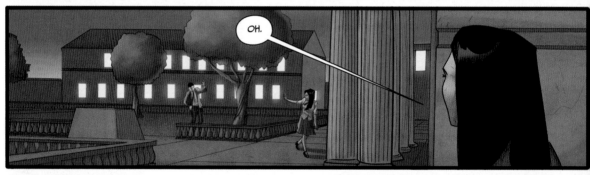

THIS IS--

THE NIGHT BEFORE, YEAH.

--BRENDAN--

GROUND RULES--YOU CAN'T *CHANGE* ANYTHING. YOU'VE ONLY GOT A *FEW* MINUTES. HE'S THE ONLY ONE YOU CAN SEE, NOT THAT YOU PROBABLY *MIND* THAT PART.

I KNOW IT'S NOT A LOT, VANESSA, BUT LOOK AT IT *THIS* WAY--

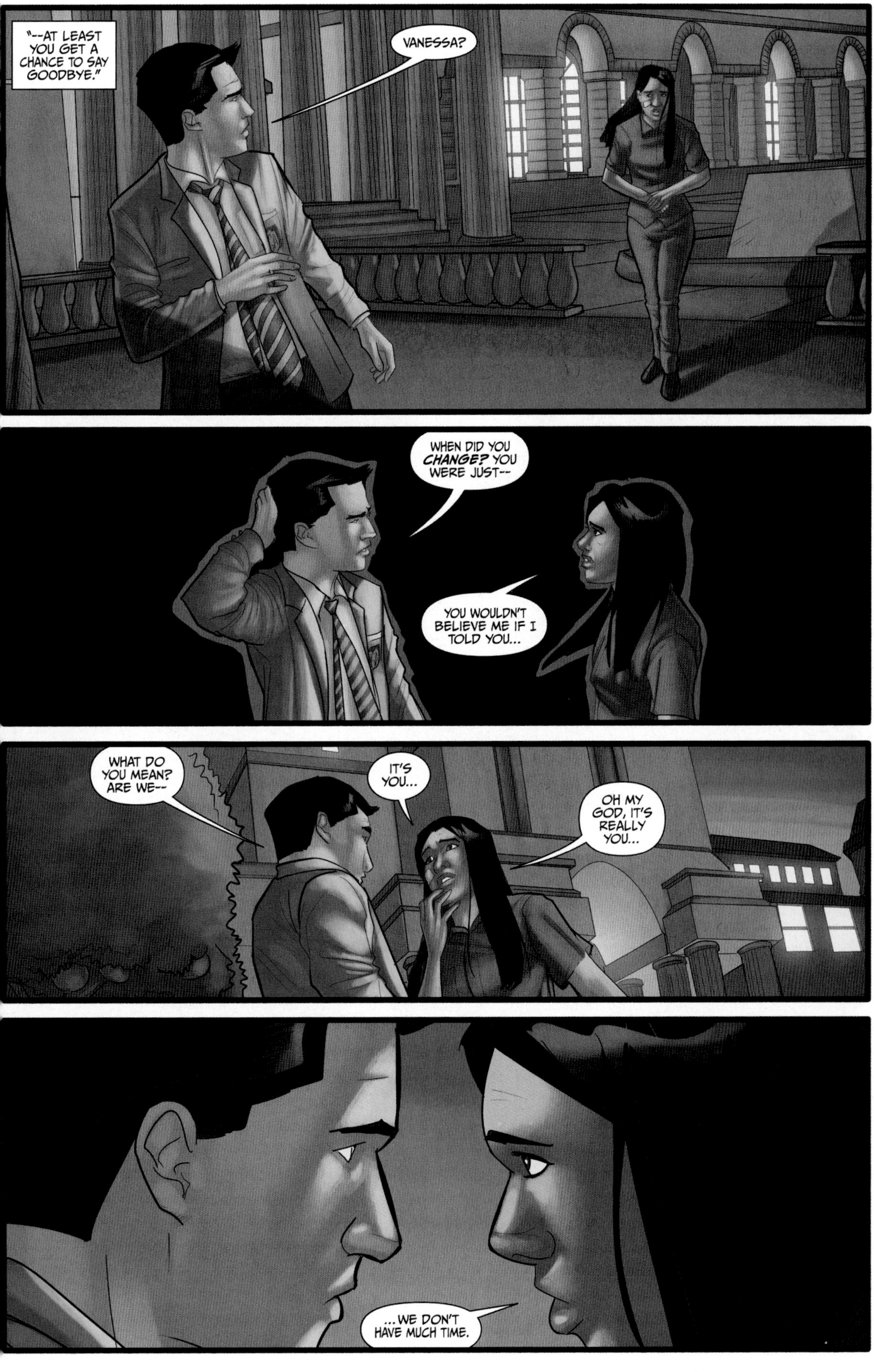
"--AT LEAST YOU GET A CHANCE TO SAY GOODBYE."
VANESSA?
WHEN DID YOU CHANGE? YOU WERE JUST--
YOU WOULDN'T BELIEVE ME IF I TOLD YOU...
WHAT DO YOU MEAN? ARE WE--
IT'S YOU...
OH MY GOD, IT'S REALLY YOU...
...WE DON'T HAVE MUCH TIME.

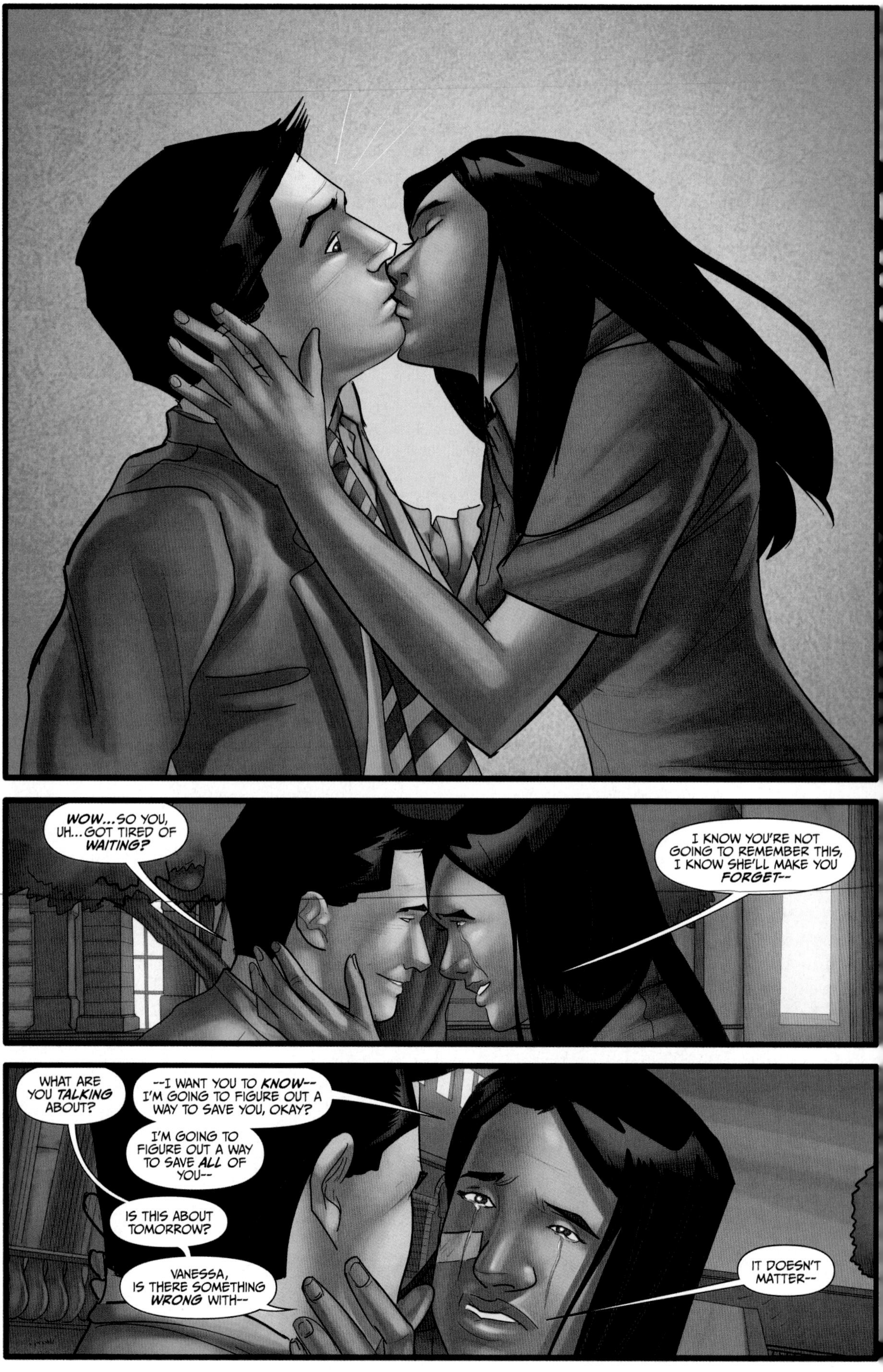
WOW...SO YOU, UH...GOT TIRED OF WAITING?
I KNOW YOU'RE NOT GOING TO REMEMBER THIS, I KNOW SHE'LL MAKE YOU FORGET--
WHAT ARE YOU TALKING ABOUT?
--I WANT YOU TO KNOW-- I'M GOING TO FIGURE OUT A WAY TO SAVE YOU, OKAY?
I'M GOING TO FIGURE OUT A WAY TO SAVE ALL OF YOU--
IS THIS ABOUT TOMORROW?
VANESSA, IS THERE SOMETHING WRONG WITH--
IT DOESN'T MATTER--

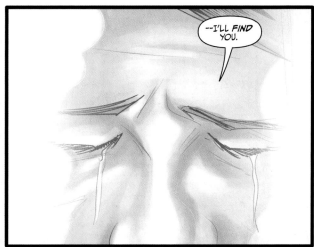

--I'LL *FIND* YOU.

I LOVE YOU *SO MUCH,* BRENDAN. I DON'T KNOW WHY I WAS SO SCARED, WHY I DIDN'T TELL YOU--I *SHOULD* HAVE-- WE WASTED *SO MUCH* TIME--

WHEN WE SAY GOODBYE TOMORROW I WANT YOU TO KISS ME AGAIN AND I WANT YOU TO TELL ME YOU'LL *FIND* ME--

--YOU *REMEMBER* THAT, BRENDAN? YOU REMEMBER WHEN WE FIRST MET, WHAT I SAID?

IT'S TRUE--

VANESSA!!!

VANESSA?!!

SHE'S GONE.

HODGE!

HEY, BRENDAN. I'M SO *SORRY*--

--I WISH IT *HAD,* I REALLY DO, BUT THIS--

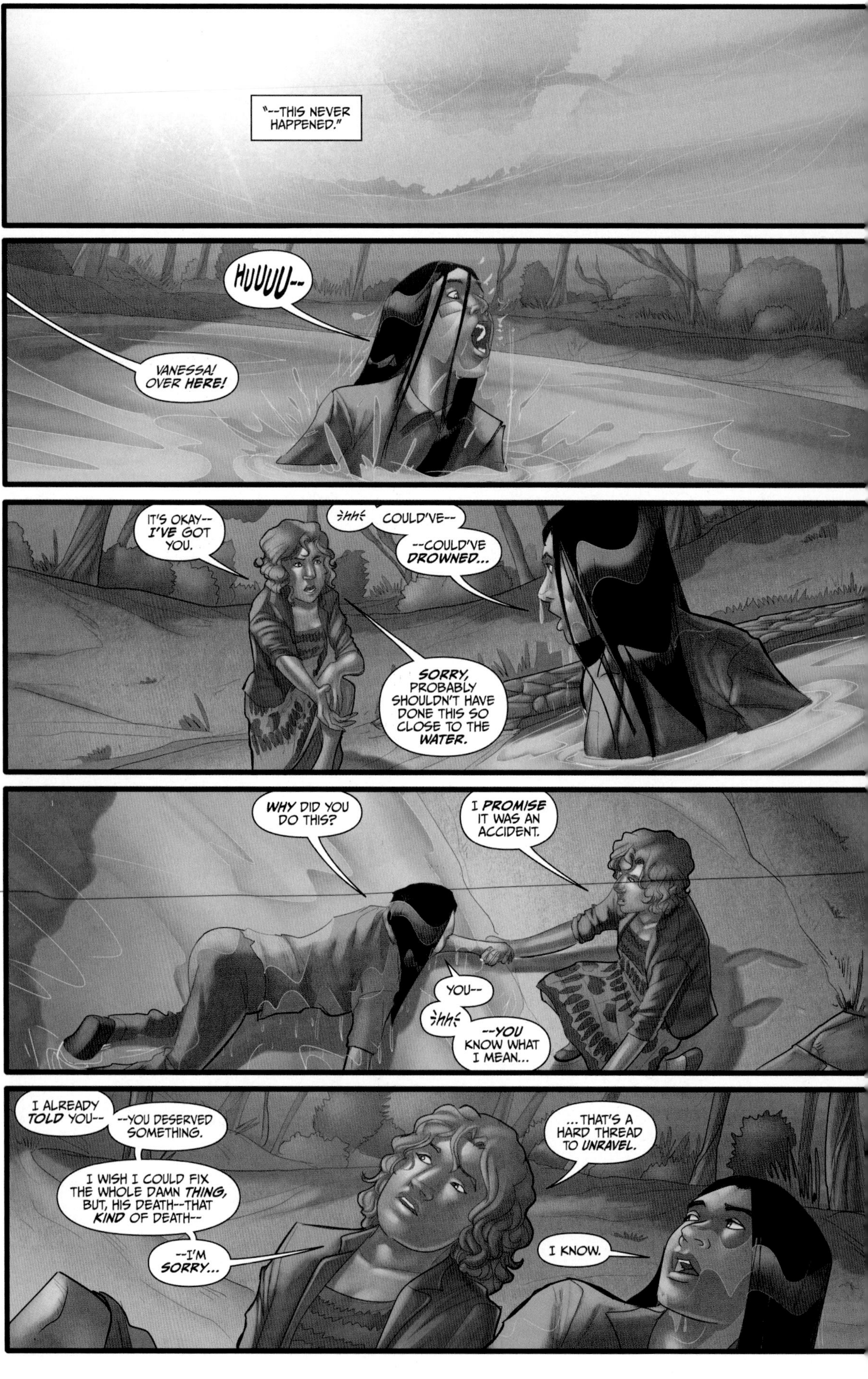
"--THIS NEVER HAPPENED."
HUUUU--
VANESSA! OVER HERE!
IT'S OKAY-- I'VE GOT YOU.
shh
COULD'VE--
--COULD'VE DROWNED...
SORRY, PROBABLY SHOULDN'T HAVE DONE THIS SO CLOSE TO THE WATER.
WHY DID YOU DO THIS?
I PROMISE IT WAS AN ACCIDENT.
YOU--
shh
--YOU KNOW WHAT I MEAN...
I ALREADY TOLD YOU--
--YOU DESERVED SOMETHING.
I WISH I COULD FIX THE WHOLE DAMN THING, BUT, HIS DEATH--THAT KIND OF DEATH--
--I'M SORRY...
...THAT'S A HARD THREAD TO UNRAVEL.
I KNOW.

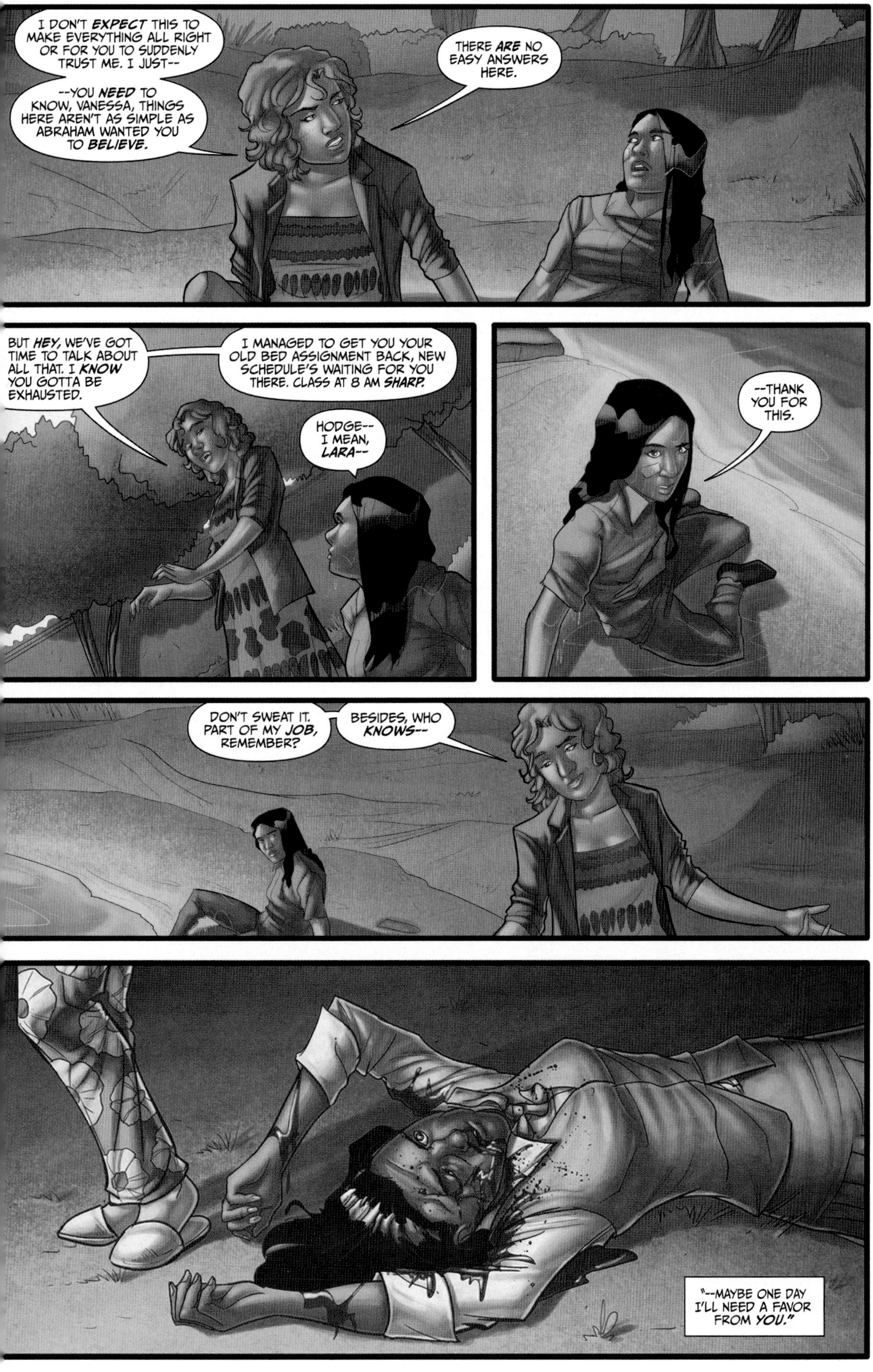
I DON'T *EXPECT* THIS TO MAKE EVERYTHING ALL RIGHT OR FOR YOU TO SUDDENLY TRUST ME. I JUST--
--YOU *NEED* TO KNOW, VANESSA, THINGS HERE AREN'T AS SIMPLE AS ABRAHAM WANTED YOU TO *BELIEVE.*
THERE *ARE* NO EASY ANSWERS HERE.
BUT *HEY,* WE'VE GOT TIME TO TALK ABOUT ALL THAT. I *KNOW* YOU GOTTA BE EXHAUSTED.
I MANAGED TO GET YOU YOUR OLD BED ASSIGNMENT BACK, NEW SCHEDULE'S WAITING FOR YOU THERE. CLASS AT 8 AM *SHARP.*
HODGE-- I MEAN, *LARA--*
--THANK YOU FOR THIS.
DON'T SWEAT IT. PART OF MY *JOB,* REMEMBER?
BESIDES, WHO *KNOWS--*
"--MAYBE ONE DAY I'LL NEED A FAVOR FROM *YOU.*"

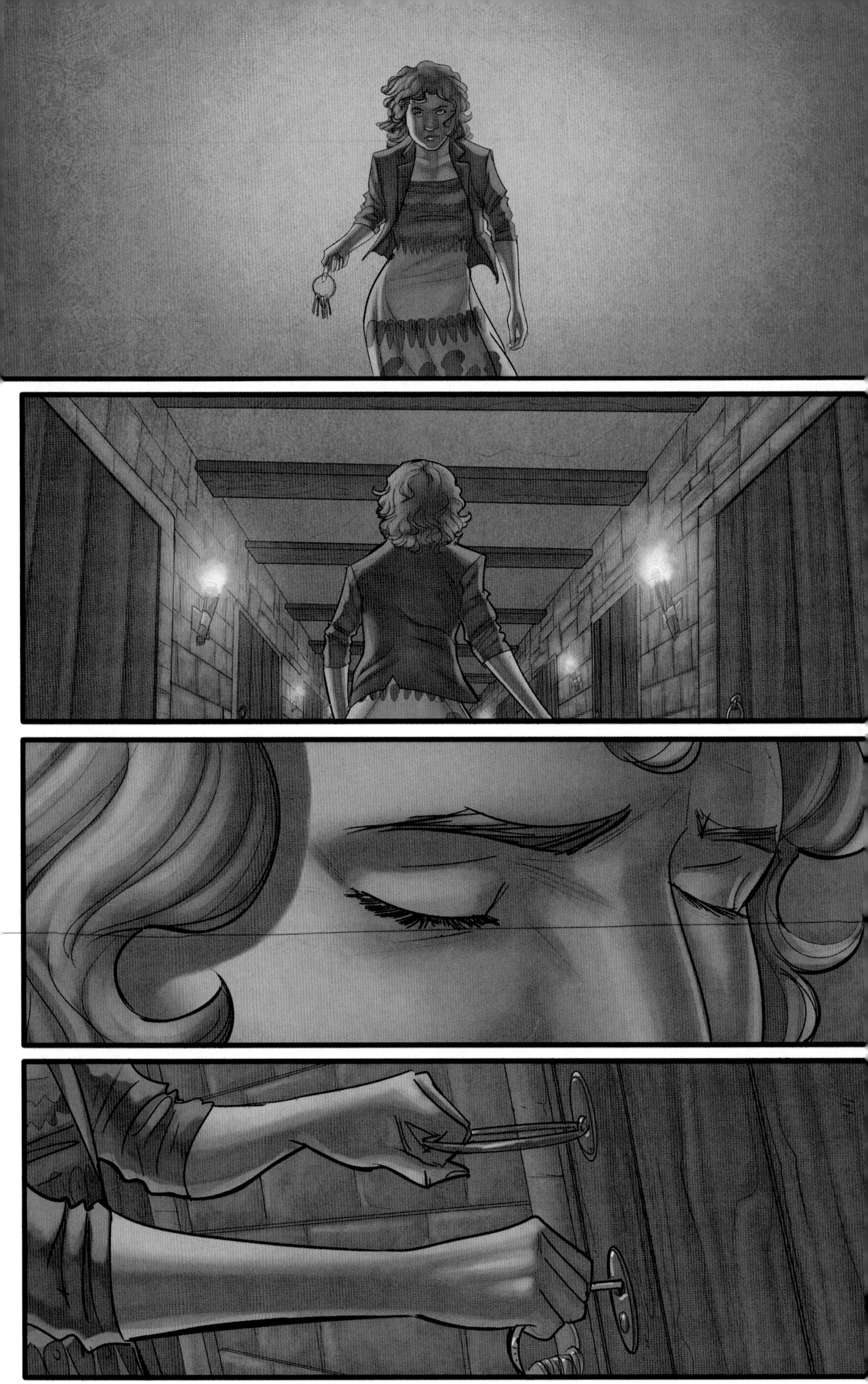

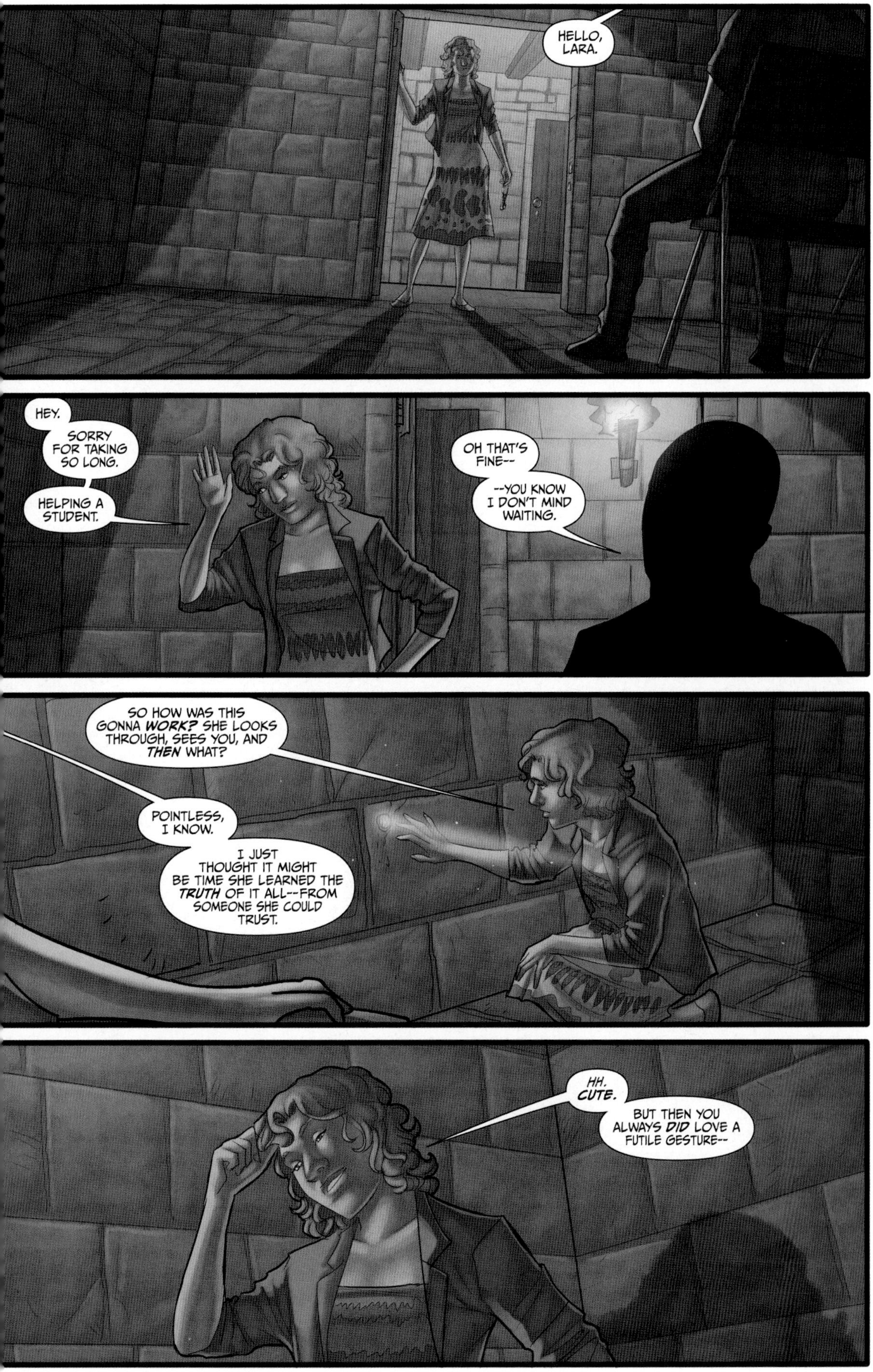
HELLO, LARA.
HEY.
SORRY FOR TAKING SO LONG.
HELPING A STUDENT.
OH THAT'S FINE--
--YOU KNOW I DON'T MIND WAITING.
SO HOW WAS THIS GONNA **WORK?** SHE LOOKS THROUGH, SEES YOU, AND **THEN** WHAT?
POINTLESS, I KNOW.
I JUST THOUGHT IT MIGHT BE TIME SHE LEARNED THE **TRUTH** OF IT ALL--FROM SOMEONE SHE COULD TRUST.
HH. **CUTE.**
BUT THEN YOU ALWAYS **DID** LOVE A FUTILE GESTURE--

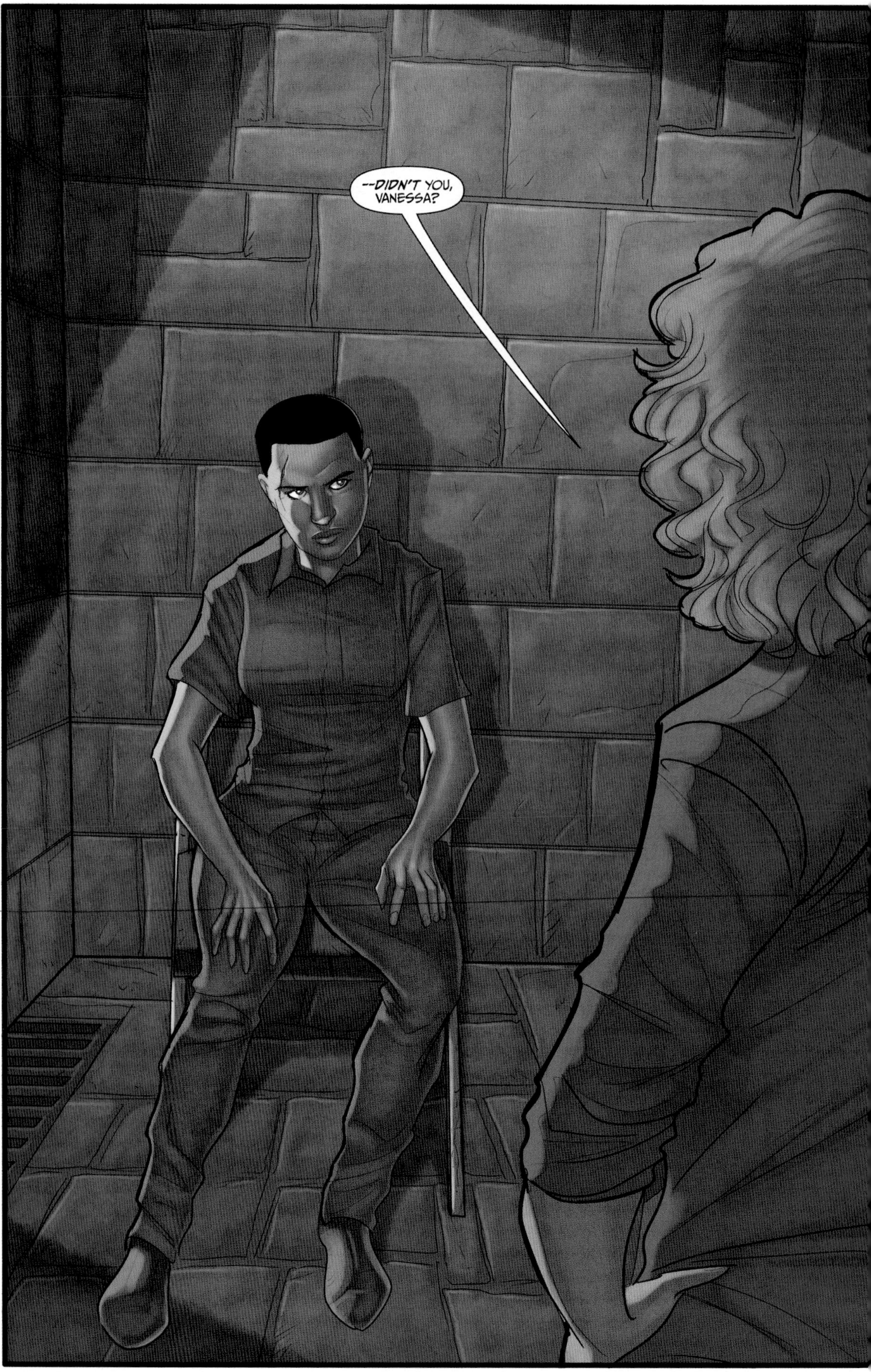
--DIDN'T YOU, VANESSA?

thirty**three**

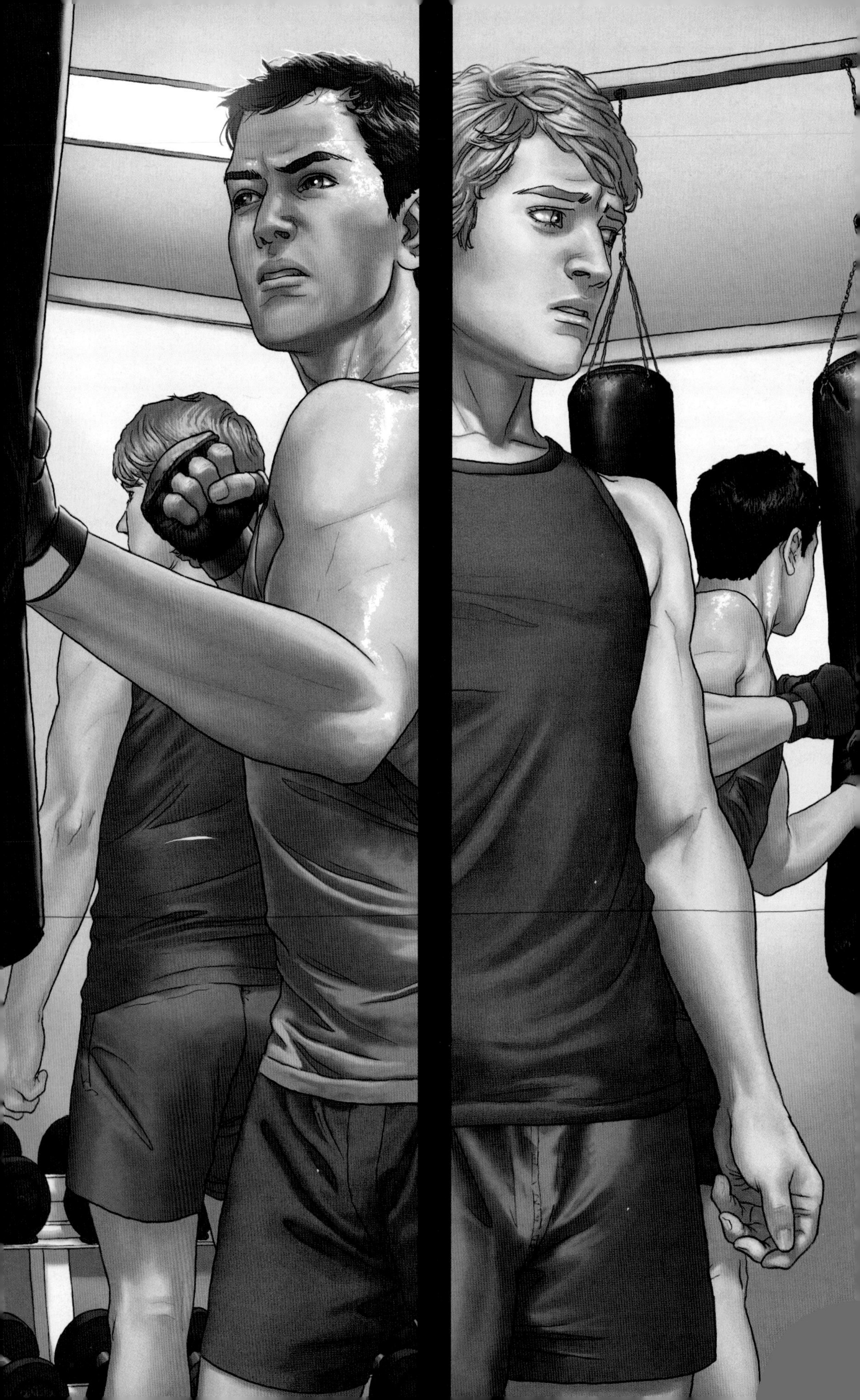

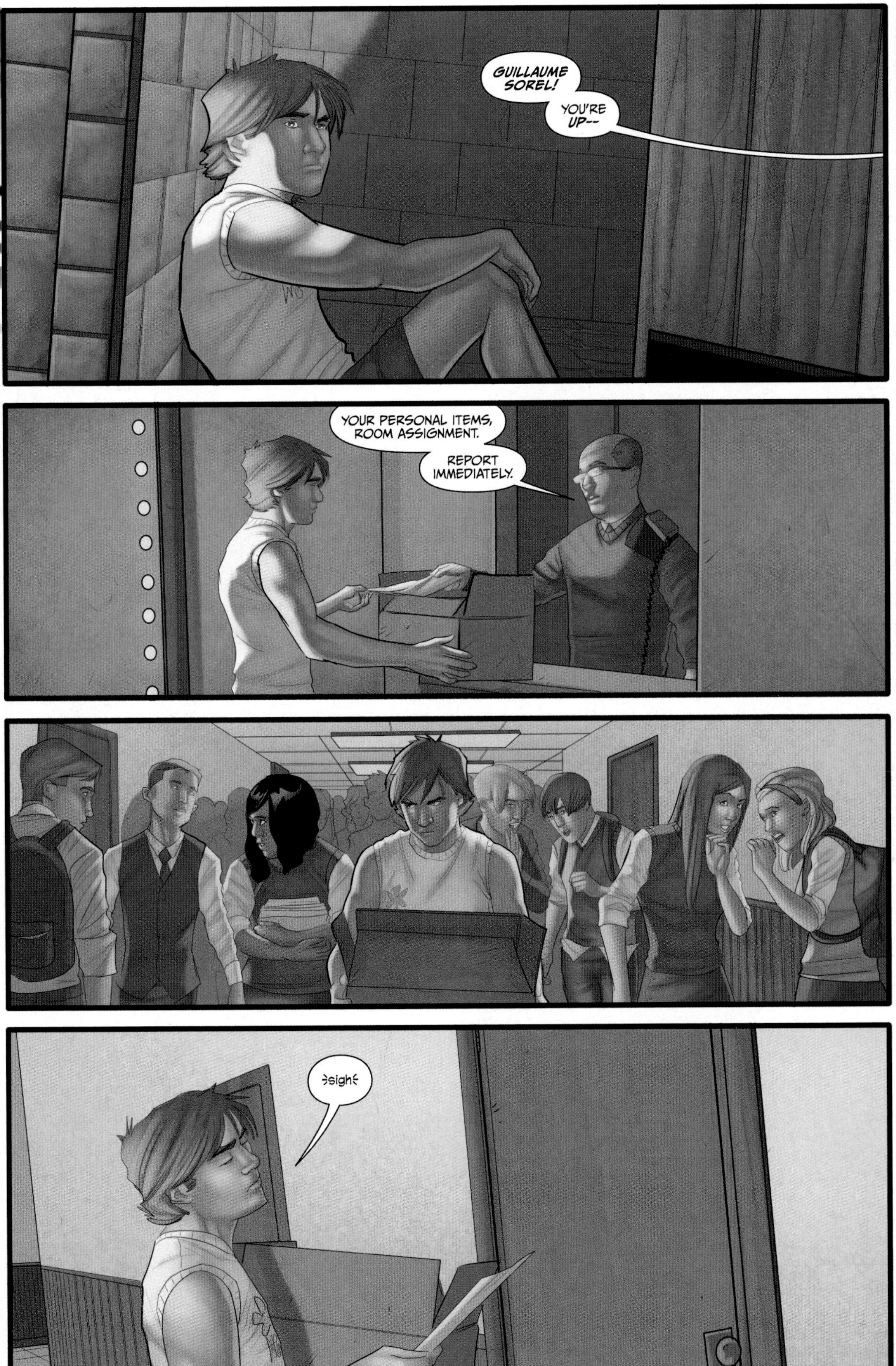
GUILLAUME SOREL!
YOU'RE UP--
YOUR PERSONAL ITEMS, ROOM ASSIGNMENT.
REPORT IMMEDIATELY.
sigh

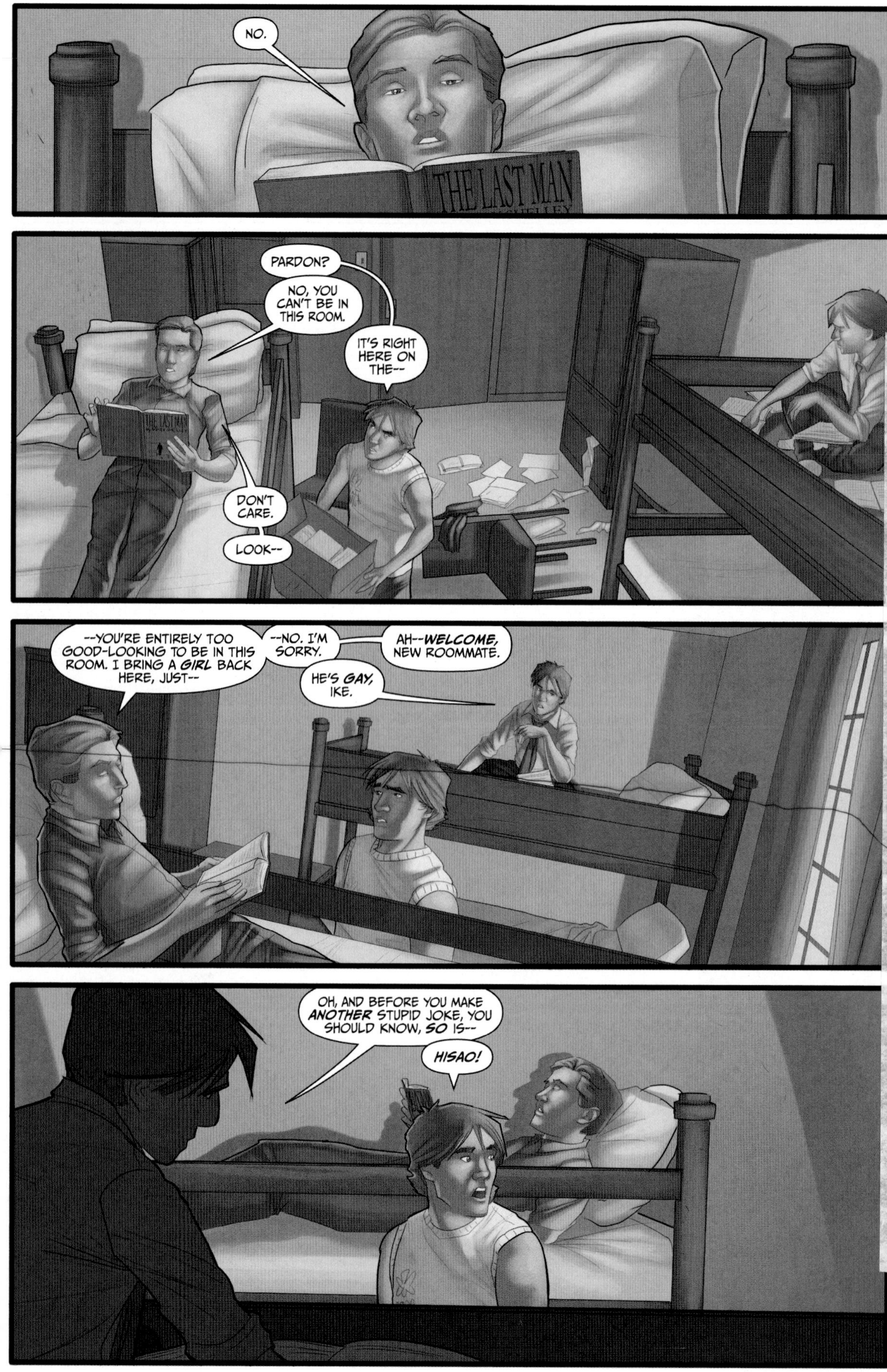
NO.
THE LAST MAN
PARDON?
NO, YOU CAN'T BE IN THIS ROOM.
IT'S RIGHT HERE ON THE--
DON'T CARE.
LOOK--
--YOU'RE ENTIRELY TOO GOOD-LOOKING TO BE IN THIS ROOM. I BRING A GIRL BACK HERE, JUST--
--NO. I'M SORRY.
AH--WELCOME, NEW ROOMMATE.
HE'S GAY, IKE.
OH, AND BEFORE YOU MAKE ANOTHER STUPID JOKE, YOU SHOULD KNOW, SO IS--
HISAO!

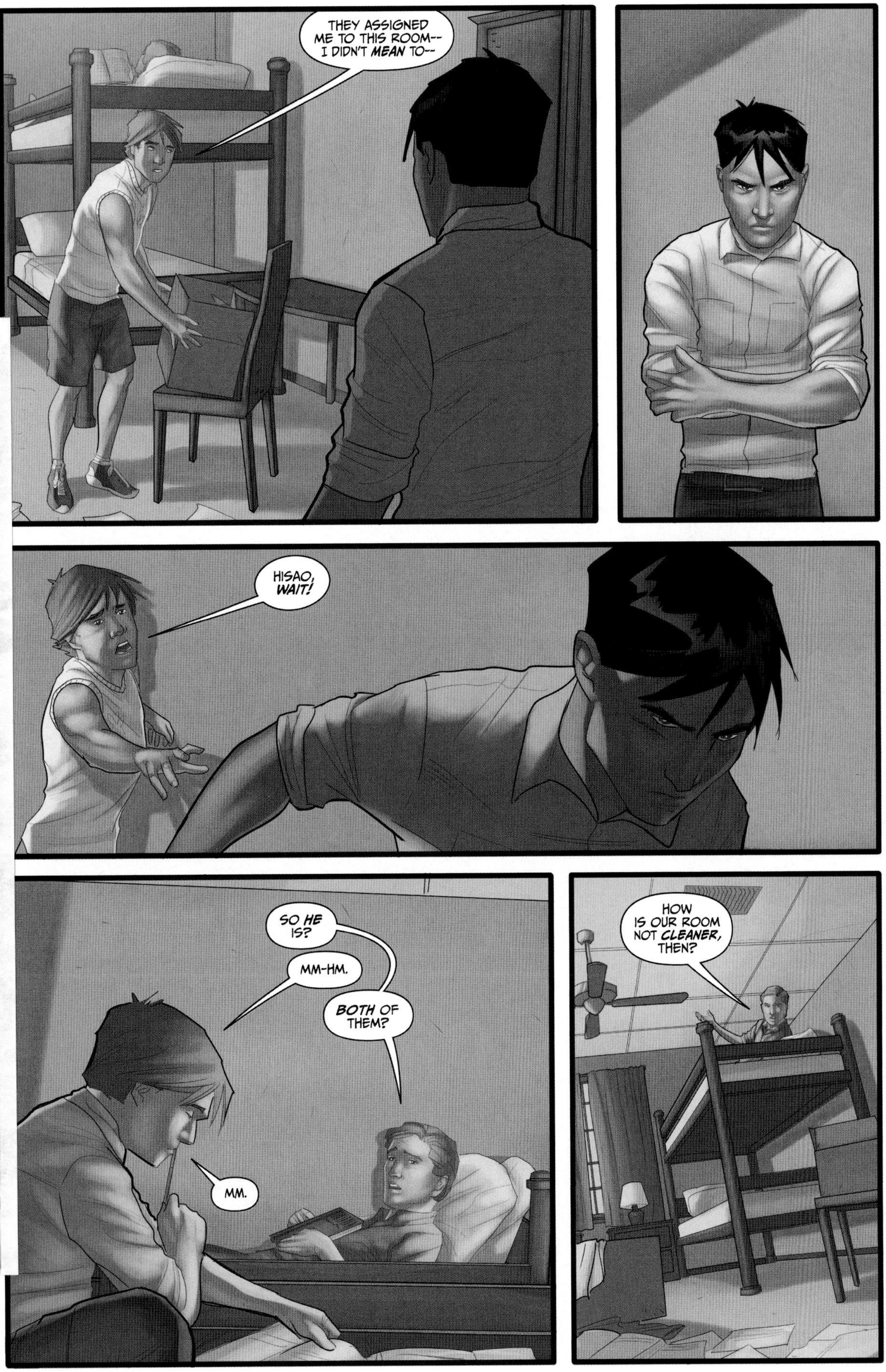
THEY ASSIGNED ME TO THIS ROOM-- I DIDN'T *MEAN* TO--
HISAO, *WAIT!*
SO *HE* IS?
MM-HM.
BOTH OF THEM?
MM.
HOW IS OUR ROOM NOT *CLEANER,* THEN?

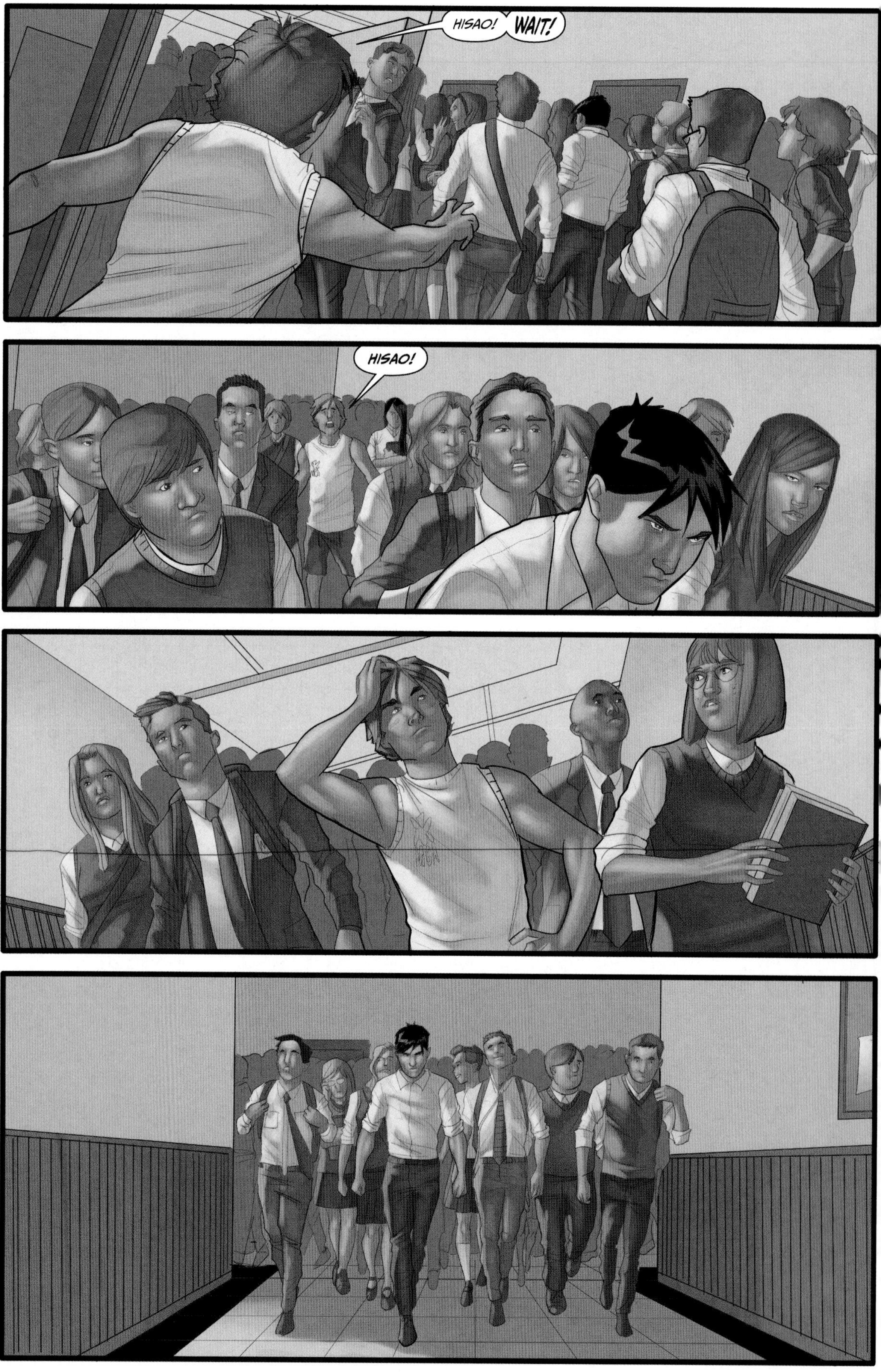
HISAO!
WAIT!
HISAO!

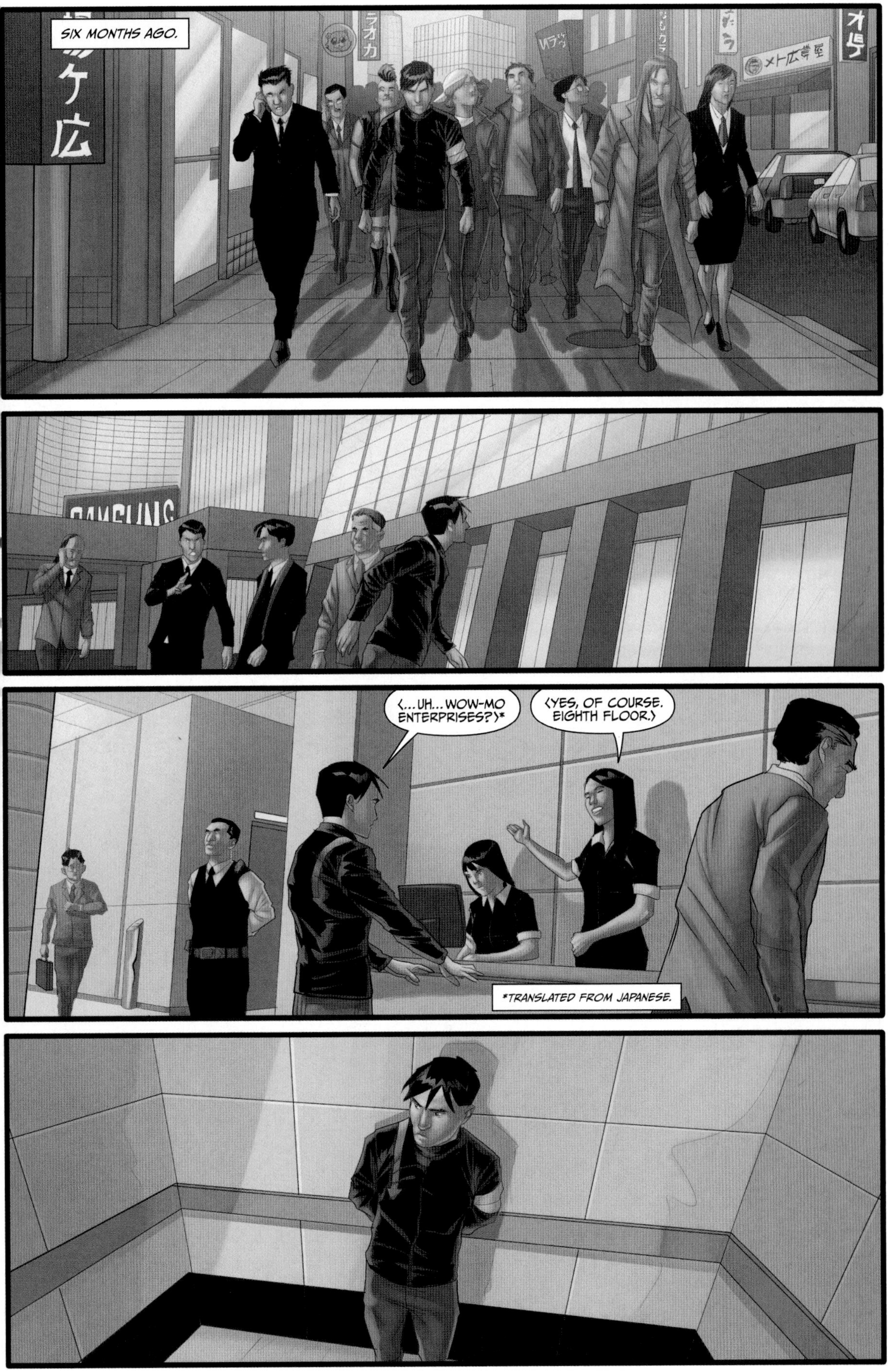
SIX MONTHS AGO.
‹...UH...WOW-MO ENTERPRISES?›*
‹YES, OF COURSE. EIGHTH FLOOR.›
*TRANSLATED FROM JAPANESE.

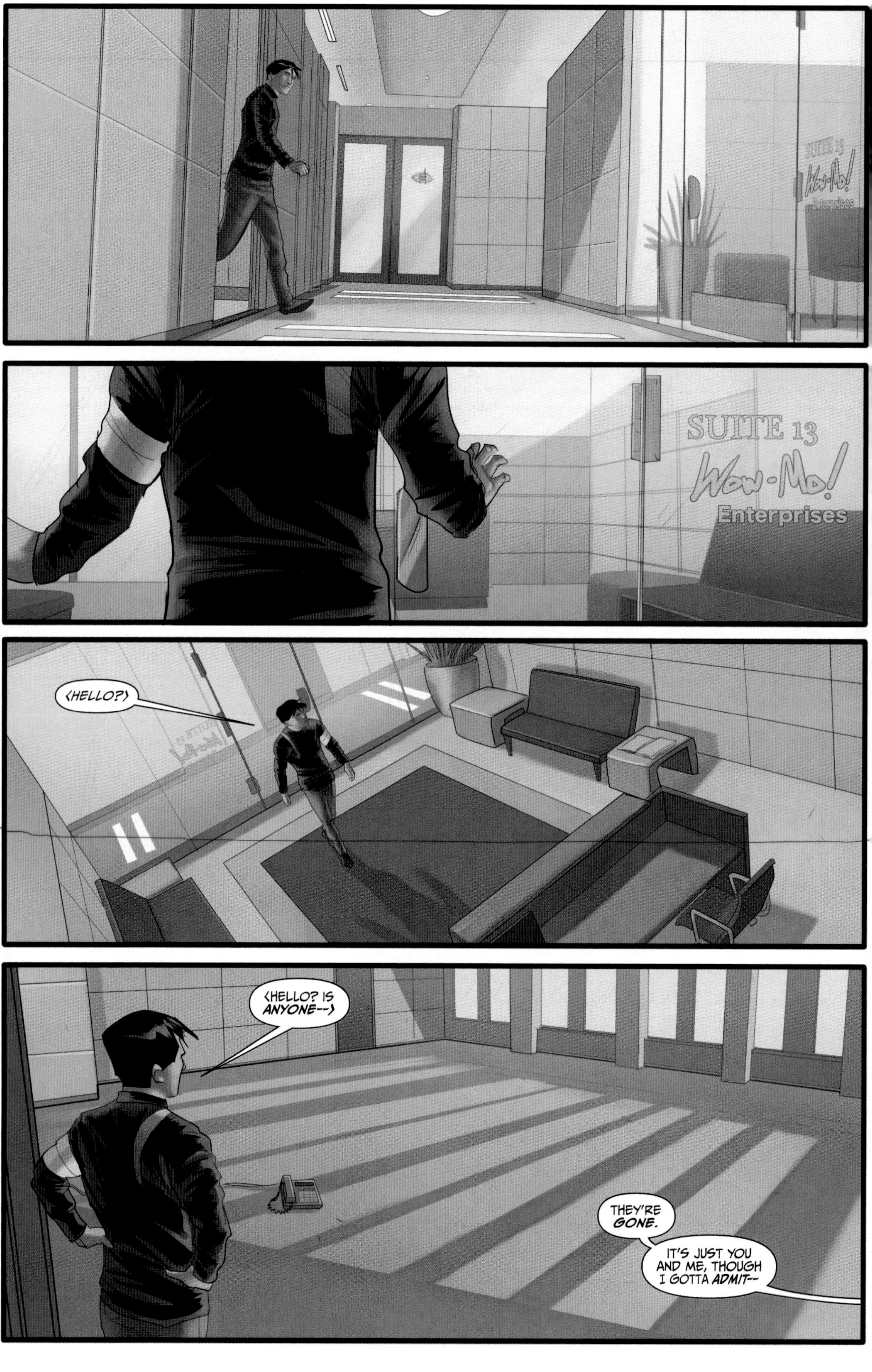
SUITE 13
Wow-Mo!
Enterprises
SUITE 13
Wow-Mo!
Enterprises
‹HELLO?›
‹HELLO? IS ANYONE--›
THEY'RE GONE.
IT'S JUST YOU AND ME, THOUGH I GOTTA ADMIT--

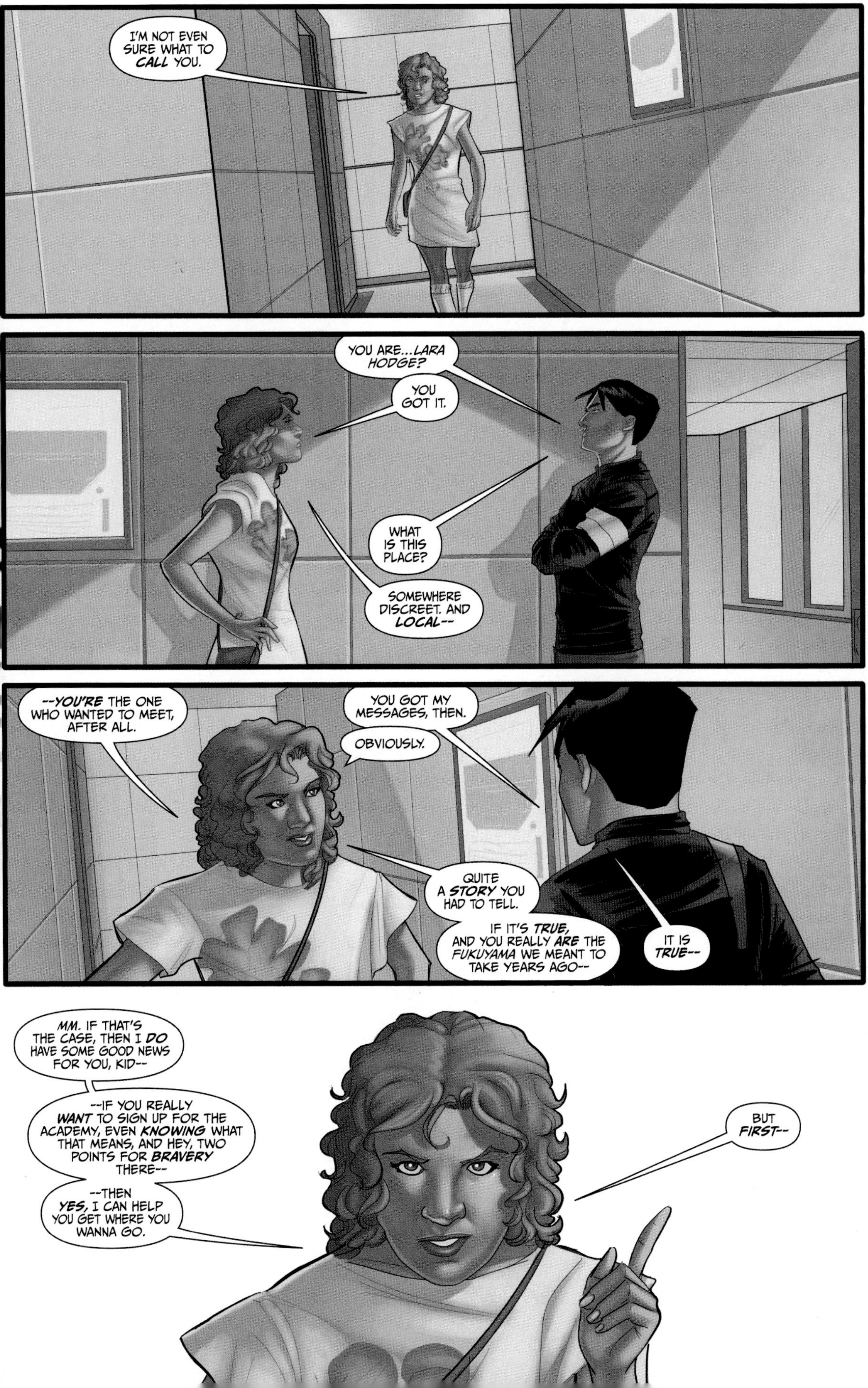
I'M NOT EVEN SURE WHAT TO CALL YOU.
YOU ARE...LARA HODGE?
YOU GOT IT.
WHAT IS THIS PLACE?
SOMEWHERE DISCREET. AND LOCAL--
--YOU'RE THE ONE WHO WANTED TO MEET, AFTER ALL.
YOU GOT MY MESSAGES, THEN.
OBVIOUSLY.
QUITE A STORY YOU HAD TO TELL.
IF IT'S TRUE, AND YOU REALLY ARE THE FUKUYAMA WE MEANT TO TAKE YEARS AGO--
IT IS TRUE--
MM. IF THAT'S THE CASE, THEN I DO HAVE SOME GOOD NEWS FOR YOU, KID--
--IF YOU REALLY WANT TO SIGN UP FOR THE ACADEMY, EVEN KNOWING WHAT THAT MEANS, AND HEY, TWO POINTS FOR BRAVERY THERE--
--THEN YES, I CAN HELP YOU GET WHERE YOU WANNA GO.
BUT FIRST--

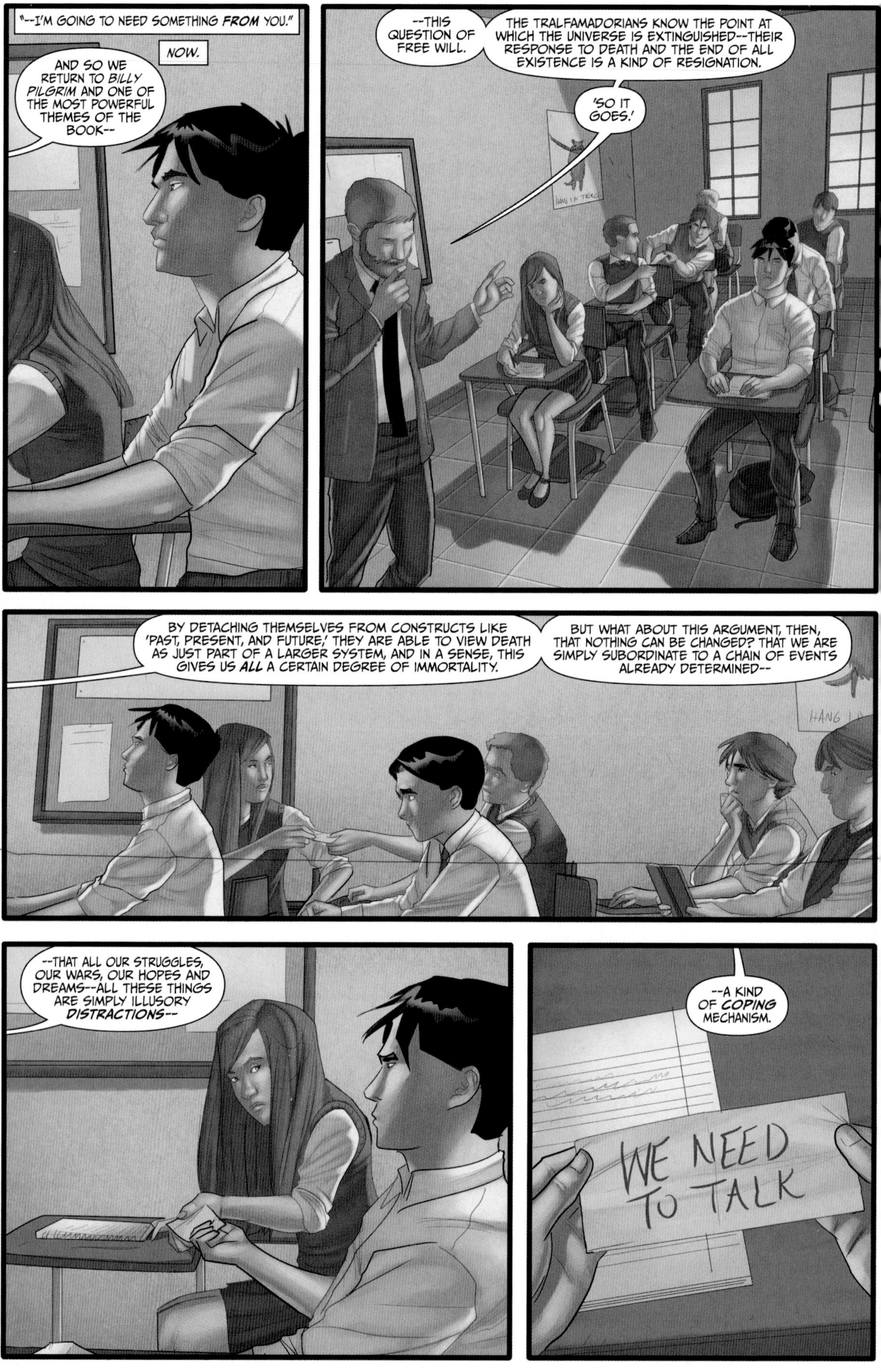
"--I'M GOING TO NEED SOMETHING FROM YOU."
NOW.
AND SO WE RETURN TO BILLY PILGRIM AND ONE OF THE MOST POWERFUL THEMES OF THE BOOK--
--THIS QUESTION OF FREE WILL.
THE TRALFAMADORIANS KNOW THE POINT AT WHICH THE UNIVERSE IS EXTINGUISHED--THEIR RESPONSE TO DEATH AND THE END OF ALL EXISTENCE IS A KIND OF RESIGNATION.
'SO IT GOES.'
BY DETACHING THEMSELVES FROM CONSTRUCTS LIKE 'PAST, PRESENT, AND FUTURE,' THEY ARE ABLE TO VIEW DEATH AS JUST PART OF A LARGER SYSTEM, AND IN A SENSE, THIS GIVES US ALL A CERTAIN DEGREE OF IMMORTALITY.
BUT WHAT ABOUT THIS ARGUMENT, THEN, THAT NOTHING CAN BE CHANGED? THAT WE ARE SIMPLY SUBORDINATE TO A CHAIN OF EVENTS ALREADY DETERMINED--
--THAT ALL OUR STRUGGLES, OUR WARS, OUR HOPES AND DREAMS--ALL THESE THINGS ARE SIMPLY ILLUSORY DISTRACTIONS--
--A KIND OF COPING MECHANISM.
WE NEED TO TALK

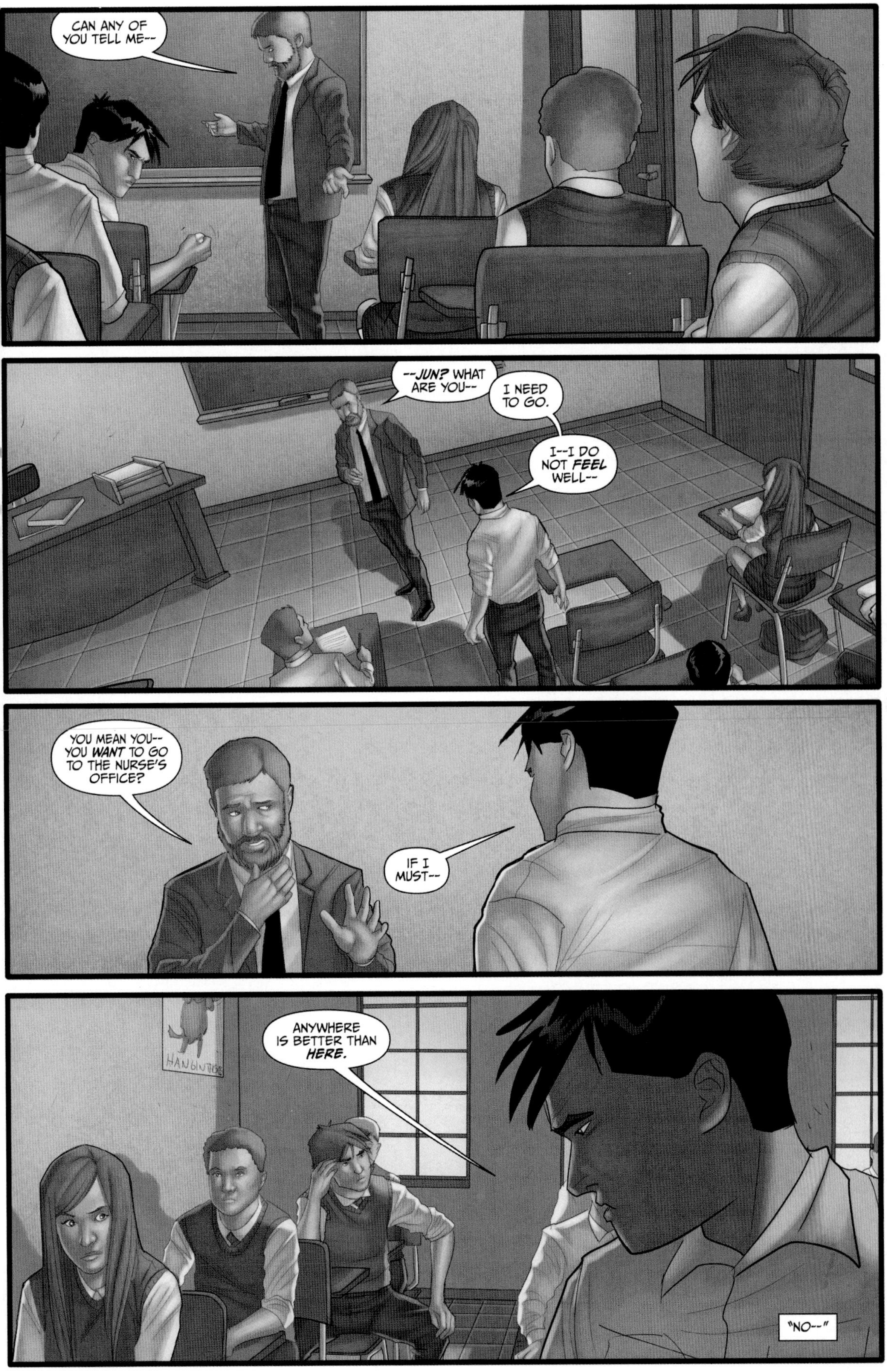
CAN ANY OF YOU TELL ME--
--JUN? WHAT ARE YOU--
I NEED TO GO.
I--I DO NOT FEEL WELL--
YOU MEAN YOU--YOU WANT TO GO TO THE NURSE'S OFFICE?
IF I MUST--
ANYWHERE IS BETTER THAN HERE.
"NO--"

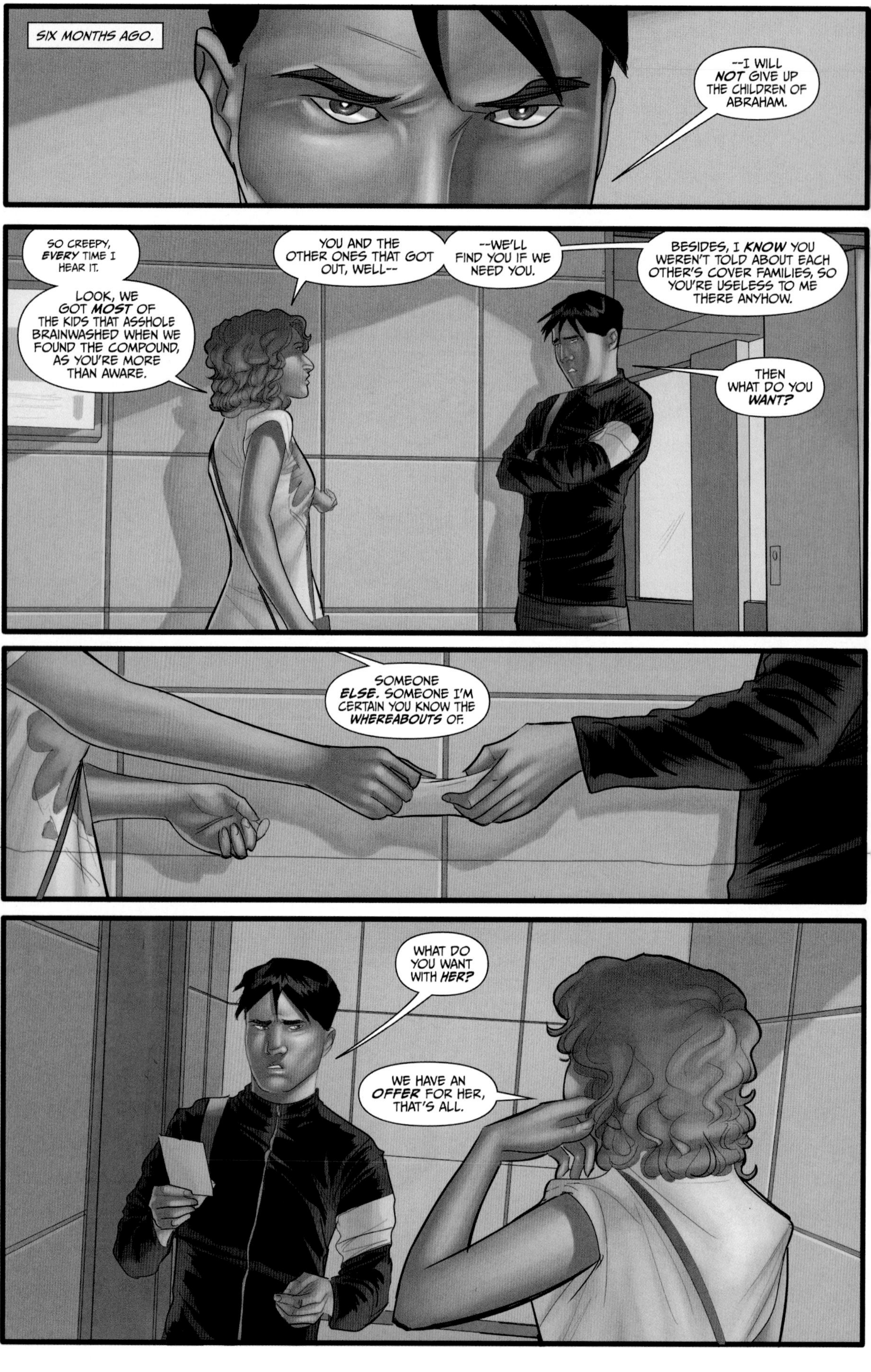

SIX MONTHS AGO.
--I WILL NOT GIVE UP THE CHILDREN OF ABRAHAM.
SO CREEPY, EVERY TIME I HEAR IT.
LOOK, WE GOT MOST OF THE KIDS THAT ASSHOLE BRAINWASHED WHEN WE FOUND THE COMPOUND, AS YOU'RE MORE THAN AWARE.
YOU AND THE OTHER ONES THAT GOT OUT, WELL--
--WE'LL FIND YOU IF WE NEED YOU.
BESIDES, I KNOW YOU WEREN'T TOLD ABOUT EACH OTHER'S COVER FAMILIES, SO YOU'RE USELESS TO ME THERE ANYHOW.
THEN WHAT DO YOU WANT?
SOMEONE ELSE. SOMEONE I'M CERTAIN YOU KNOW THE WHEREABOUTS OF.
WHAT DO YOU WANT WITH HER?
WE HAVE AN OFFER FOR HER, THAT'S ALL.

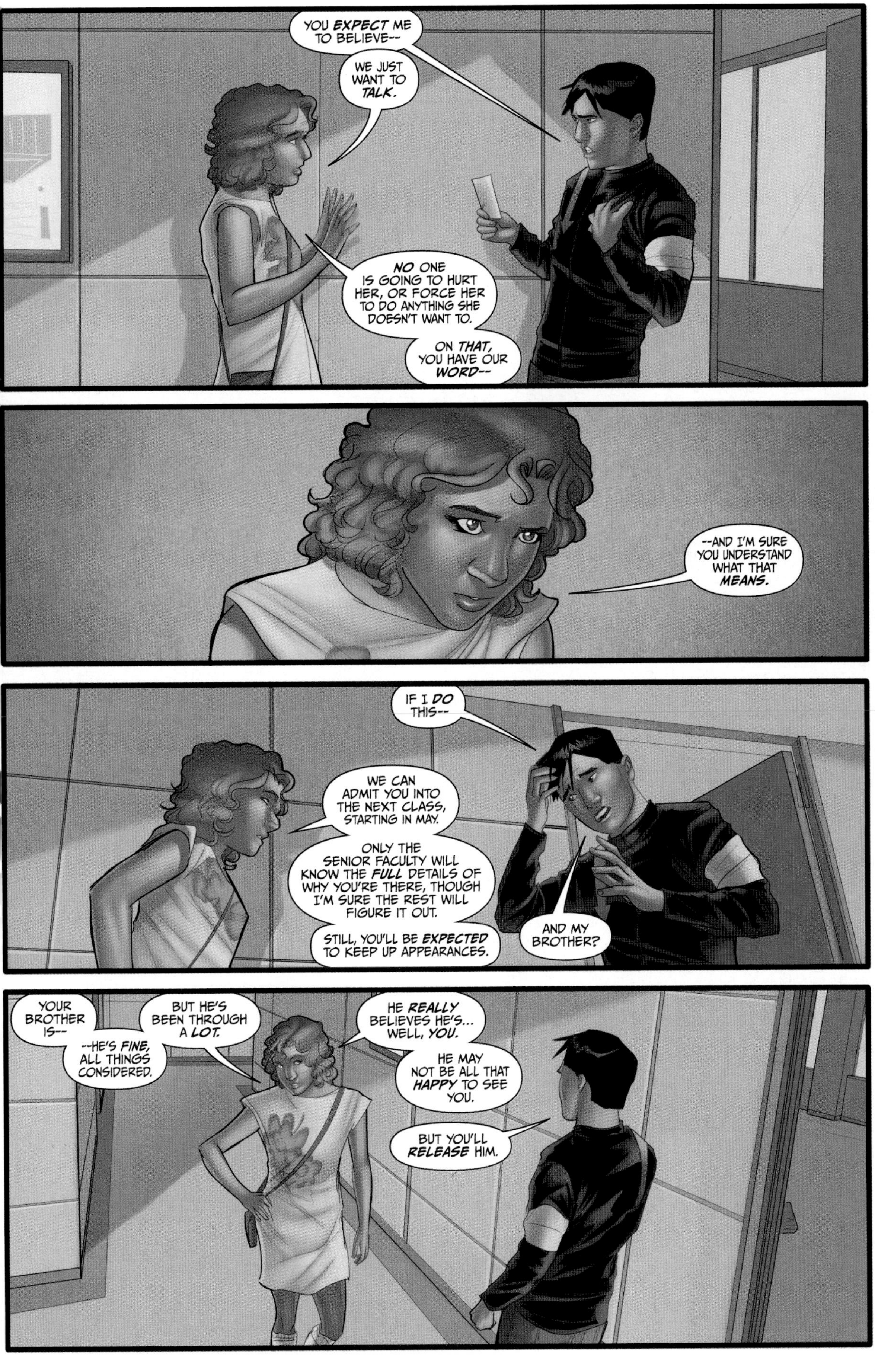
YOU EXPECT ME TO BELIEVE--
WE JUST WANT TO TALK.
NO ONE IS GOING TO HURT HER, OR FORCE HER TO DO ANYTHING SHE DOESN'T WANT TO.
ON THAT, YOU HAVE OUR WORD--
--AND I'M SURE YOU UNDERSTAND WHAT THAT MEANS.
IF I DO THIS--
WE CAN ADMIT YOU INTO THE NEXT CLASS, STARTING IN MAY.
ONLY THE SENIOR FACULTY WILL KNOW THE FULL DETAILS OF WHY YOU'RE THERE, THOUGH I'M SURE THE REST WILL FIGURE IT OUT.
STILL, YOU'LL BE EXPECTED TO KEEP UP APPEARANCES.
AND MY BROTHER?
YOUR BROTHER IS--
--HE'S FINE, ALL THINGS CONSIDERED.
BUT HE'S BEEN THROUGH A LOT.
HE REALLY BELIEVES HE'S... WELL, YOU.
HE MAY NOT BE ALL THAT HAPPY TO SEE YOU.
BUT YOU'LL RELEASE HIM.

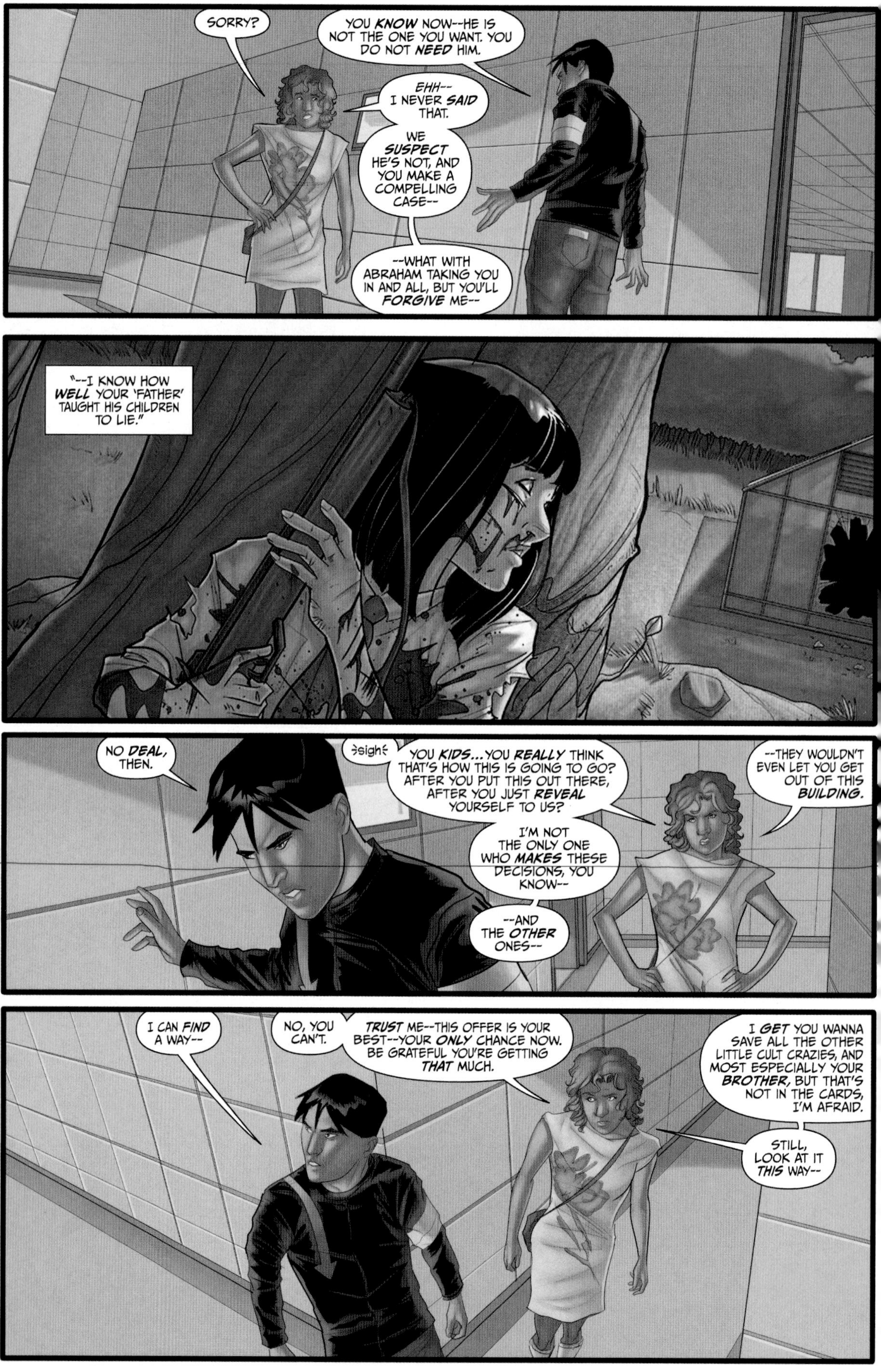
SORRY?
YOU KNOW NOW--HE IS NOT THE ONE YOU WANT. YOU DO NOT NEED HIM.
EHH-- I NEVER SAID THAT.
WE SUSPECT HE'S NOT, AND YOU MAKE A COMPELLING CASE--
--WHAT WITH ABRAHAM TAKING YOU IN AND ALL, BUT YOU'LL FORGIVE ME--
"--I KNOW HOW WELL YOUR 'FATHER' TAUGHT HIS CHILDREN TO LIE."
NO DEAL, THEN.
sigh
YOU KIDS... YOU REALLY THINK THAT'S HOW THIS IS GOING TO GO? AFTER YOU PUT THIS OUT THERE, AFTER YOU JUST REVEAL YOURSELF TO US?
I'M NOT THE ONLY ONE WHO MAKES THESE DECISIONS, YOU KNOW--
--AND THE OTHER ONES--
--THEY WOULDN'T EVEN LET YOU GET OUT OF THIS BUILDING.
I CAN FIND A WAY--
NO, YOU CAN'T.
TRUST ME--THIS OFFER IS YOUR BEST--YOUR ONLY CHANCE NOW. BE GRATEFUL YOU'RE GETTING THAT MUCH.
I GET YOU WANNA SAVE ALL THE OTHER LITTLE CULT CRAZIES, AND MOST ESPECIALLY YOUR BROTHER, BUT THAT'S NOT IN THE CARDS, I'M AFRAID.
STILL, LOOK AT IT THIS WAY--

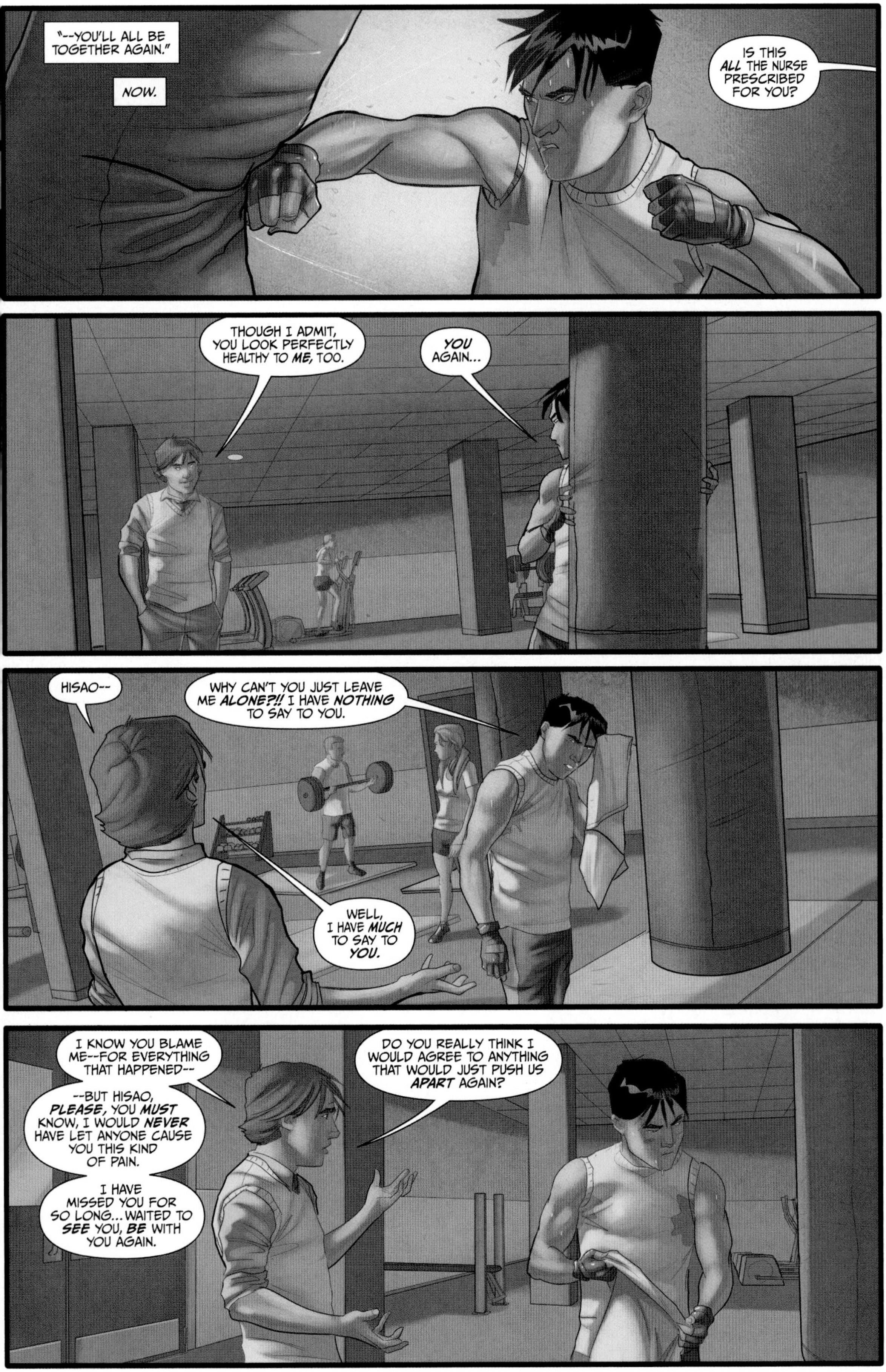
"--YOU'LL ALL BE TOGETHER AGAIN."
NOW.
IS THIS ALL THE NURSE PRESCRIBED FOR YOU?
THOUGH I ADMIT, YOU LOOK PERFECTLY HEALTHY TO ME, TOO.
YOU AGAIN...
HISAO--
WHY CAN'T YOU JUST LEAVE ME ALONE?!! I HAVE NOTHING TO SAY TO YOU.
WELL, I HAVE MUCH TO SAY TO YOU.
I KNOW YOU BLAME ME--FOR EVERYTHING THAT HAPPENED--
--BUT HISAO, PLEASE, YOU MUST KNOW, I WOULD NEVER HAVE LET ANYONE CAUSE YOU THIS KIND OF PAIN.
I HAVE MISSED YOU FOR SO LONG...WAITED TO SEE YOU, BE WITH YOU AGAIN.
DO YOU REALLY THINK I WOULD AGREE TO ANYTHING THAT WOULD JUST PUSH US APART AGAIN?

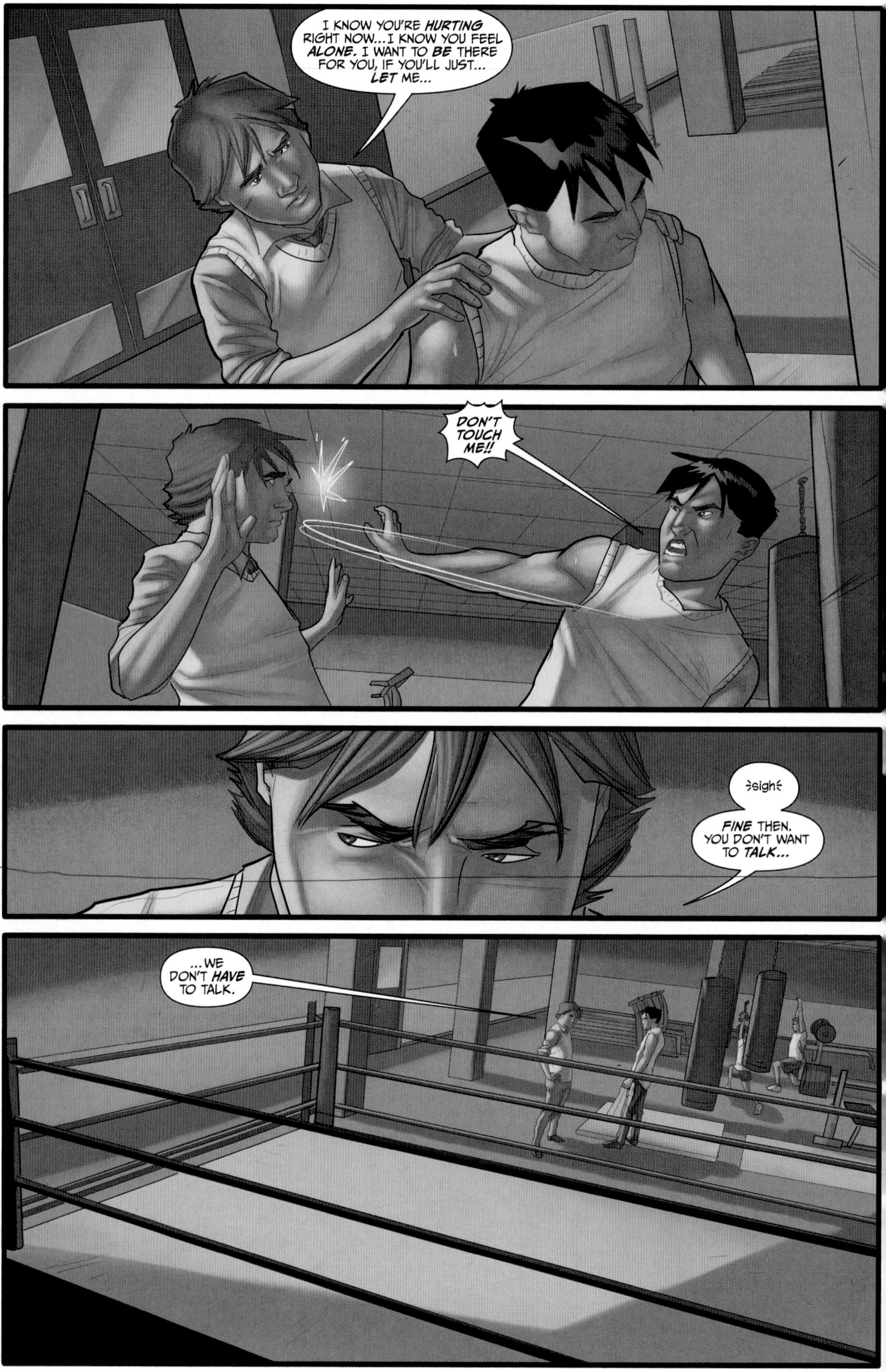
I KNOW YOU'RE HURTING RIGHT NOW...I KNOW YOU FEEL ALONE. I WANT TO BE THERE FOR YOU, IF YOU'LL JUST... LET ME...
DON'T TOUCH ME!!
sigh
FINE THEN. YOU DON'T WANT TO TALK...
...WE DON'T HAVE TO TALK.

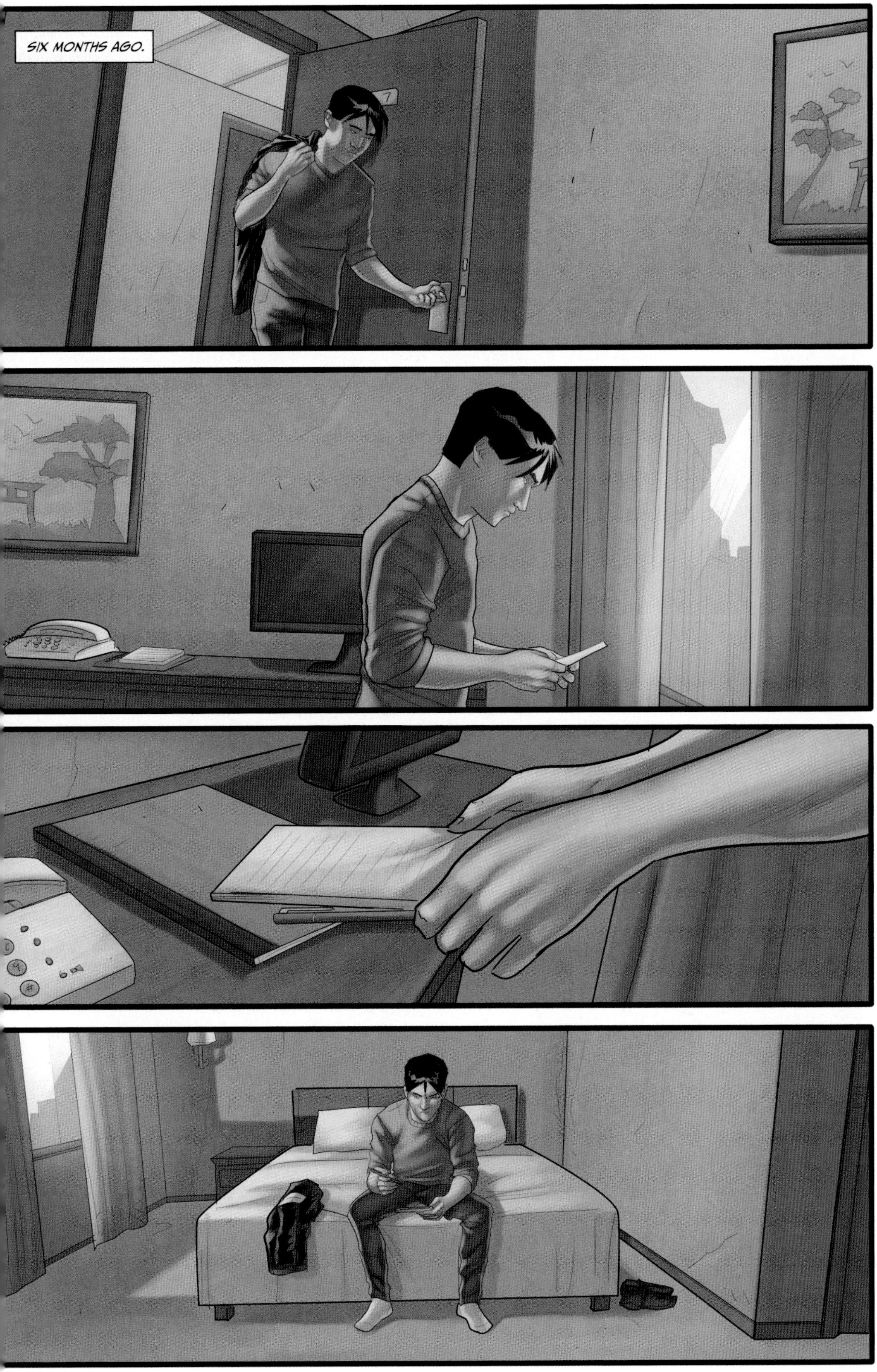
SIX MONTHS AGO.

Dear Guillaume,

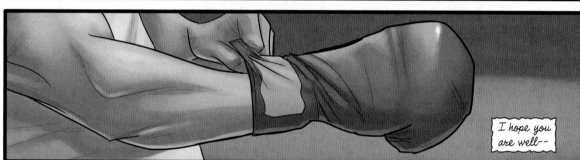

I hope you are well--

--though I know you are not.

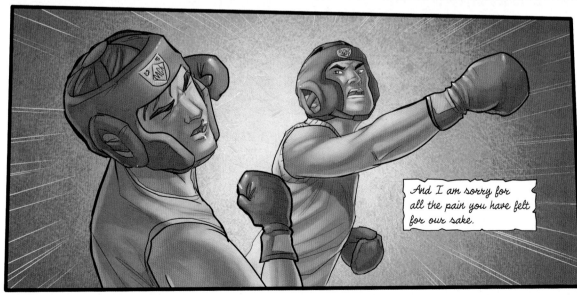

And I am sorry for all the pain you have felt for our sake.

We were taught much about sacrifice-- its virtues, the glory that comes from it--

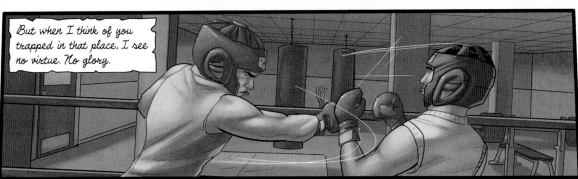

But when I think of you trapped in that place, I see no virtue. No glory.

It only makes me want to give up.

And maybe I have.

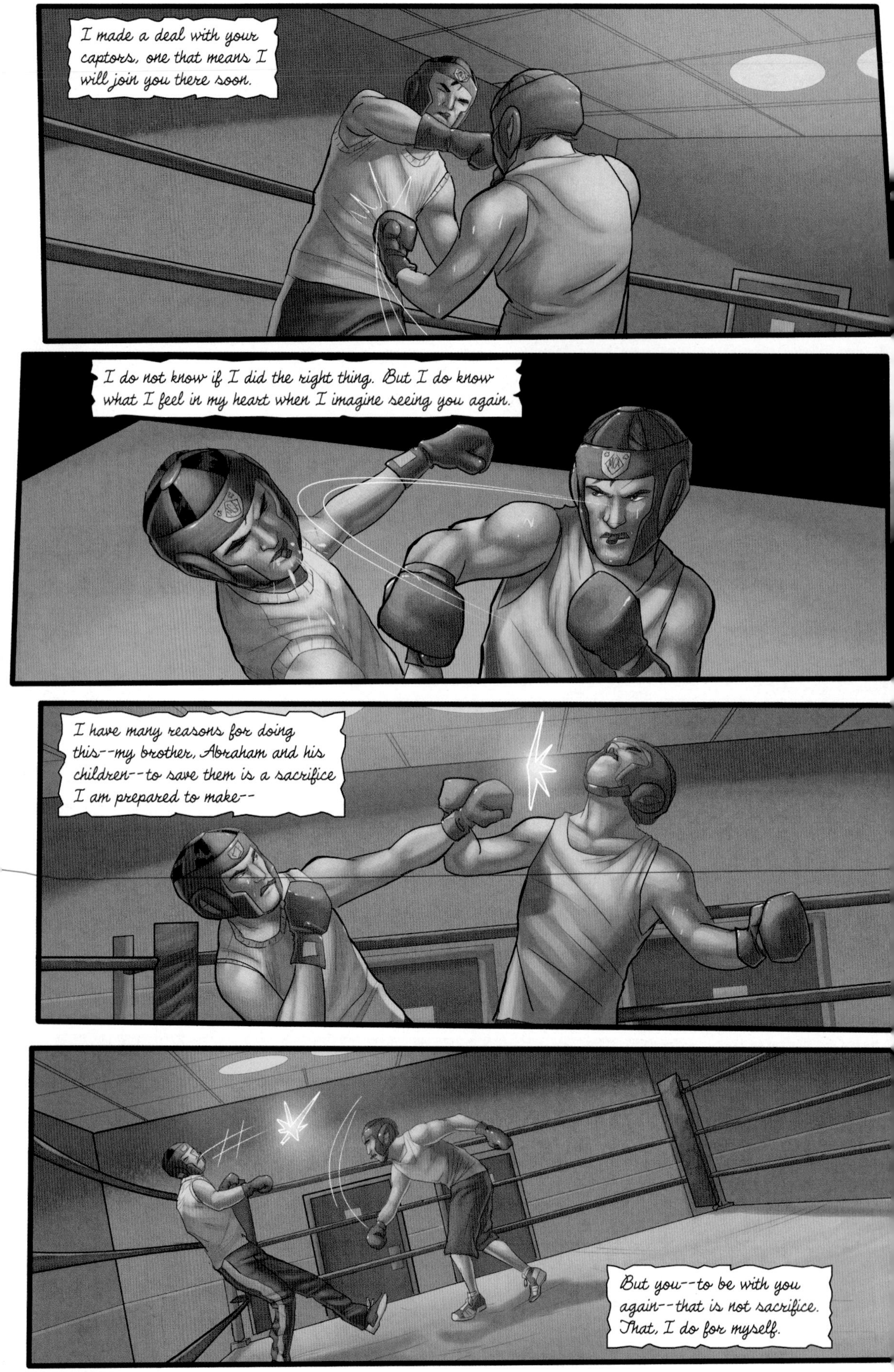
I made a deal with your captors, one that means I will join you there soon.
I do not know if I did the right thing. But I do know what I feel in my heart when I imagine seeing you again.
I have many reasons for doing this--my brother, Abraham and his children--to save them is a sacrifice I am prepared to make--
But you--to be with you again--that is not sacrifice. That, I do for myself.

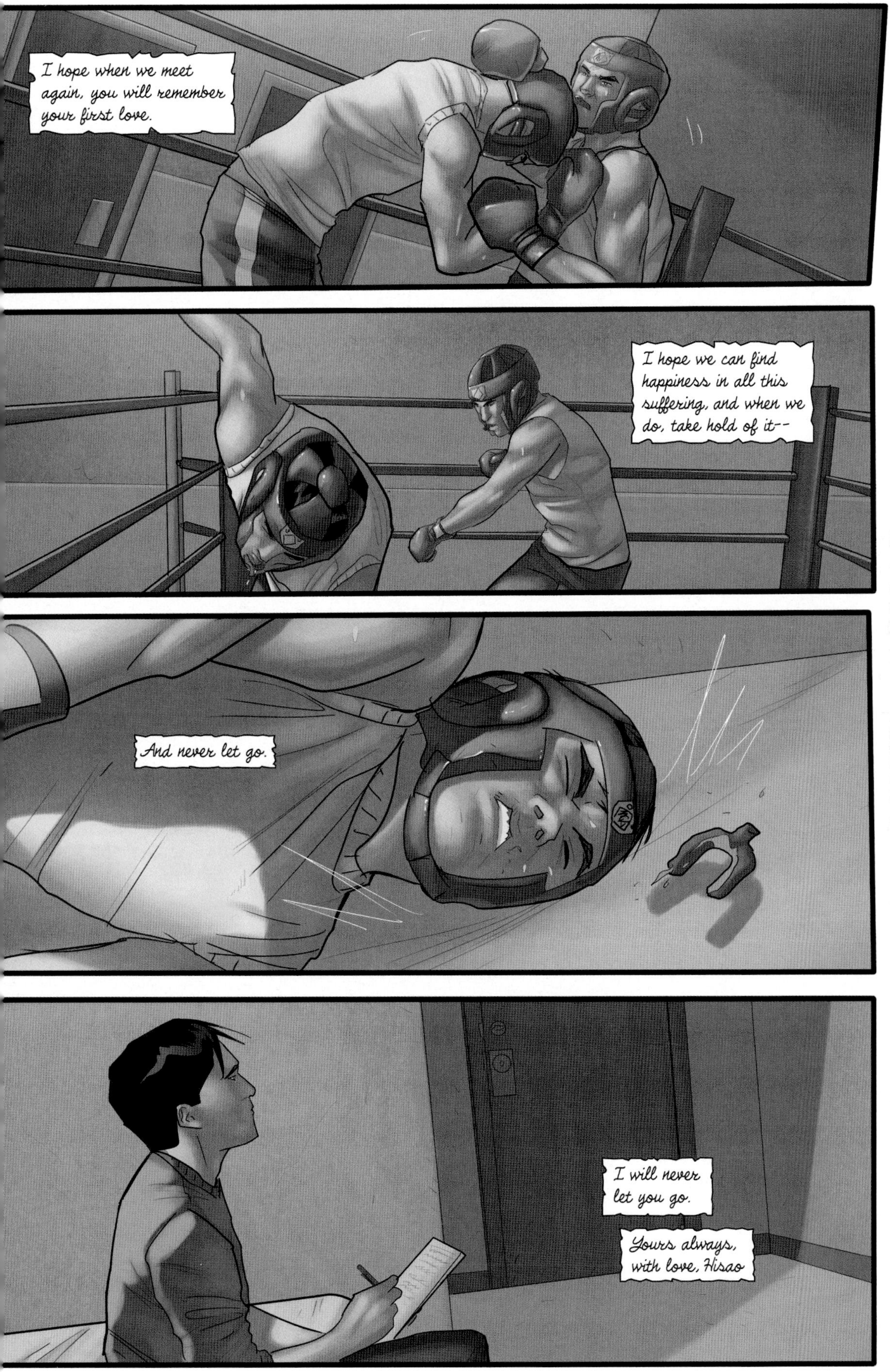
I hope when we meet again, you will remember your first love.
I hope we can find happiness in all this suffering, and when we do, take hold of it--
And never let go.
I will never let you go.
Yours always, with love, Hisao

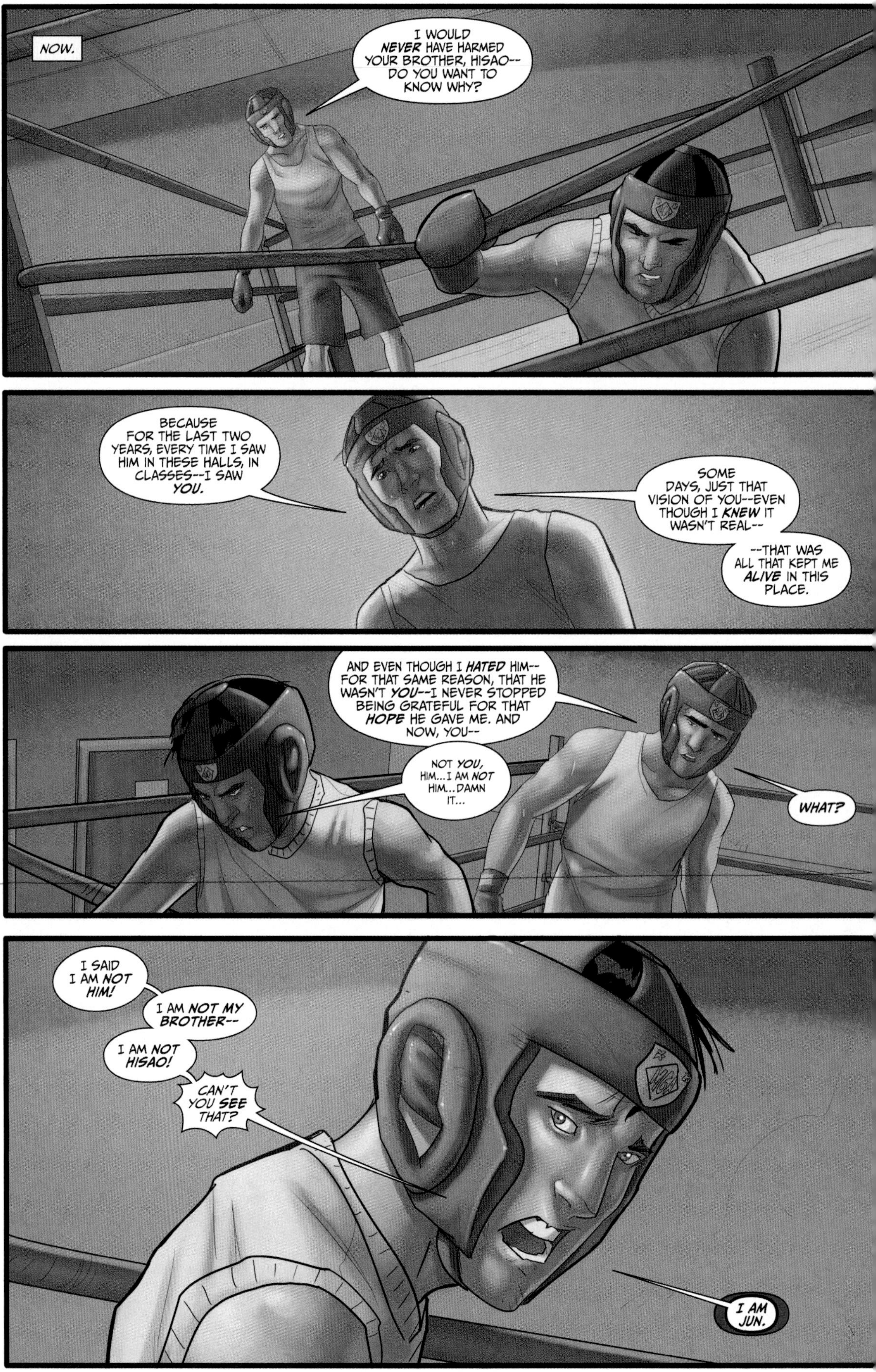
NOW.
I WOULD NEVER HAVE HARMED YOUR BROTHER, HISAO-- DO YOU WANT TO KNOW WHY?
BECAUSE FOR THE LAST TWO YEARS, EVERY TIME I SAW HIM IN THESE HALLS, IN CLASSES--I SAW YOU.
SOME DAYS, JUST THAT VISION OF YOU--EVEN THOUGH I KNEW IT WASN'T REAL--
--THAT WAS ALL THAT KEPT ME ALIVE IN THIS PLACE.
AND EVEN THOUGH I HATED HIM-- FOR THAT SAME REASON, THAT HE WASN'T YOU--I NEVER STOPPED BEING GRATEFUL FOR THAT HOPE HE GAVE ME. AND NOW, YOU--
NOT YOU, HIM...I AM NOT HIM...DAMN IT...
WHAT?
I SAID I AM NOT HIM!
I AM NOT MY BROTHER--
I AM NOT HISAO!
CAN'T YOU SEE THAT?
I AM JUN.

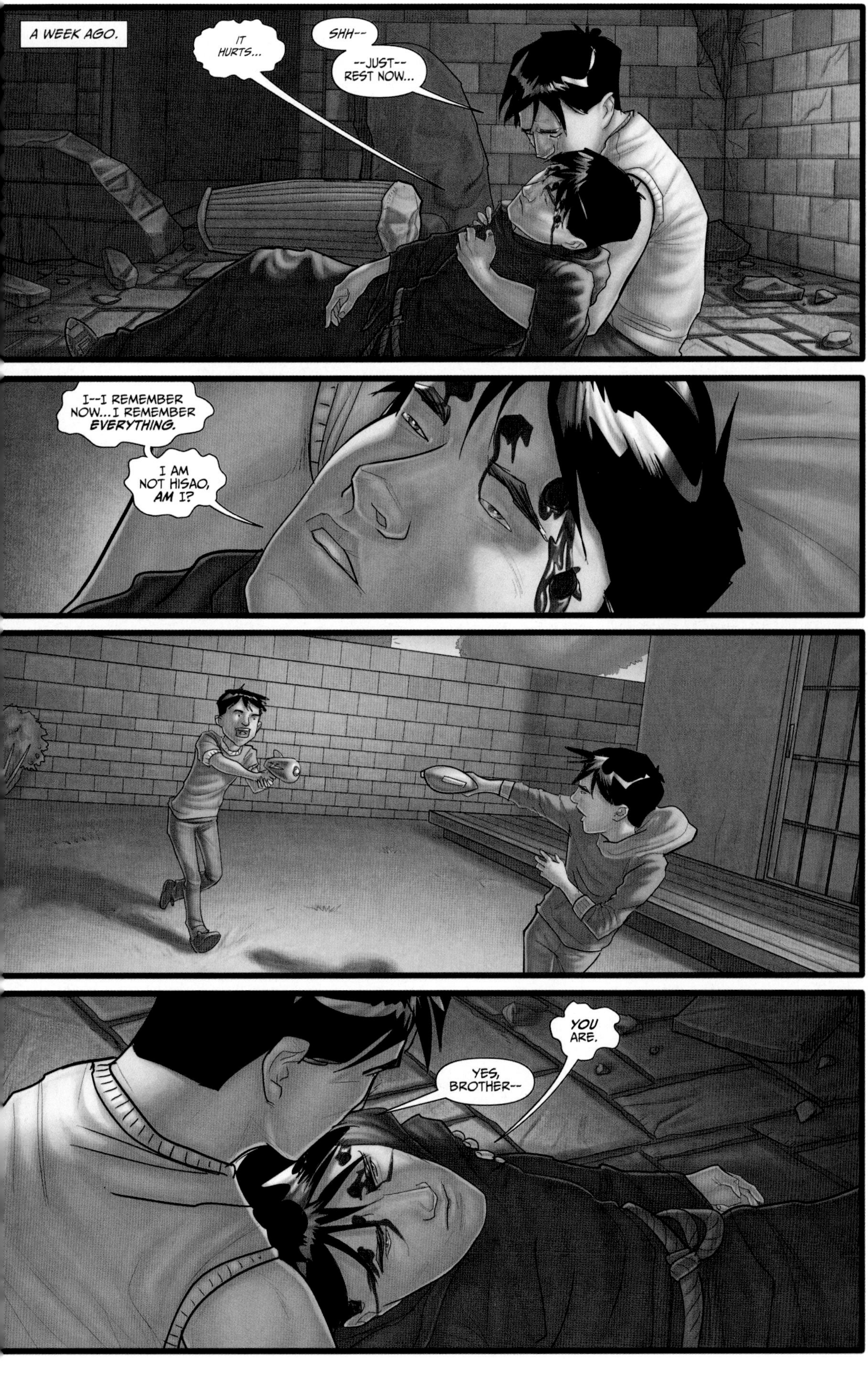
A WEEK AGO.
IT HURTS...
SHH--
--JUST-- REST NOW...
I--I REMEMBER NOW...I REMEMBER **EVERYTHING.**
I AM NOT HISAO, **AM** I?
YES, BROTHER--
YOU ARE.

YOU *SAVED* ME. YOU SAVED MY LIFE.

AND YOU CAME *BACK* FOR *ME*...

I--I TRIED-- BUT...I HAVE *FAILED* YOU, BROTHER--I AM *TOO LATE*--

NO... NO...

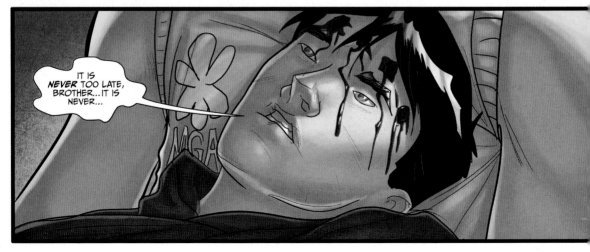

IT IS *NEVER* TOO LATE, BROTHER...IT IS NEVER...

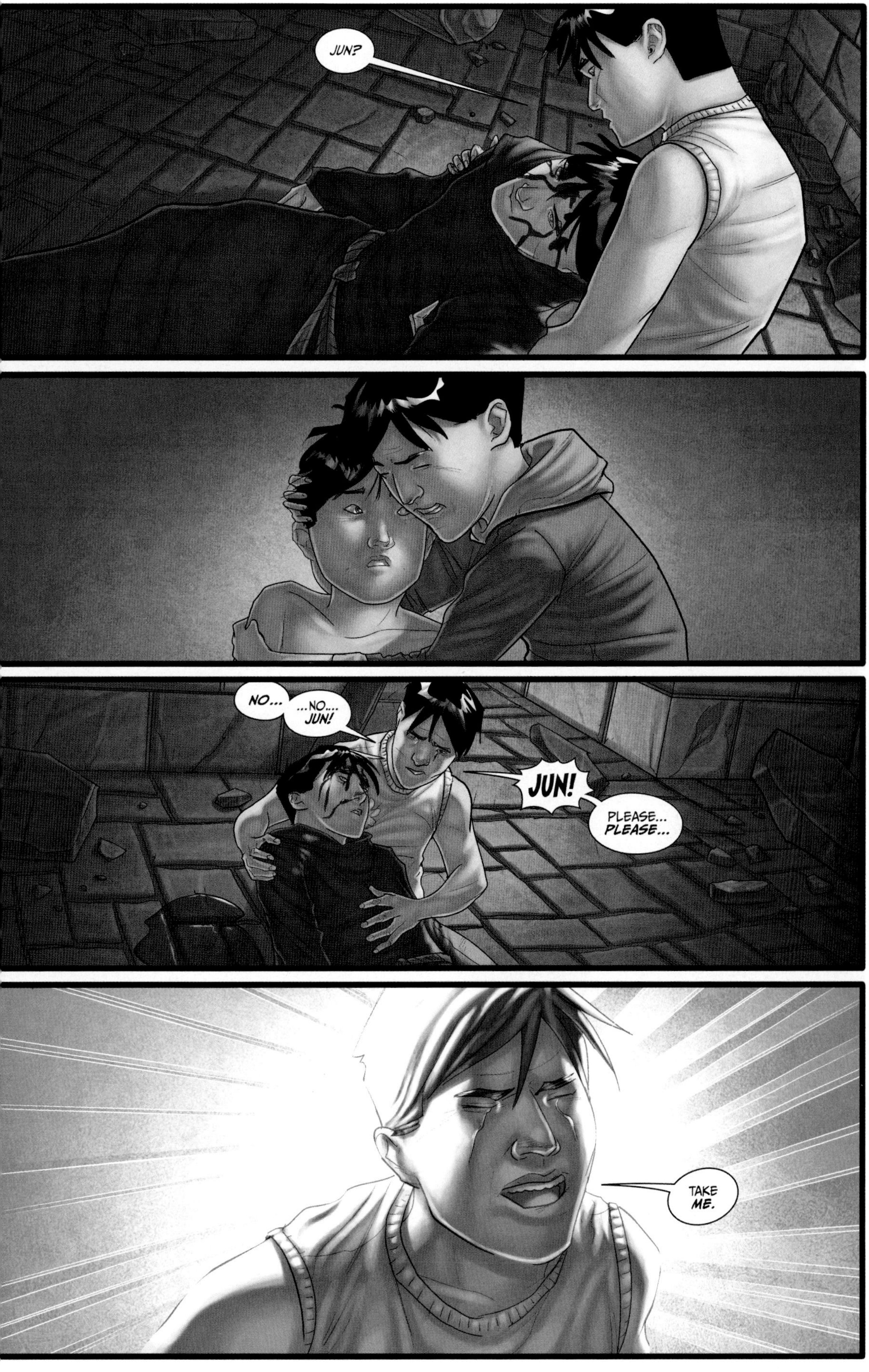
JUN?
NO...
...NO....
JUN!
JUN!
PLEASE...
PLEASE...
TAKE
ME.

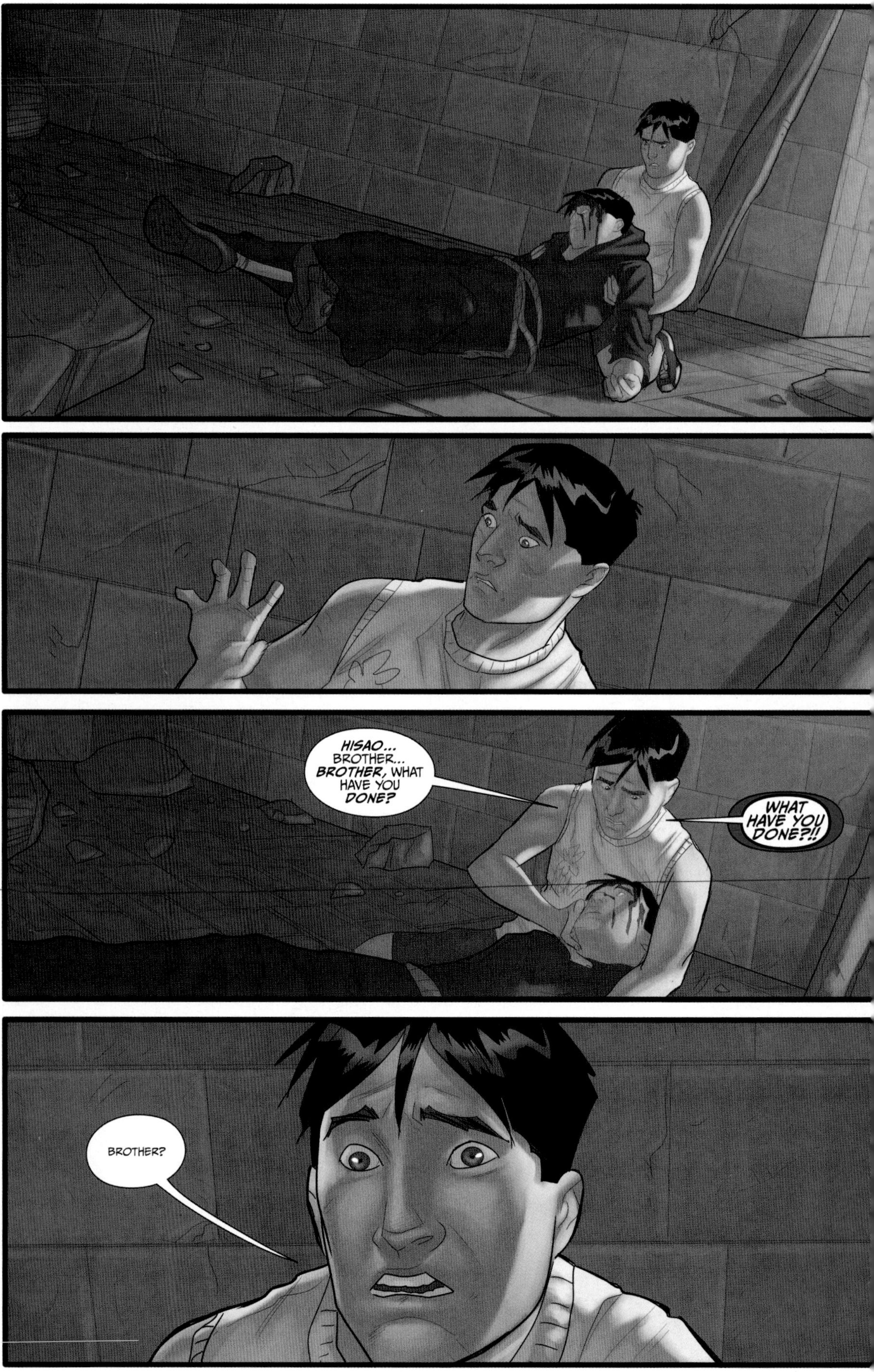
HISAO... BROTHER... BROTHER, WHAT HAVE YOU DONE?
WHAT HAVE YOU DONE?!!
BROTHER?

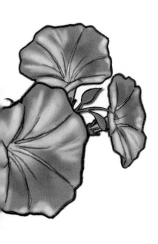

thirty**four**

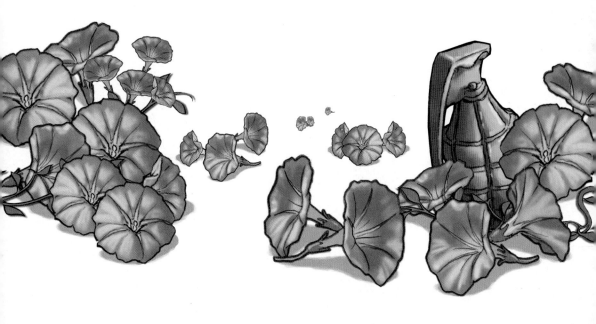

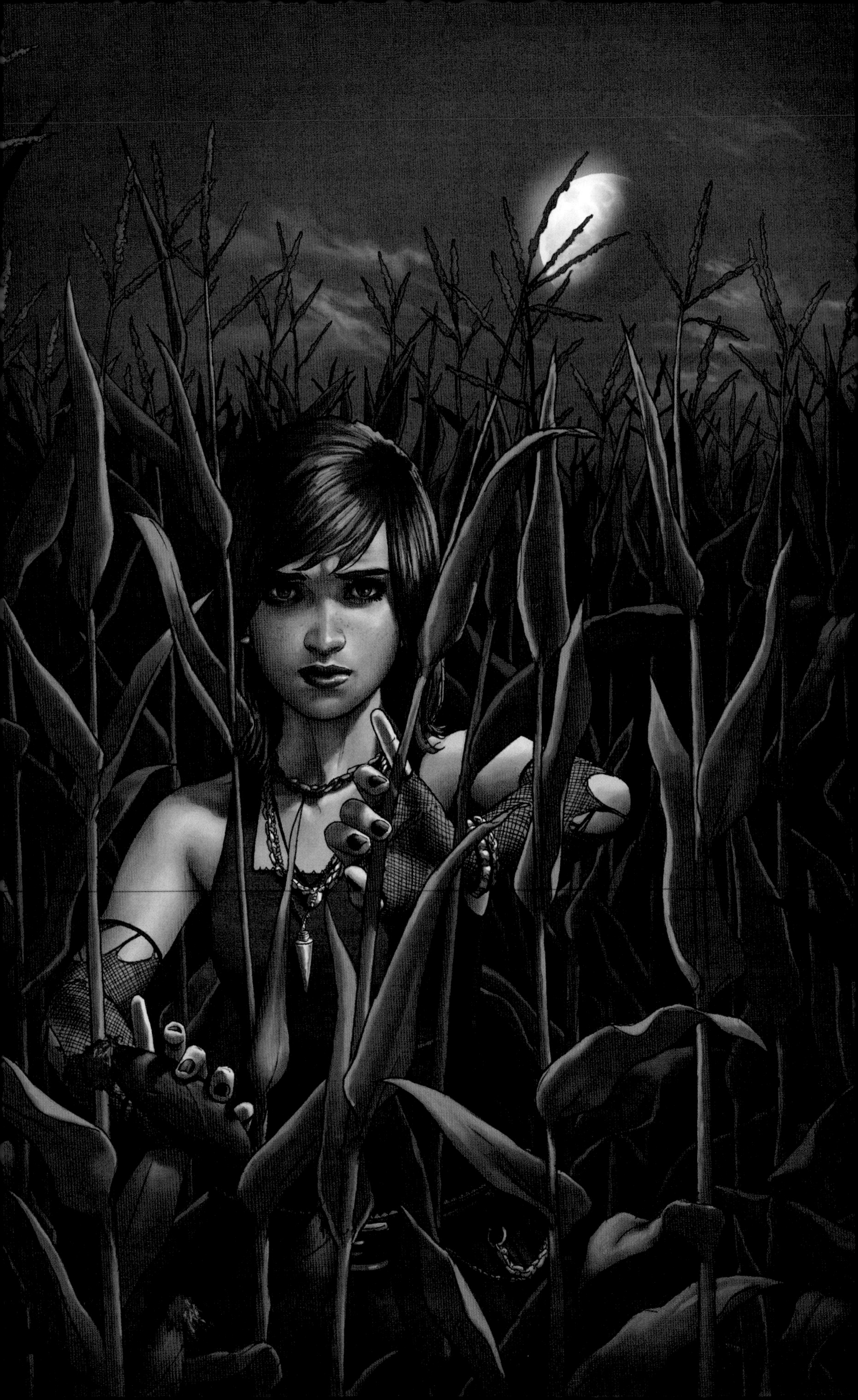

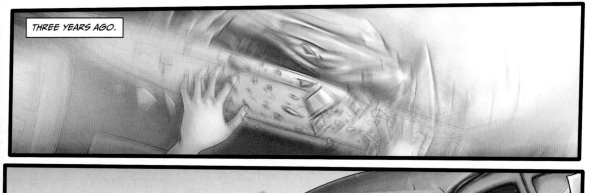

THREE YEARS AGO.

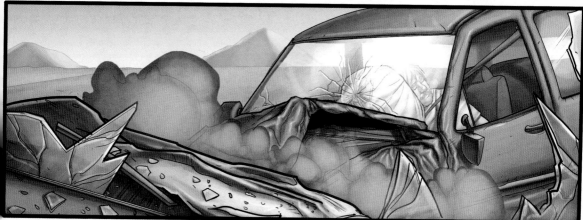

MOM?

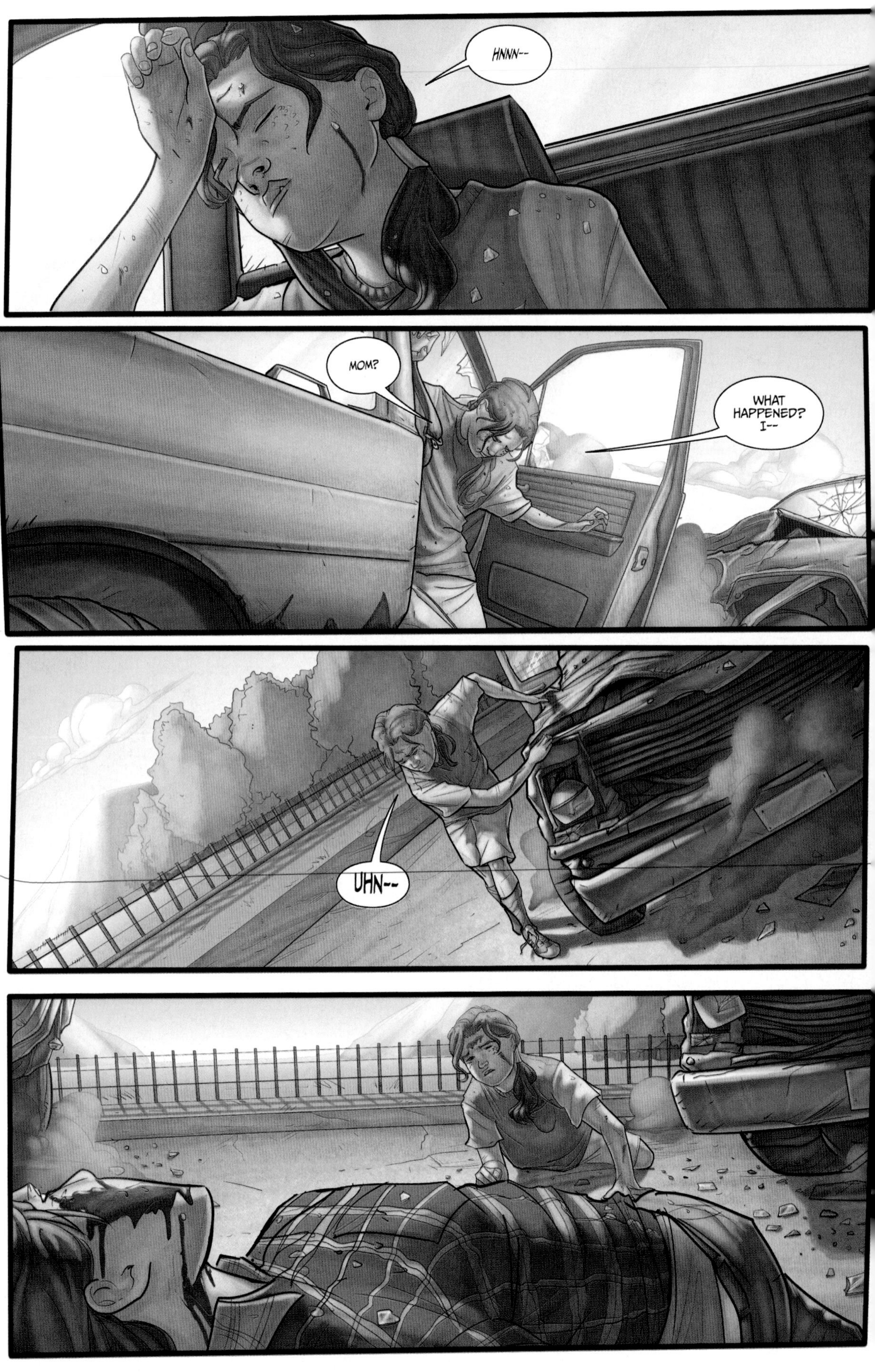
HNNN--
MOM?
WHAT HAPPENED? I--
UHN--

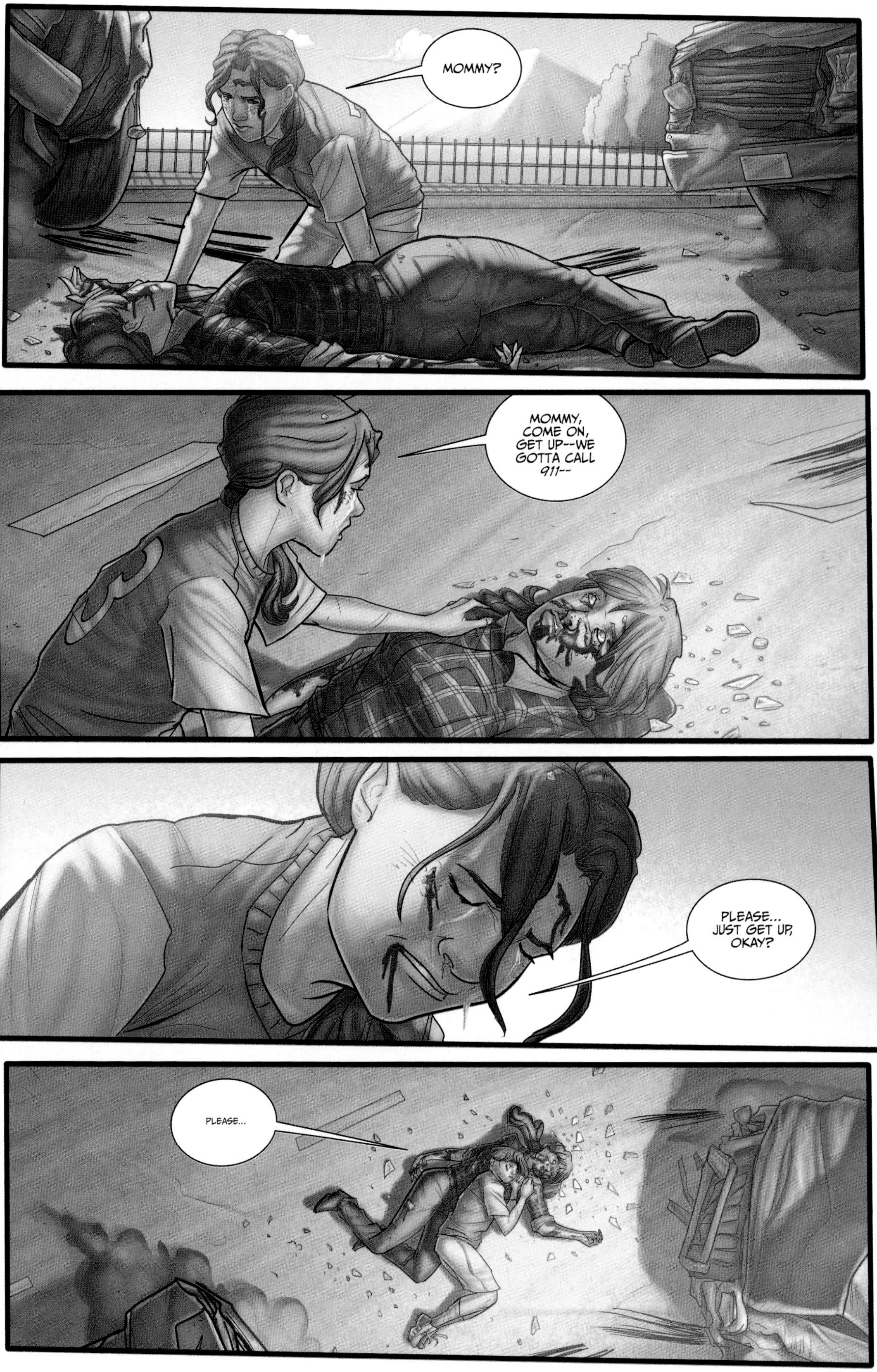
MOMMY?
MOMMY, COME ON, GET UP--WE GOTTA CALL 911--
PLEASE... JUST GET UP, OKAY?
PLEASE...

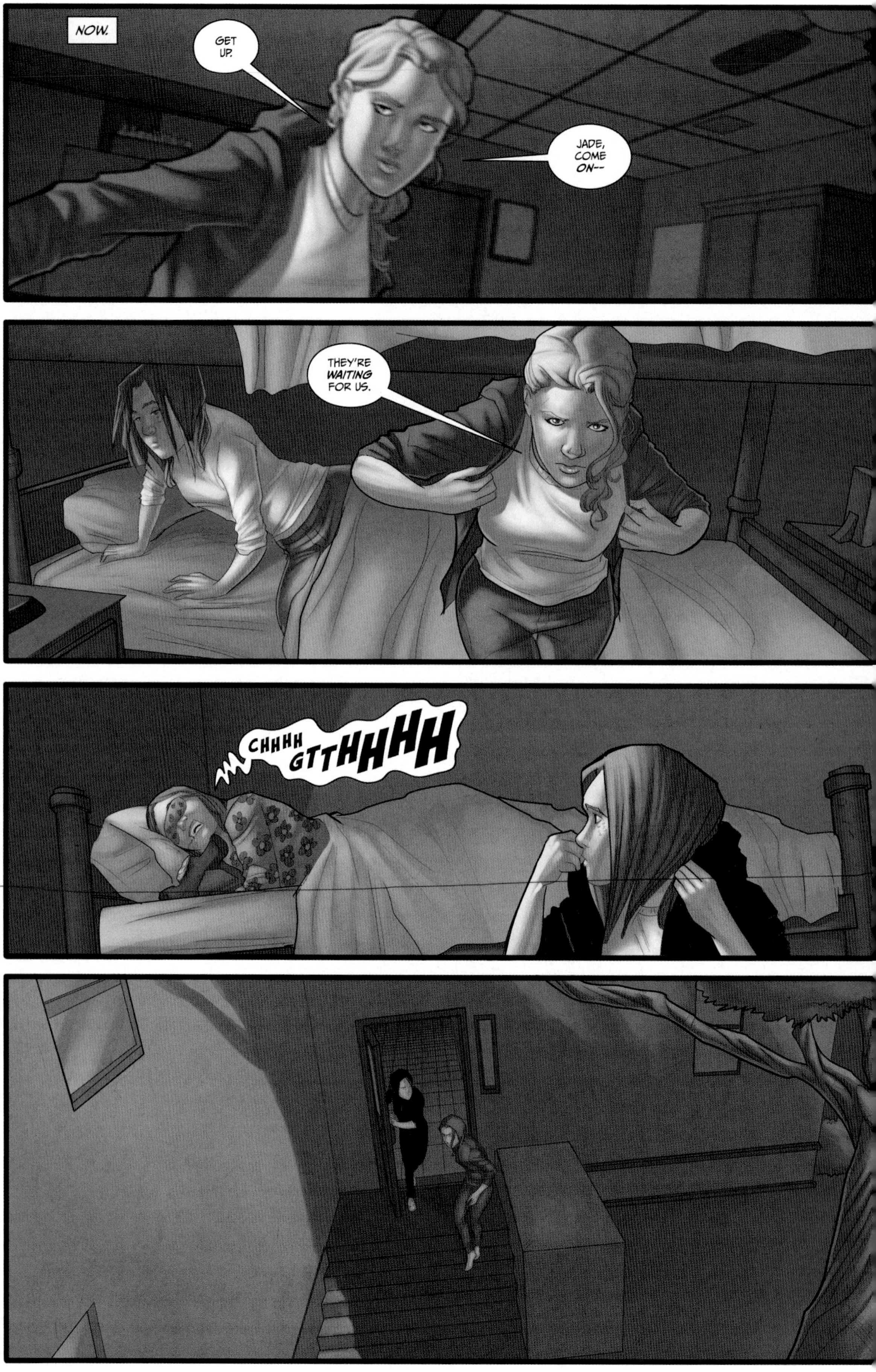
NOW.
GET UP.
JADE, COME ON--
THEY'RE WAITING FOR US.
CHHHH GTTHHHH

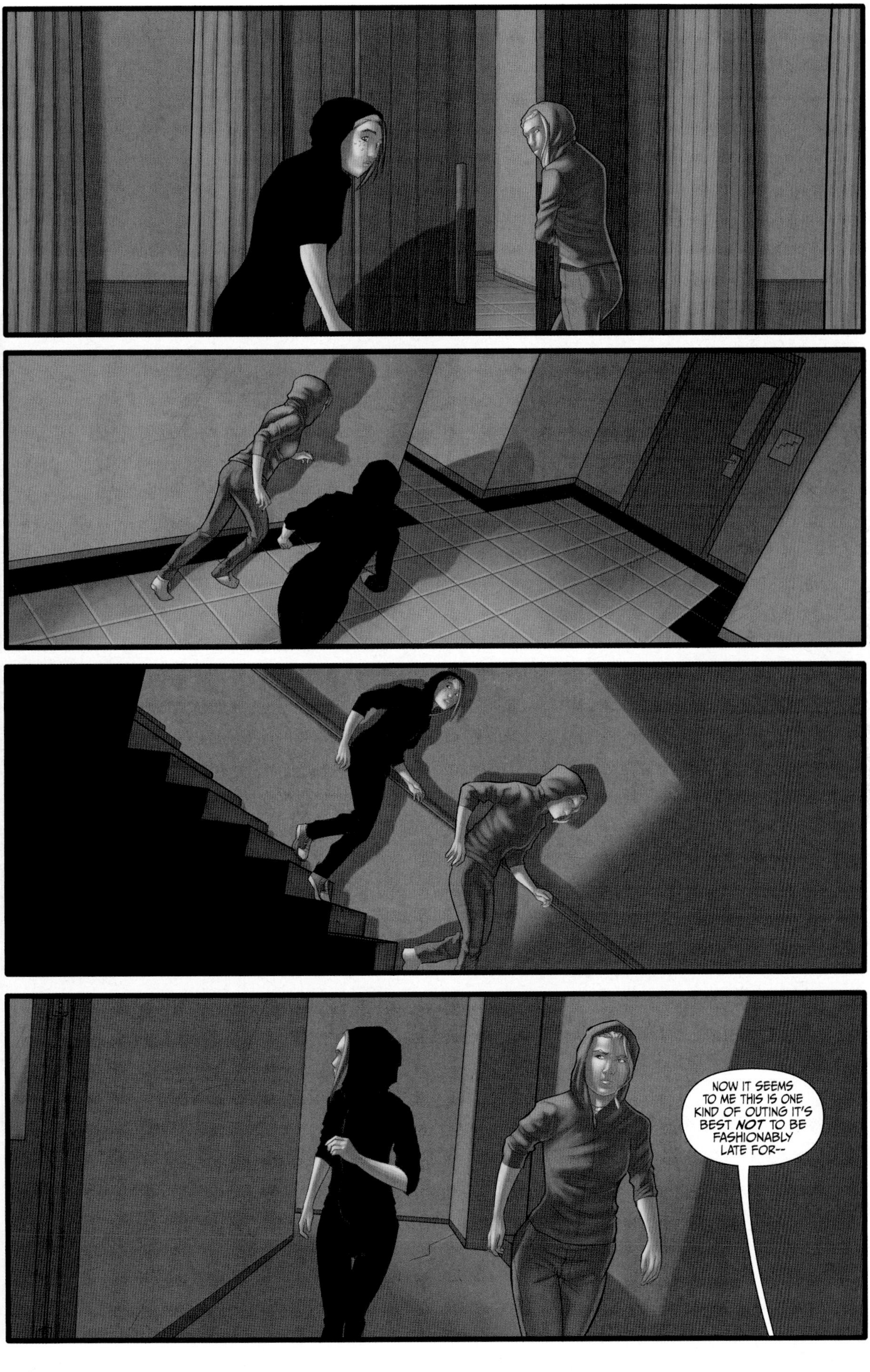
NOW IT SEEMS TO ME THIS IS ONE KIND OF OUTING IT'S BEST *NOT* TO BE FASHIONABLY LATE FOR--

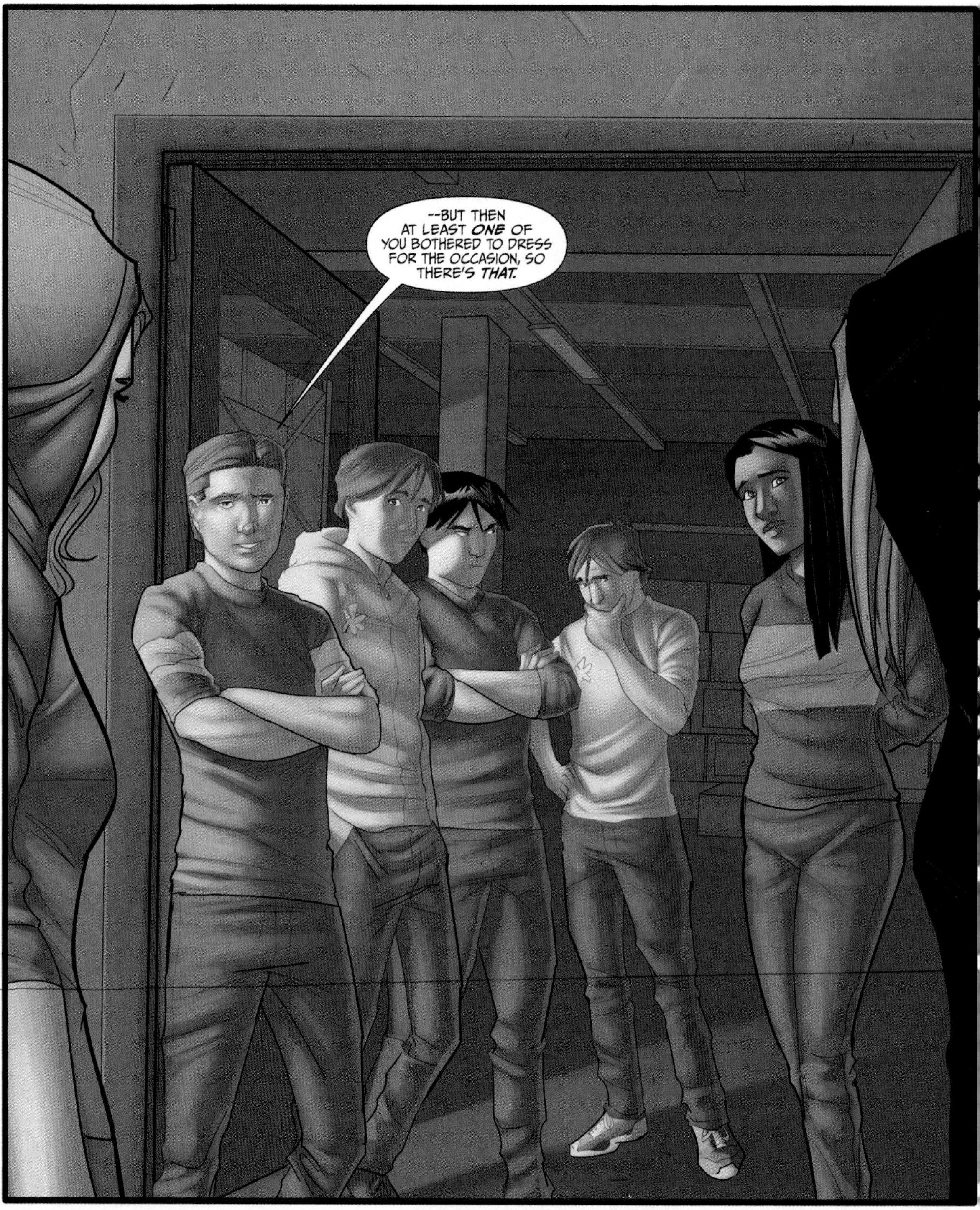
--BUT THEN AT LEAST ONE OF YOU BOTHERED TO DRESS FOR THE OCCASION, SO THERE'S THAT.

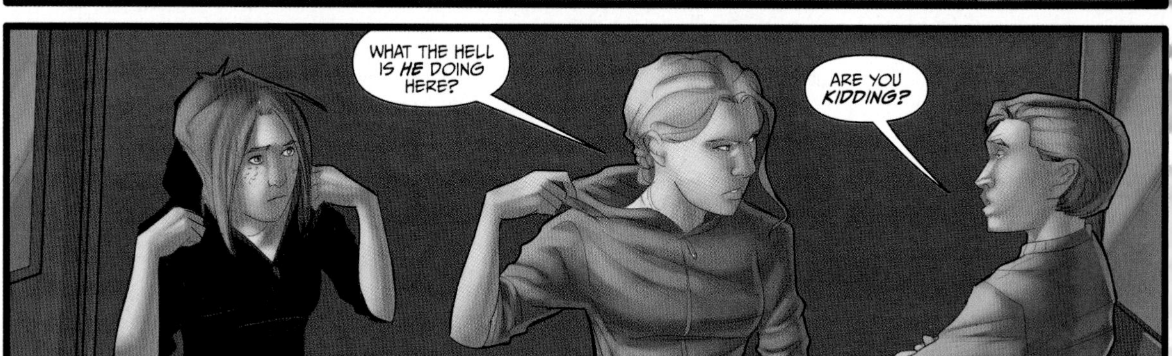
WHAT THE HELL IS HE DOING HERE?
ARE YOU KIDDING?

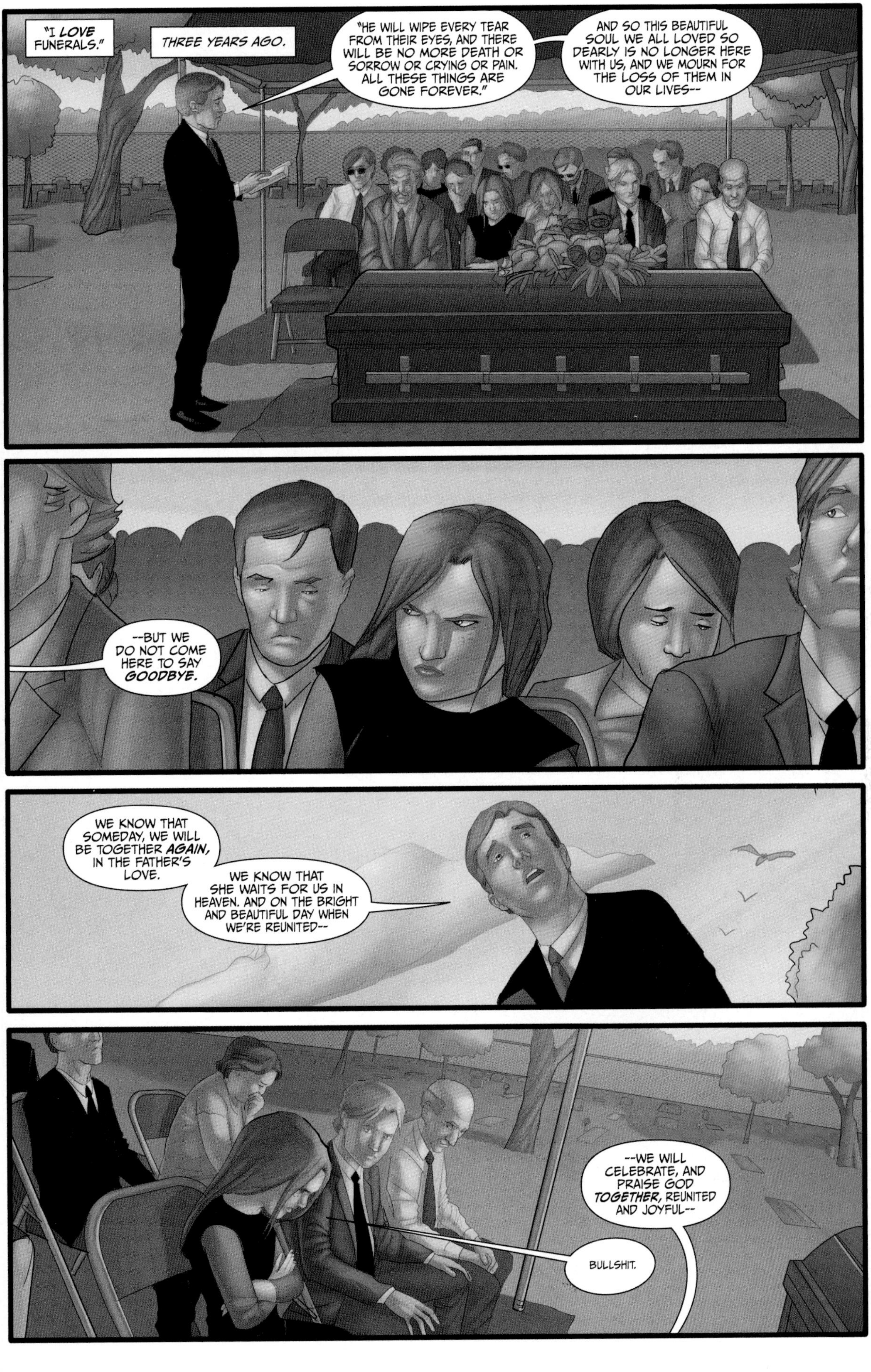
"I LOVE FUNERALS."
THREE YEARS AGO.
"HE WILL WIPE EVERY TEAR FROM THEIR EYES, AND THERE WILL BE NO MORE DEATH OR SORROW OR CRYING OR PAIN. ALL THESE THINGS ARE GONE FOREVER."
AND SO THIS BEAUTIFUL SOUL WE ALL LOVED SO DEARLY IS NO LONGER HERE WITH US, AND WE MOURN FOR THE LOSS OF THEM IN OUR LIVES--
--BUT WE DO NOT COME HERE TO SAY GOODBYE.
WE KNOW THAT SOMEDAY, WE WILL BE TOGETHER AGAIN, IN THE FATHER'S LOVE.
WE KNOW THAT SHE WAITS FOR US IN HEAVEN. AND ON THE BRIGHT AND BEAUTIFUL DAY WHEN WE'RE REUNITED--
--WE WILL CELEBRATE, AND PRAISE GOD TOGETHER, REUNITED AND JOYFUL--
BULLSHIT.

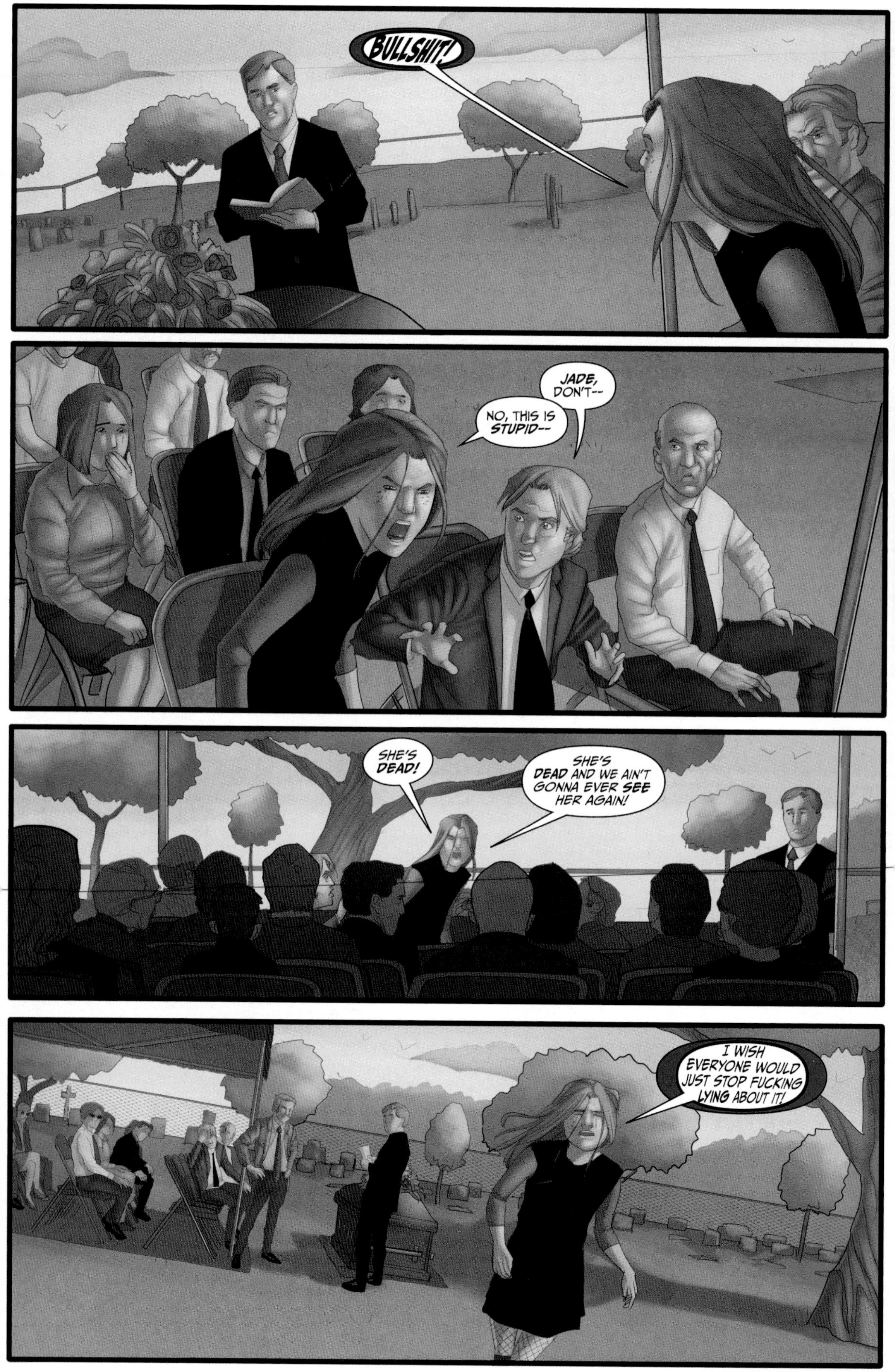
BULLSHIT!
JADE, DON'T--
NO, THIS IS STUPID--
SHE'S DEAD!
SHE'S DEAD AND WE AIN'T GONNA EVER SEE HER AGAIN!
I WISH EVERYONE WOULD JUST STOP FUCKING LYING ABOUT IT!

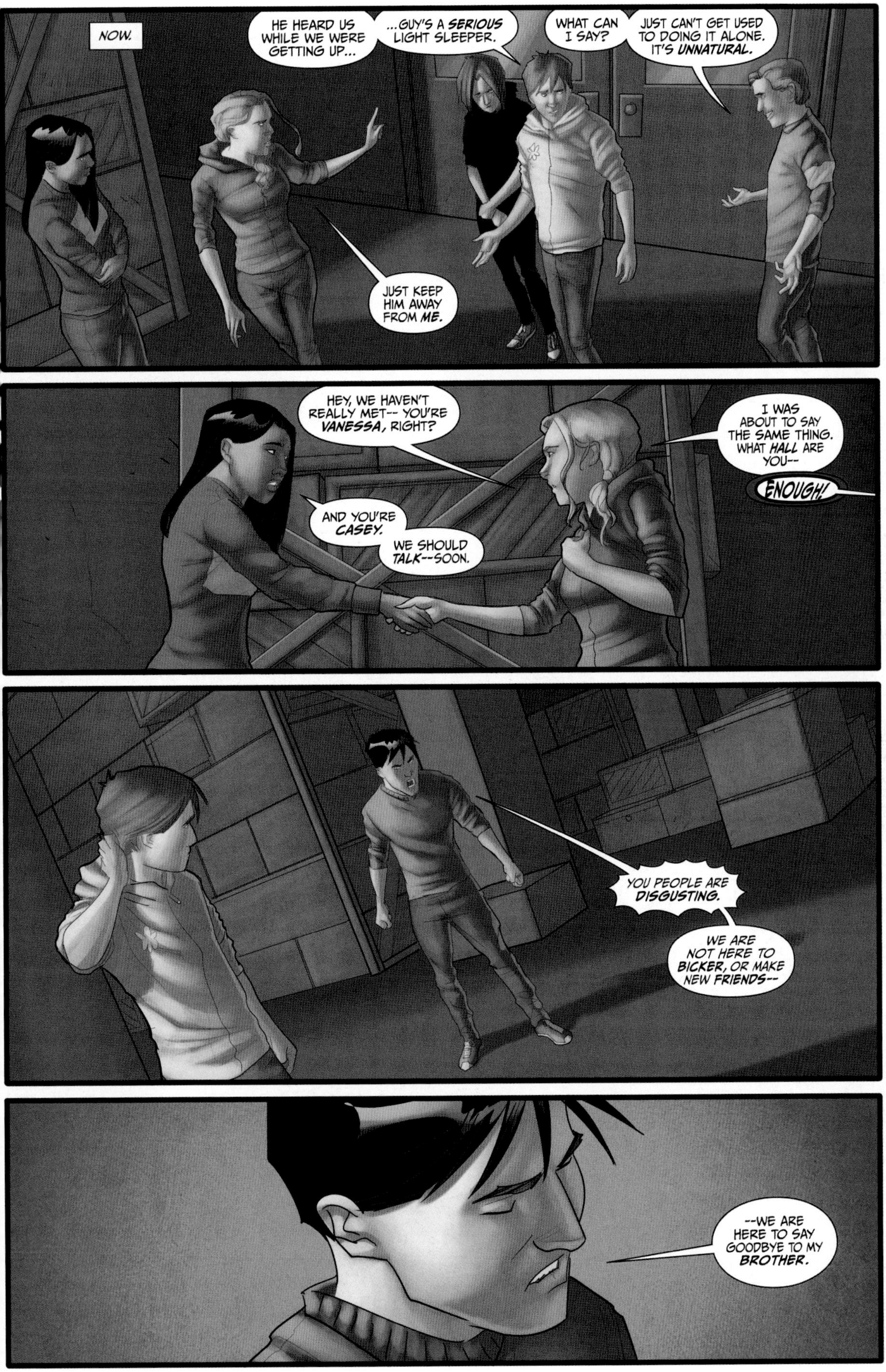
NOW.
HE HEARD US WHILE WE WERE GETTING UP...
...GUY'S A SERIOUS LIGHT SLEEPER.
WHAT CAN I SAY?
JUST CAN'T GET USED TO DOING IT ALONE. IT'S UNNATURAL.
JUST KEEP HIM AWAY FROM ME.
HEY, WE HAVEN'T REALLY MET-- YOU'RE VANESSA, RIGHT?
AND YOU'RE CASEY.
WE SHOULD TALK--SOON.
I WAS ABOUT TO SAY THE SAME THING. WHAT HALL ARE YOU--
ENOUGH!
YOU PEOPLE ARE DISGUSTING.
WE ARE NOT HERE TO BICKER, OR MAKE NEW FRIENDS--
--WE ARE HERE TO SAY GOODBYE TO MY BROTHER.

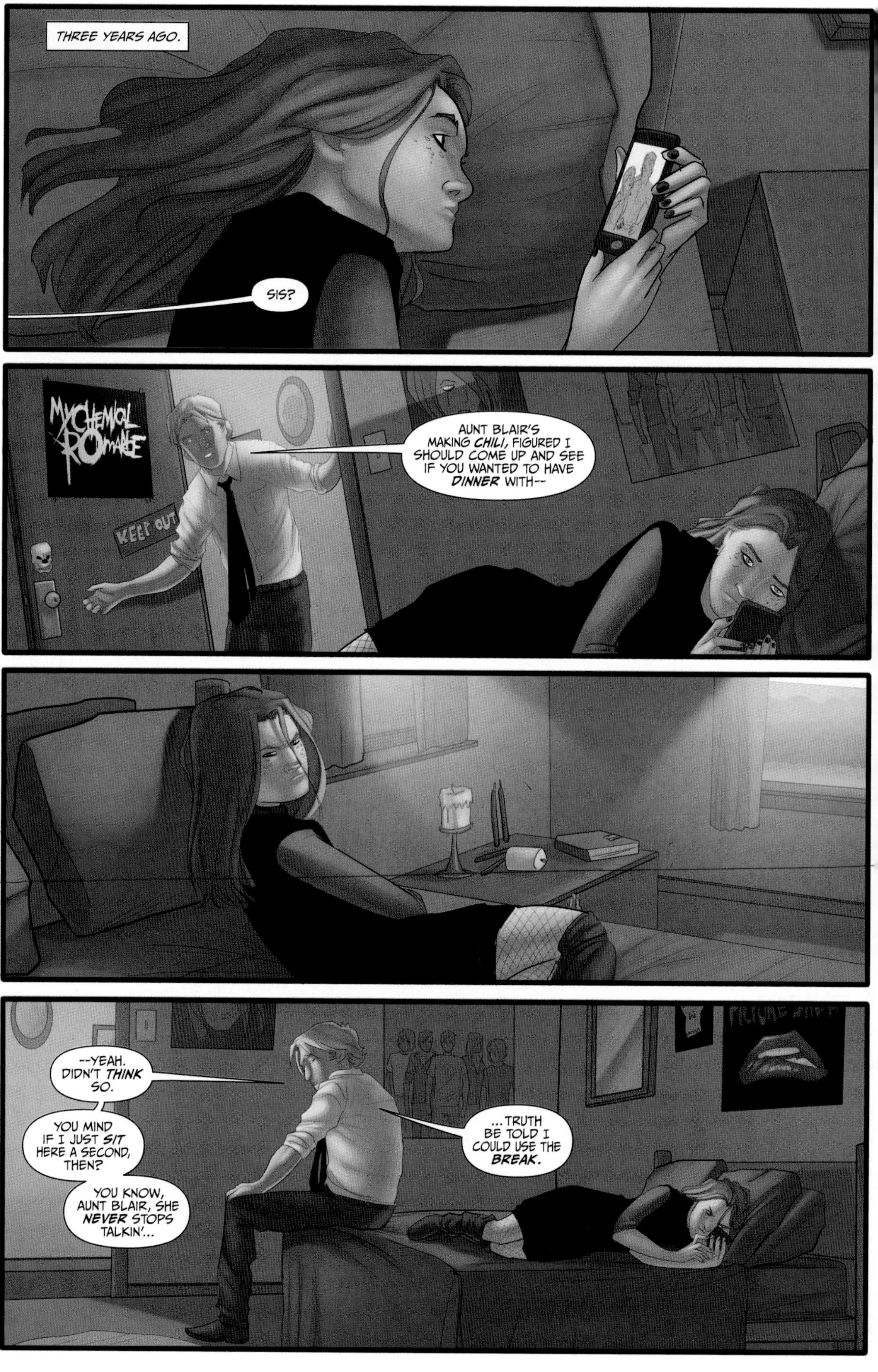
THREE YEARS AGO.
SIS?
AUNT BLAIR'S MAKING CHILI, FIGURED I SHOULD COME UP AND SEE IF YOU WANTED TO HAVE DINNER WITH--
MY CHEMICAL ROMANCE
KEEP OUT
--YEAH. DIDN'T THINK SO.
YOU MIND IF I JUST SIT HERE A SECOND, THEN?
YOU KNOW, AUNT BLAIR, SHE NEVER STOPS TALKIN'...
...TRUTH BE TOLD I COULD USE THE BREAK.

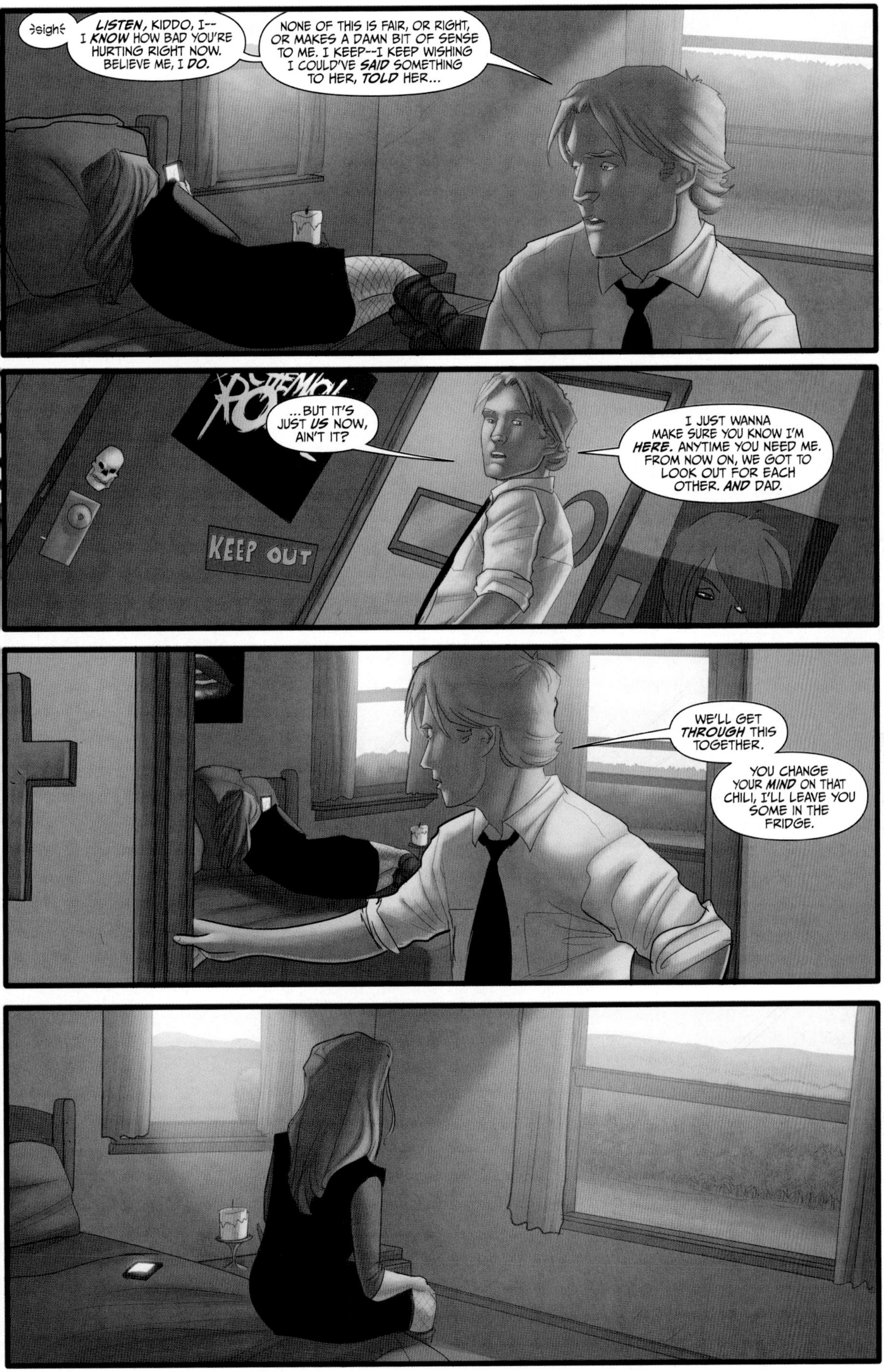
sigh
LISTEN, KIDDO, I-- I KNOW HOW BAD YOU'RE HURTING RIGHT NOW. BELIEVE ME, I DO.
NONE OF THIS IS FAIR, OR RIGHT, OR MAKES A DAMN BIT OF SENSE TO ME. I KEEP--I KEEP WISHING I COULD'VE SAID SOMETHING TO HER, TOLD HER...
...BUT IT'S JUST US NOW, AIN'T IT?
I JUST WANNA MAKE SURE YOU KNOW I'M HERE. ANYTIME YOU NEED ME. FROM NOW ON, WE GOT TO LOOK OUT FOR EACH OTHER. AND DAD.
KEEP OUT
WE'LL GET THROUGH THIS TOGETHER.
YOU CHANGE YOUR MIND ON THAT CHILI, I'LL LEAVE YOU SOME IN THE FRIDGE.

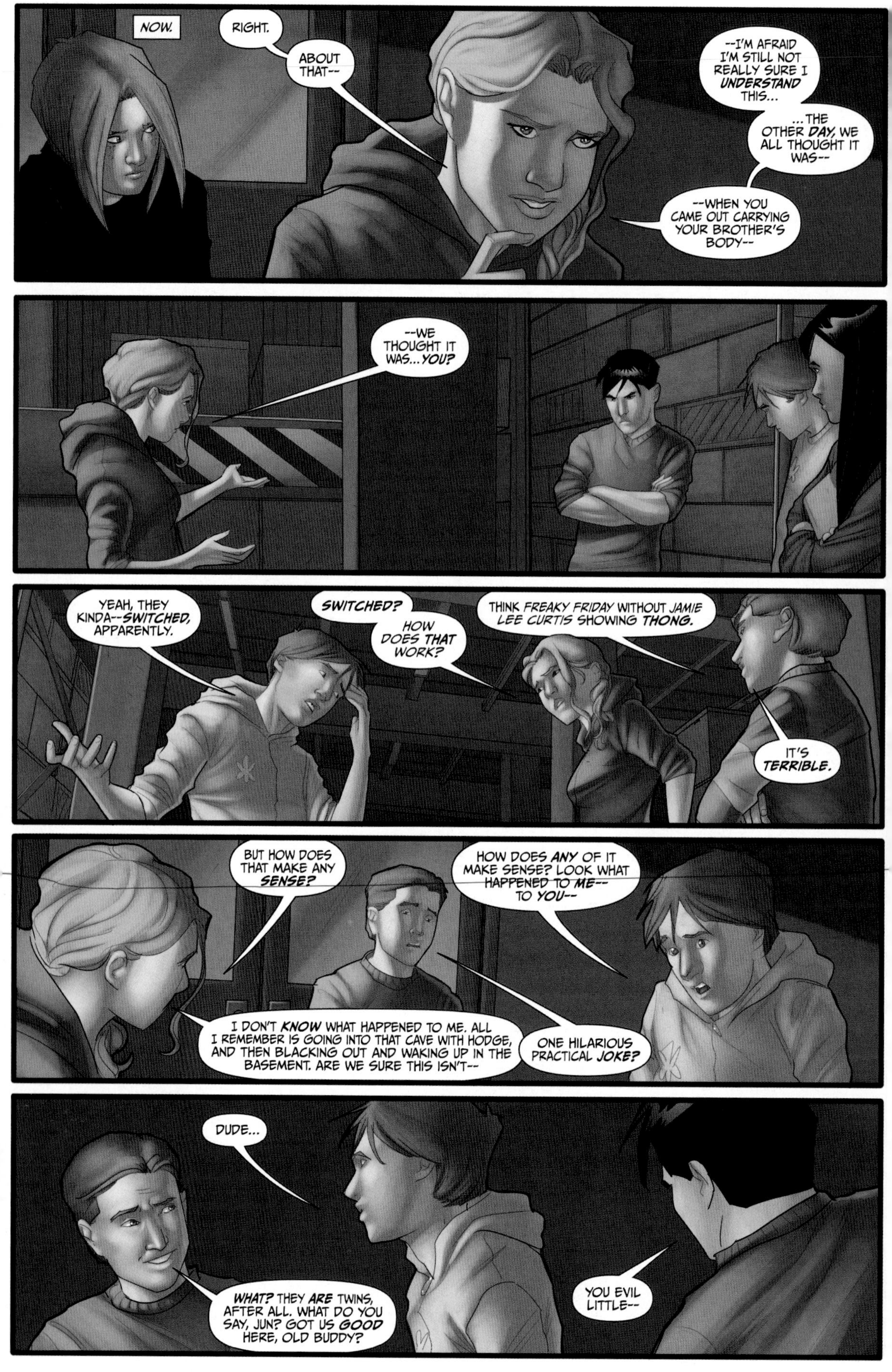
NOW.
RIGHT.
ABOUT THAT--
--I'M AFRAID I'M STILL NOT REALLY SURE I UNDERSTAND THIS...
...THE OTHER DAY, WE ALL THOUGHT IT WAS--
--WHEN YOU CAME OUT CARRYING YOUR BROTHER'S BODY--
--WE THOUGHT IT WAS...YOU?
YEAH, THEY KINDA--SWITCHED, APPARENTLY.
SWITCHED?
HOW DOES THAT WORK?
THINK FREAKY FRIDAY WITHOUT JAMIE LEE CURTIS SHOWING THONG.
IT'S TERRIBLE.
BUT HOW DOES THAT MAKE ANY SENSE?
HOW DOES ANY OF IT MAKE SENSE? LOOK WHAT HAPPENED TO ME-- TO YOU--
I DON'T KNOW WHAT HAPPENED TO ME. ALL I REMEMBER IS GOING INTO THAT CAVE WITH HODGE, AND THEN BLACKING OUT AND WAKING UP IN THE BASEMENT. ARE WE SURE THIS ISN'T--
ONE HILARIOUS PRACTICAL JOKE?
DUDE...
WHAT? THEY ARE TWINS, AFTER ALL. WHAT DO YOU SAY, JUN? GOT US GOOD HERE, OLD BUDDY?
YOU EVIL LITTLE--

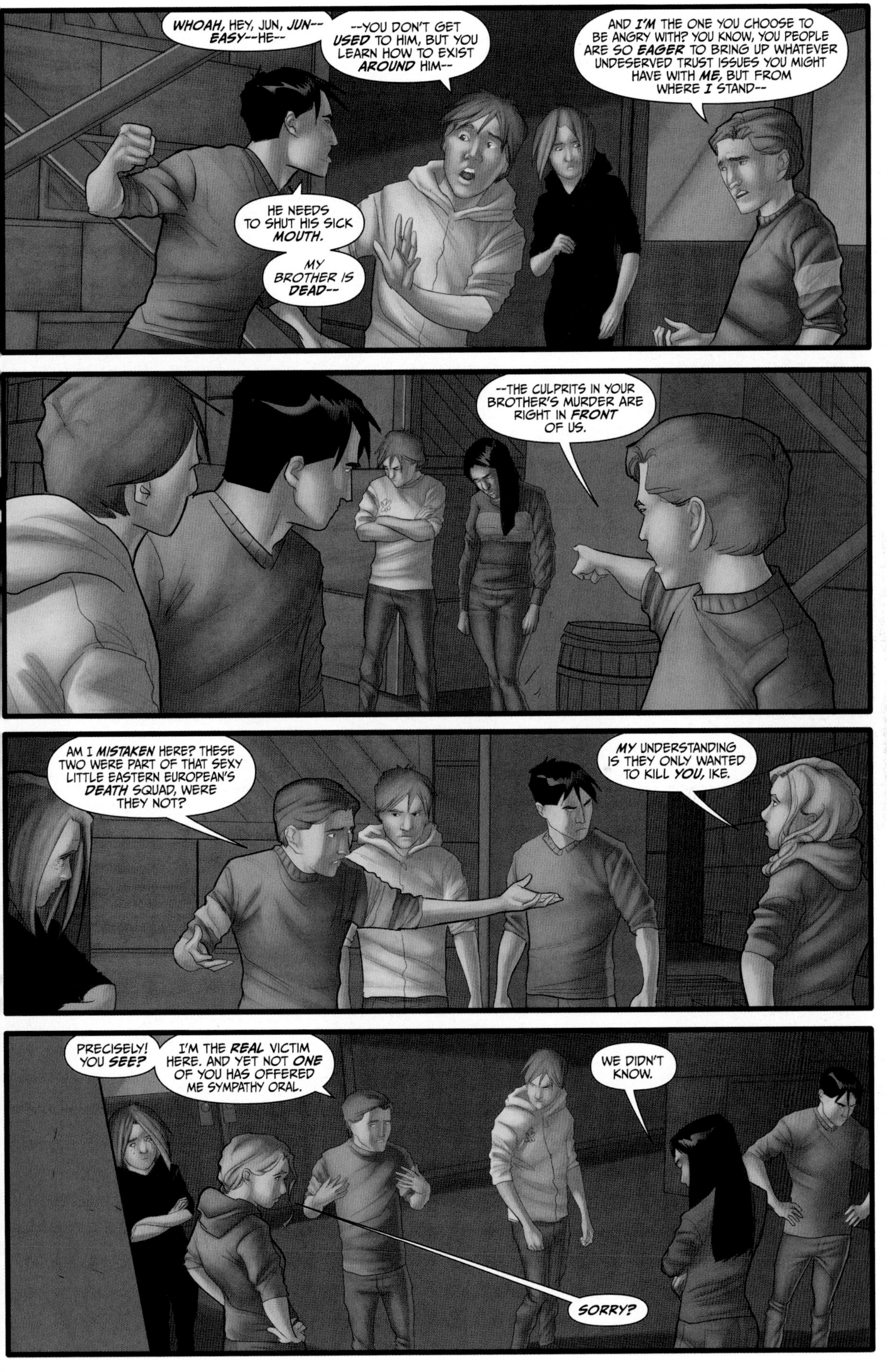
WHOAH, HEY, JUN, JUN-- EASY--HE--
--YOU DON'T GET USED TO HIM, BUT YOU LEARN HOW TO EXIST AROUND HIM--
AND I'M THE ONE YOU CHOOSE TO BE ANGRY WITH? YOU KNOW, YOU PEOPLE ARE SO EAGER TO BRING UP WHATEVER UNDESERVED TRUST ISSUES YOU MIGHT HAVE WITH ME, BUT FROM WHERE I STAND--
HE NEEDS TO SHUT HIS SICK MOUTH.
MY BROTHER IS DEAD--
--THE CULPRITS IN YOUR BROTHER'S MURDER ARE RIGHT IN FRONT OF US.
AM I MISTAKEN HERE? THESE TWO WERE PART OF THAT SEXY LITTLE EASTERN EUROPEAN'S DEATH SQUAD, WERE THEY NOT?
MY UNDERSTANDING IS THEY ONLY WANTED TO KILL YOU, IKE.
PRECISELY! YOU SEE?
I'M THE REAL VICTIM HERE. AND YET NOT ONE OF YOU HAS OFFERED ME SYMPATHY ORAL.
WE DIDN'T KNOW.
SORRY?

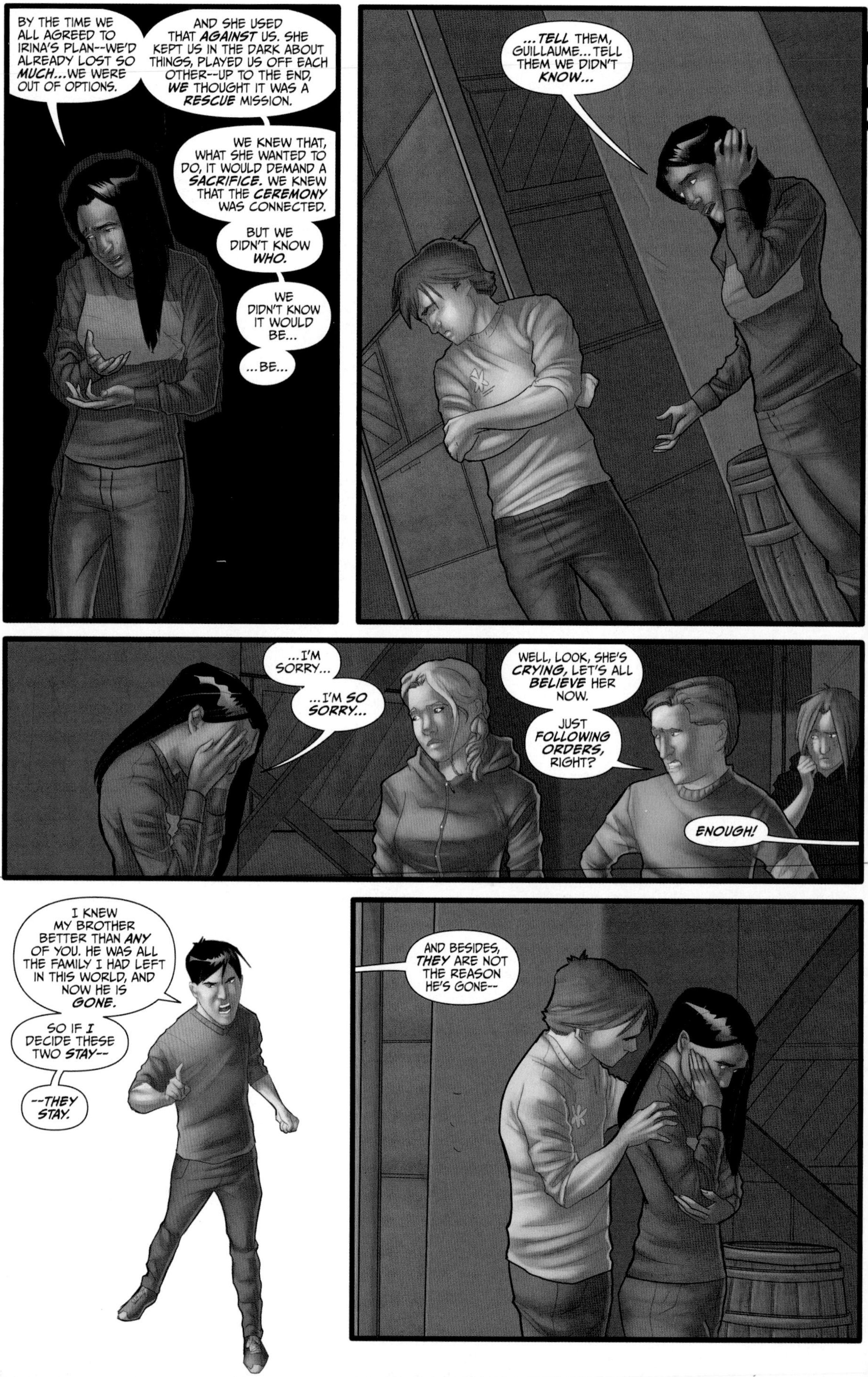
BY THE TIME WE ALL AGREED TO IRINA'S PLAN--WE'D ALREADY LOST SO MUCH...WE WERE OUT OF OPTIONS.
AND SHE USED THAT AGAINST US. SHE KEPT US IN THE DARK ABOUT THINGS, PLAYED US OFF EACH OTHER--UP TO THE END, WE THOUGHT IT WAS A RESCUE MISSION.
WE KNEW THAT, WHAT SHE WANTED TO DO, IT WOULD DEMAND A SACRIFICE. WE KNEW THAT THE CEREMONY WAS CONNECTED.
BUT WE DIDN'T KNOW WHO.
WE DIDN'T KNOW IT WOULD BE...
...BE...
...TELL THEM, GUILLAUME...TELL THEM WE DIDN'T KNOW...
...I'M SORRY...
...I'M SO SORRY...
WELL, LOOK, SHE'S CRYING, LET'S ALL BELIEVE HER NOW.
JUST FOLLOWING ORDERS, RIGHT?
ENOUGH!
I KNEW MY BROTHER BETTER THAN ANY OF YOU. HE WAS ALL THE FAMILY I HAD LEFT IN THIS WORLD, AND NOW HE IS GONE.
SO IF I DECIDE THESE TWO STAY--
--THEY STAY.
AND BESIDES, THEY ARE NOT THE REASON HE'S GONE--

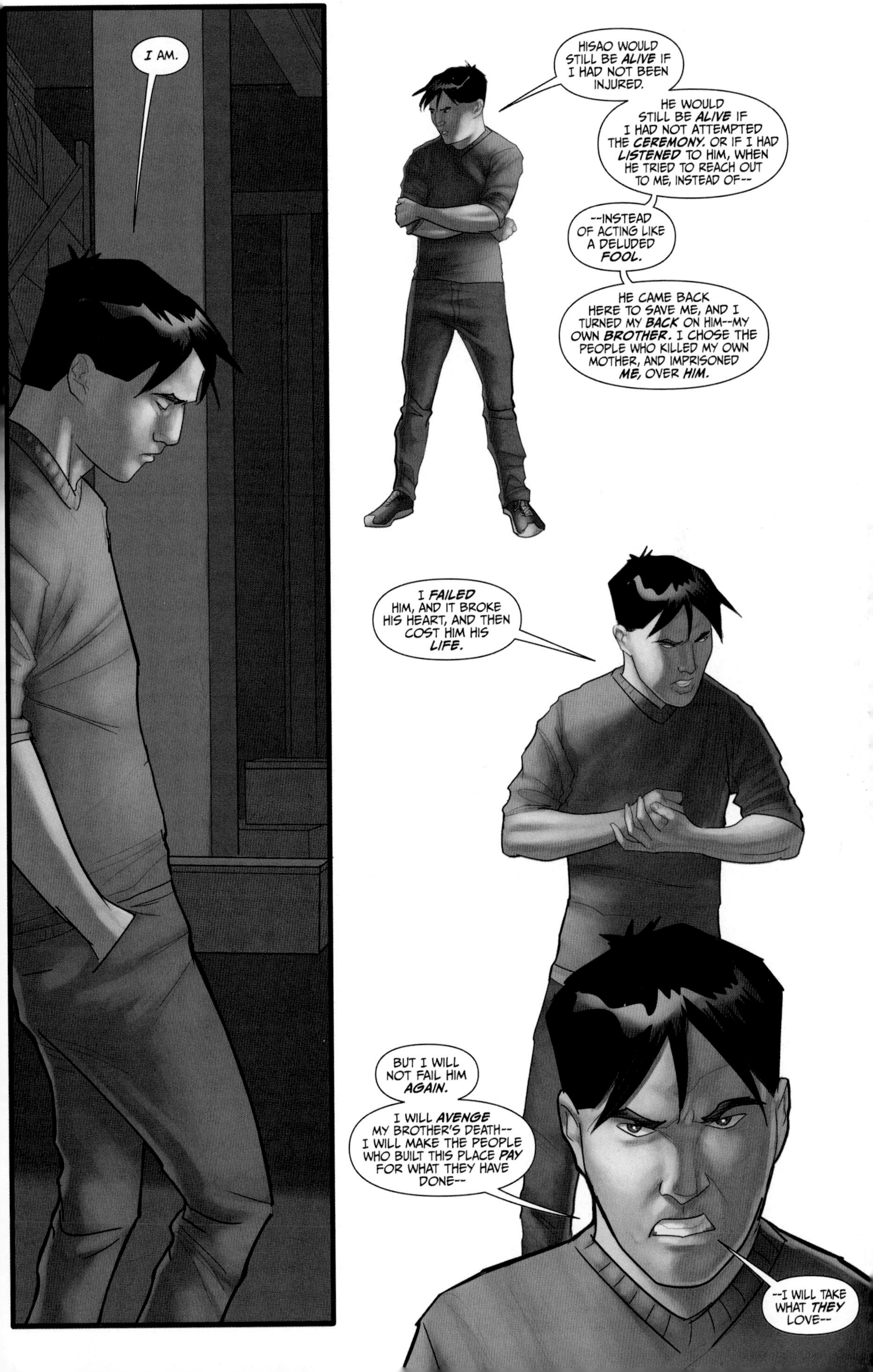
I AM.
HISAO WOULD STILL BE ALIVE IF I HAD NOT BEEN INJURED.
HE WOULD STILL BE ALIVE IF I HAD NOT ATTEMPTED THE CEREMONY. OR IF I HAD LISTENED TO HIM, WHEN HE TRIED TO REACH OUT TO ME, INSTEAD OF--
--INSTEAD OF ACTING LIKE A DELUDED FOOL.
HE CAME BACK HERE TO SAVE ME, AND I TURNED MY BACK ON HIM--MY OWN BROTHER. I CHOSE THE PEOPLE WHO KILLED MY OWN MOTHER, AND IMPRISONED ME, OVER HIM.
I FAILED HIM, AND IT BROKE HIS HEART, AND THEN COST HIM HIS LIFE.
BUT I WILL NOT FAIL HIM AGAIN.
I WILL AVENGE MY BROTHER'S DEATH-- I WILL MAKE THE PEOPLE WHO BUILT THIS PLACE PAY FOR WHAT THEY HAVE DONE--
--I WILL TAKE WHAT THEY LOVE--

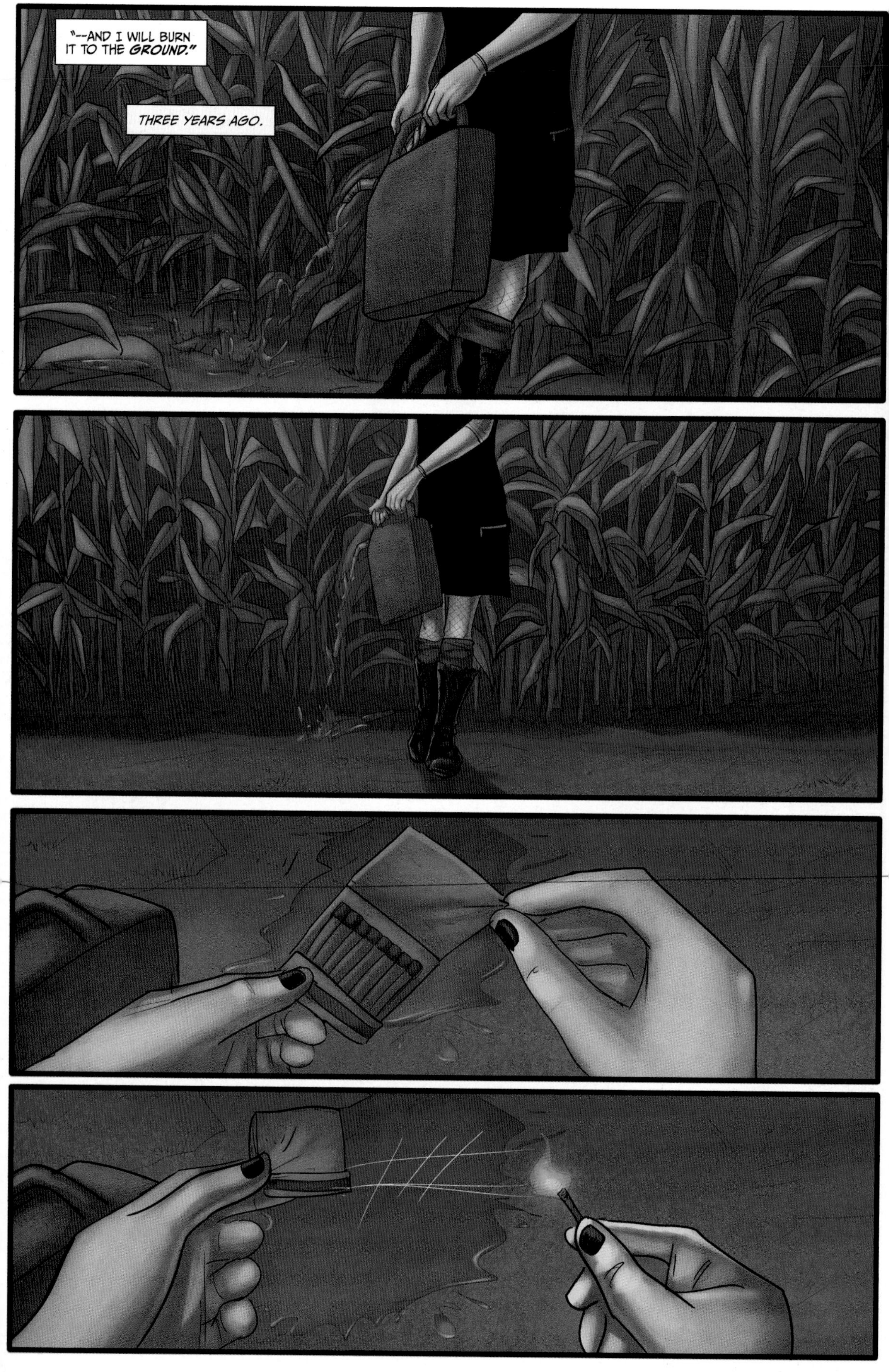
"--AND I WILL BURN IT TO THE GROUND."
THREE YEARS AGO.

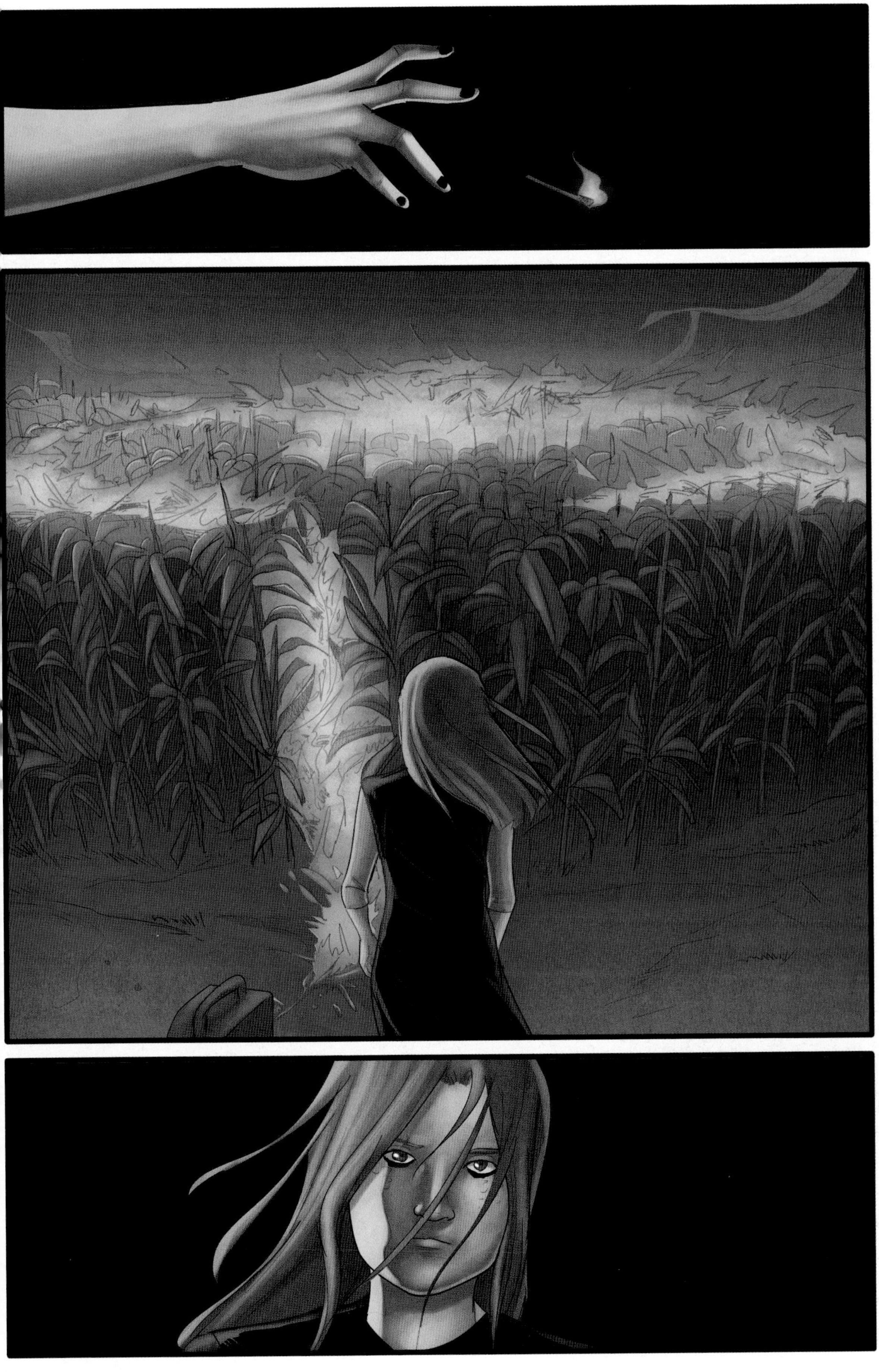

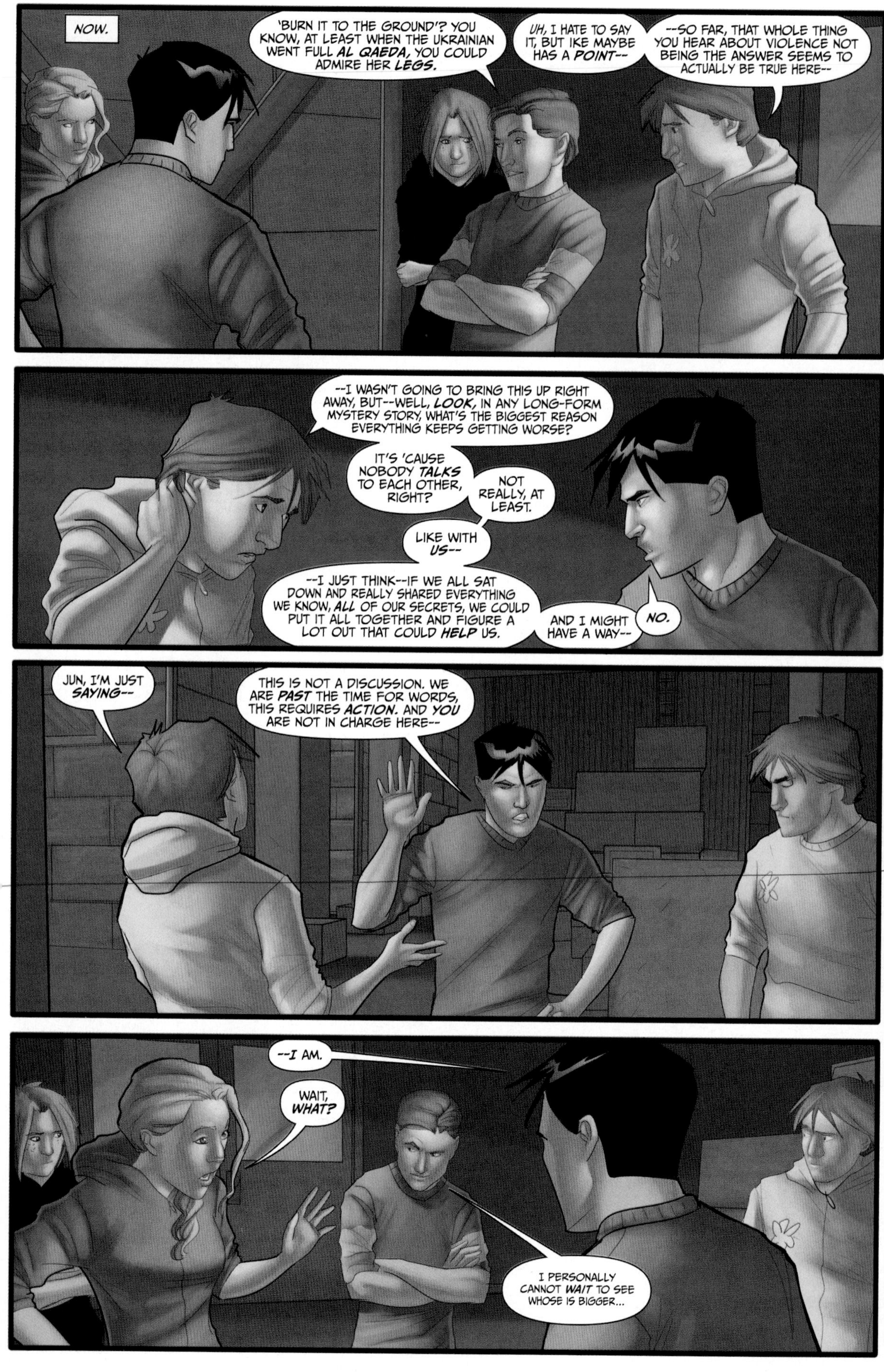
NOW.
'BURN IT TO THE GROUND'? YOU KNOW, AT LEAST WHEN THE UKRAINIAN WENT FULL AL QAEDA, YOU COULD ADMIRE HER LEGS.
UH, I HATE TO SAY IT, BUT IKE MAYBE HAS A POINT--
--SO FAR, THAT WHOLE THING YOU HEAR ABOUT VIOLENCE NOT BEING THE ANSWER SEEMS TO ACTUALLY BE TRUE HERE--
--I WASN'T GOING TO BRING THIS UP RIGHT AWAY, BUT--WELL, LOOK, IN ANY LONG-FORM MYSTERY STORY, WHAT'S THE BIGGEST REASON EVERYTHING KEEPS GETTING WORSE?
IT'S 'CAUSE NOBODY TALKS TO EACH OTHER, RIGHT?
NOT REALLY, AT LEAST.
LIKE WITH US--
--I JUST THINK--IF WE ALL SAT DOWN AND REALLY SHARED EVERYTHING WE KNOW, ALL OF OUR SECRETS, WE COULD PUT IT ALL TOGETHER AND FIGURE A LOT OUT THAT COULD HELP US.
AND I MIGHT HAVE A WAY--
NO.
JUN, I'M JUST SAYING--
THIS IS NOT A DISCUSSION. WE ARE PAST THE TIME FOR WORDS, THIS REQUIRES ACTION. AND YOU ARE NOT IN CHARGE HERE--
--I AM.
WAIT, WHAT?
I PERSONALLY CANNOT WAIT TO SEE WHOSE IS BIGGER...

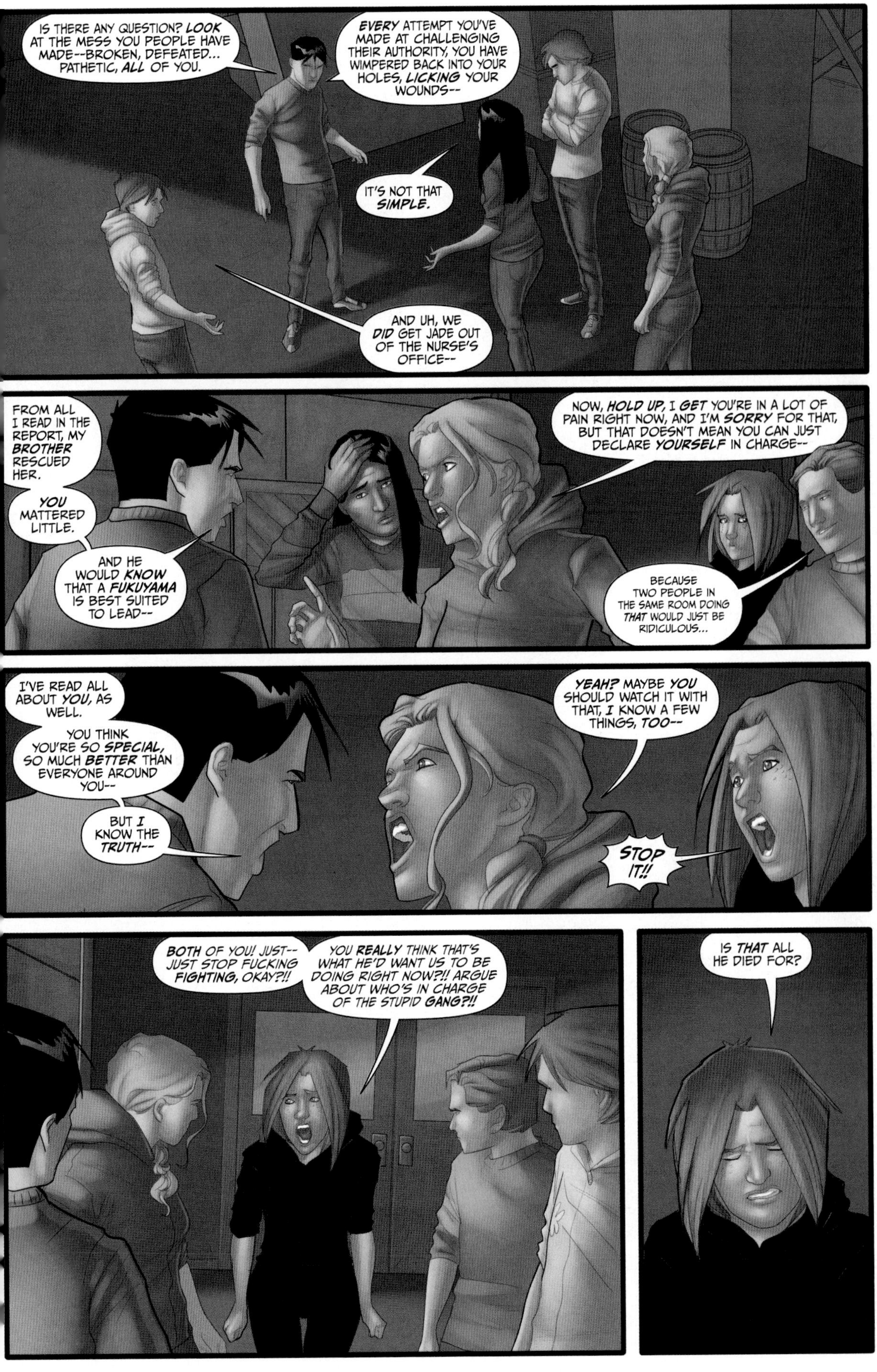
IS THERE ANY QUESTION? LOOK AT THE MESS YOU PEOPLE HAVE MADE--BROKEN, DEFEATED... PATHETIC, ALL OF YOU.
EVERY ATTEMPT YOU'VE MADE AT CHALLENGING THEIR AUTHORITY, YOU HAVE WIMPERED BACK INTO YOUR HOLES, LICKING YOUR WOUNDS--
IT'S NOT THAT SIMPLE.
AND UH, WE DID GET JADE OUT OF THE NURSE'S OFFICE--
FROM ALL I READ IN THE REPORT, MY BROTHER RESCUED HER.
YOU MATTERED LITTLE.
AND HE WOULD KNOW THAT A FUKUYAMA IS BEST SUITED TO LEAD--
NOW, HOLD UP, I GET YOU'RE IN A LOT OF PAIN RIGHT NOW, AND I'M SORRY FOR THAT, BUT THAT DOESN'T MEAN YOU CAN JUST DECLARE YOURSELF IN CHARGE--
BECAUSE TWO PEOPLE IN THE SAME ROOM DOING THAT WOULD JUST BE RIDICULOUS...
I'VE READ ALL ABOUT YOU, AS WELL.
YOU THINK YOU'RE SO SPECIAL, SO MUCH BETTER THAN EVERYONE AROUND YOU--
BUT I KNOW THE TRUTH--
YEAH? MAYBE YOU SHOULD WATCH IT WITH THAT, I KNOW A FEW THINGS, TOO--
STOP IT!!
BOTH OF YOU! JUST-- JUST STOP FUCKING FIGHTING, OKAY?!!
YOU REALLY THINK THAT'S WHAT HE'D WANT US TO BE DOING RIGHT NOW?!! ARGUE ABOUT WHO'S IN CHARGE OF THE STUPID GANG?!!
IS THAT ALL HE DIED FOR?

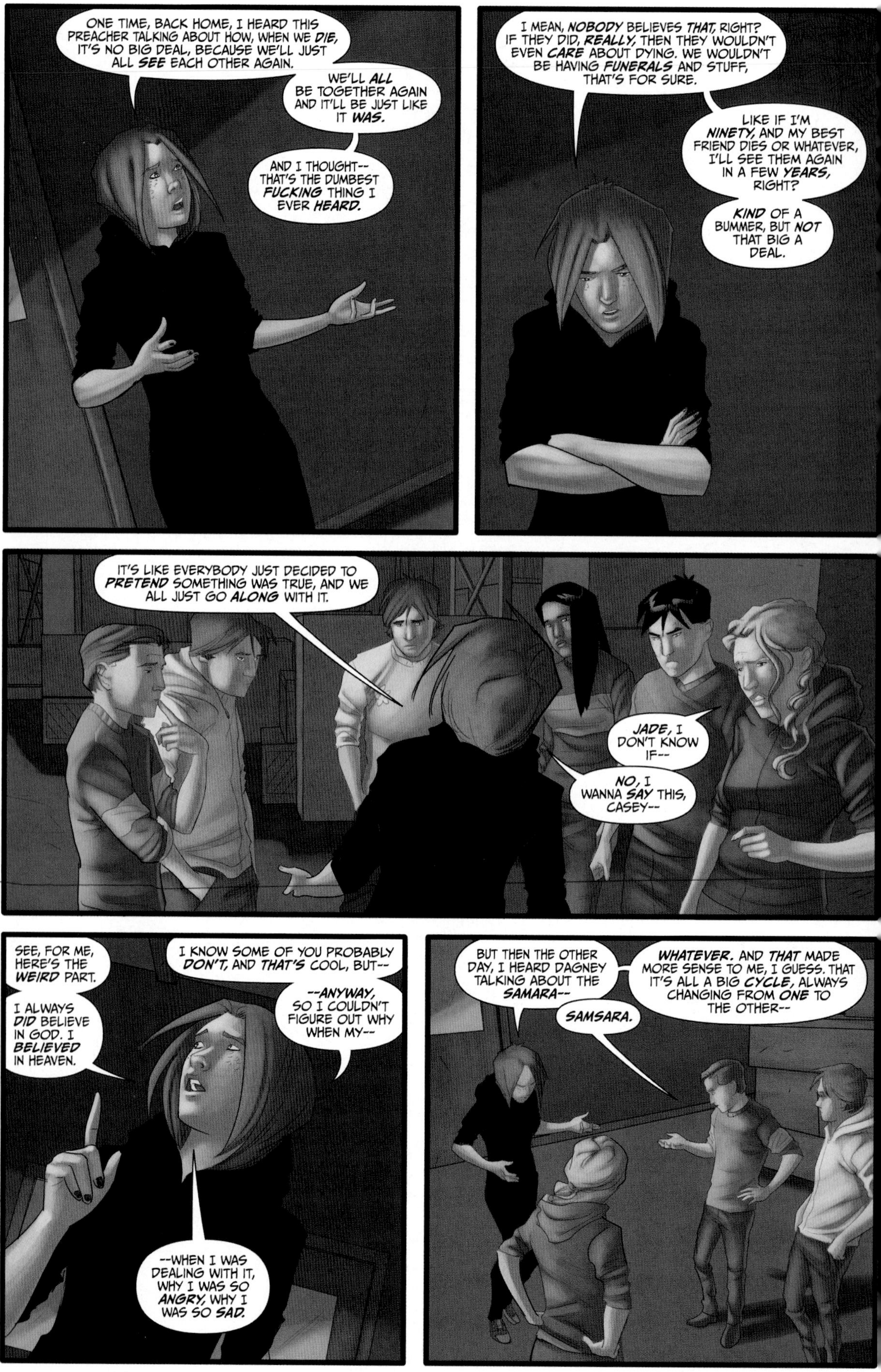
ONE TIME, BACK HOME, I HEARD THIS PREACHER TALKING ABOUT HOW, WHEN WE DIE, IT'S NO BIG DEAL, BECAUSE WE'LL JUST ALL SEE EACH OTHER AGAIN.
WE'LL ALL BE TOGETHER AGAIN AND IT'LL BE JUST LIKE IT WAS.
AND I THOUGHT-- THAT'S THE DUMBEST FUCKING THING I EVER HEARD.
I MEAN, NOBODY BELIEVES THAT, RIGHT? IF THEY DID, REALLY, THEN THEY WOULDN'T EVEN CARE ABOUT DYING. WE WOULDN'T BE HAVING FUNERALS AND STUFF, THAT'S FOR SURE.
LIKE IF I'M NINETY, AND MY BEST FRIEND DIES OR WHATEVER, I'LL SEE THEM AGAIN IN A FEW YEARS, RIGHT?
KIND OF A BUMMER, BUT NOT THAT BIG A DEAL.
IT'S LIKE EVERYBODY JUST DECIDED TO PRETEND SOMETHING WAS TRUE, AND WE ALL JUST GO ALONG WITH IT.
JADE, I DON'T KNOW IF--
NO, I WANNA SAY THIS, CASEY--
SEE, FOR ME, HERE'S THE WEIRD PART.
I ALWAYS DID BELIEVE IN GOD. I BELIEVED IN HEAVEN.
I KNOW SOME OF YOU PROBABLY DON'T, AND THAT'S COOL, BUT--
--ANYWAY, SO I COULDN'T FIGURE OUT WHY WHEN MY--
--WHEN I WAS DEALING WITH IT, WHY I WAS SO ANGRY, WHY I WAS SO SAD.
BUT THEN THE OTHER DAY, I HEARD DAGNEY TALKING ABOUT THE SAMARA--
SAMSARA.
WHATEVER. AND THAT MADE MORE SENSE TO ME, I GUESS. THAT IT'S ALL A BIG CYCLE, ALWAYS CHANGING FROM ONE TO THE OTHER--

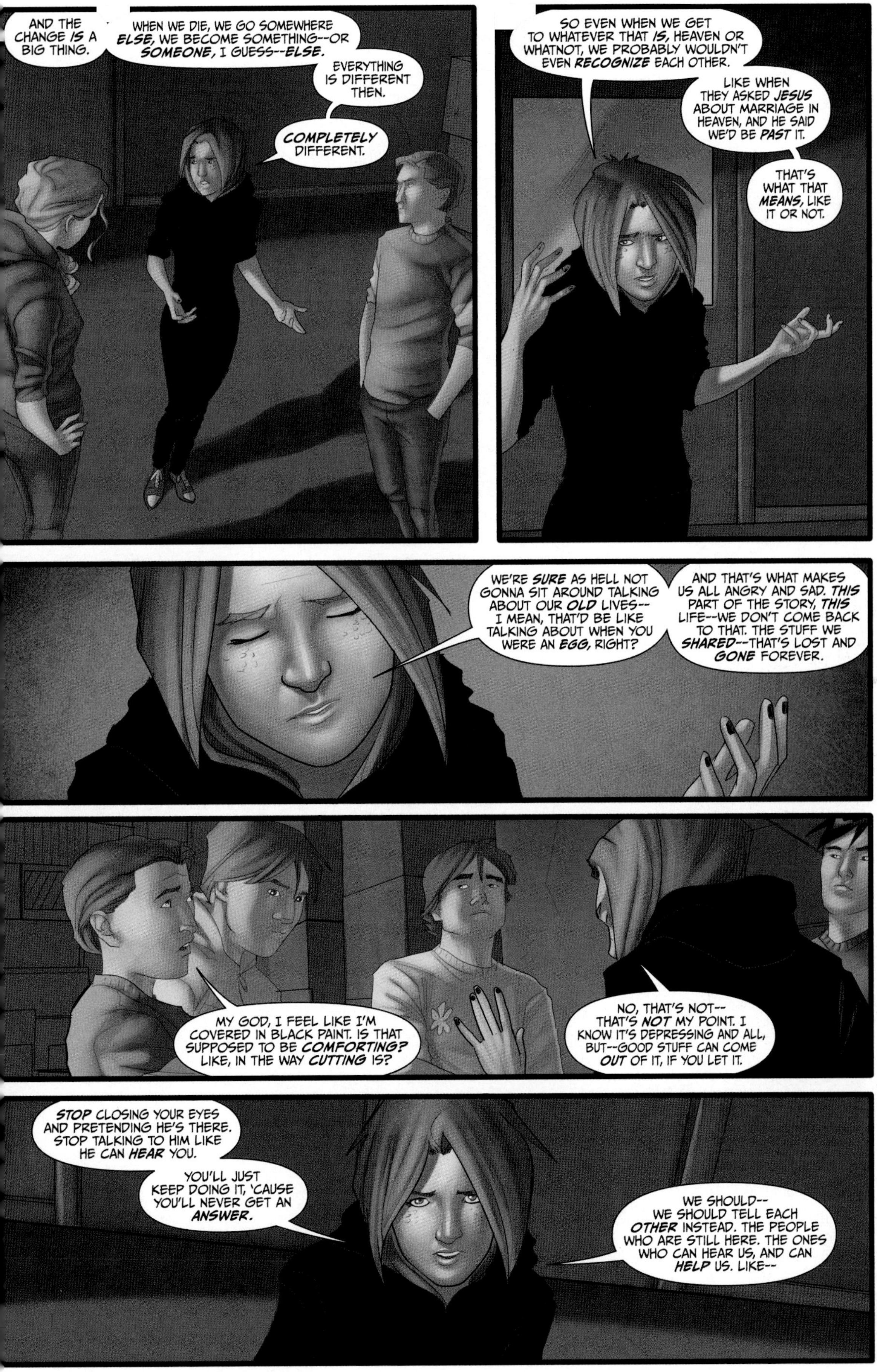
AND THE CHANGE IS A BIG THING.
WHEN WE DIE, WE GO SOMEWHERE ELSE, WE BECOME SOMETHING--OR SOMEONE, I GUESS--ELSE.
EVERYTHING IS DIFFERENT THEN.
COMPLETELY DIFFERENT.
SO EVEN WHEN WE GET TO WHATEVER THAT IS, HEAVEN OR WHATNOT, WE PROBABLY WOULDN'T EVEN RECOGNIZE EACH OTHER.
LIKE WHEN THEY ASKED JESUS ABOUT MARRIAGE IN HEAVEN, AND HE SAID WE'D BE PAST IT.
THAT'S WHAT THAT MEANS, LIKE IT OR NOT.
WE'RE SURE AS HELL NOT GONNA SIT AROUND TALKING ABOUT OUR OLD LIVES-- I MEAN, THAT'D BE LIKE TALKING ABOUT WHEN YOU WERE AN EGG, RIGHT?
AND THAT'S WHAT MAKES US ALL ANGRY AND SAD. THIS PART OF THE STORY, THIS LIFE--WE DON'T COME BACK TO THAT. THE STUFF WE SHARED--THAT'S LOST AND GONE FOREVER.
MY GOD, I FEEL LIKE I'M COVERED IN BLACK PAINT. IS THAT SUPPOSED TO BE COMFORTING? LIKE, IN THE WAY CUTTING IS?
NO, THAT'S NOT-- THAT'S NOT MY POINT. I KNOW IT'S DEPRESSING AND ALL, BUT--GOOD STUFF CAN COME OUT OF IT, IF YOU LET IT.
STOP CLOSING YOUR EYES AND PRETENDING HE'S THERE. STOP TALKING TO HIM LIKE HE CAN HEAR YOU.
YOU'LL JUST KEEP DOING IT, 'CAUSE YOU'LL NEVER GET AN ANSWER.
WE SHOULD-- WE SHOULD TELL EACH OTHER INSTEAD. THE PEOPLE WHO ARE STILL HERE. THE ONES WHO CAN HEAR US, AND CAN HELP US. LIKE--

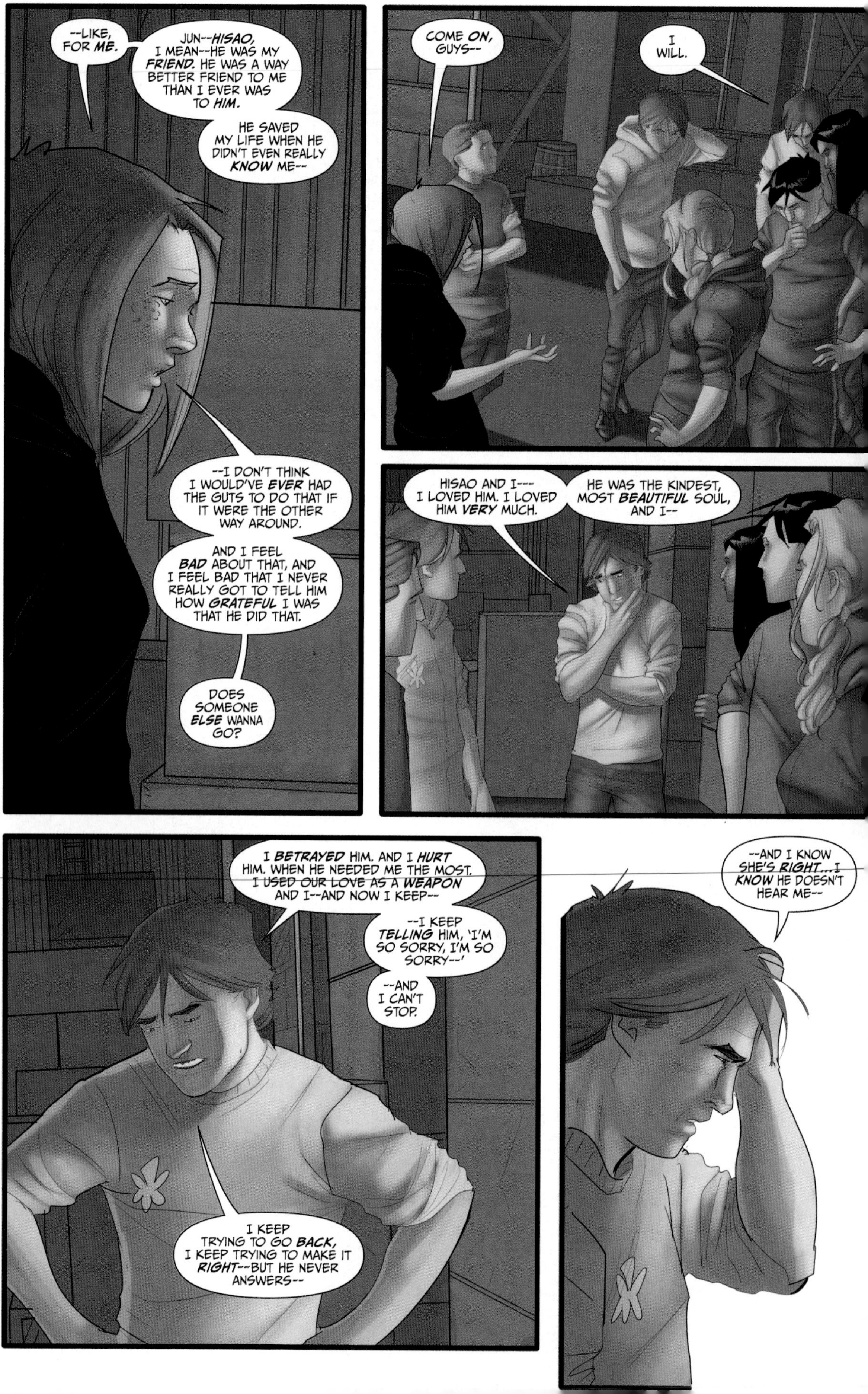

--LIKE, FOR ME.
JUN--HISAO, I MEAN--HE WAS MY FRIEND. HE WAS A WAY BETTER FRIEND TO ME THAN I EVER WAS TO HIM.
HE SAVED MY LIFE WHEN HE DIDN'T EVEN REALLY KNOW ME--
--I DON'T THINK I WOULD'VE EVER HAD THE GUTS TO DO THAT IF IT WERE THE OTHER WAY AROUND.
AND I FEEL BAD ABOUT THAT, AND I FEEL BAD THAT I NEVER REALLY GOT TO TELL HIM HOW GRATEFUL I WAS THAT HE DID THAT.
DOES SOMEONE ELSE WANNA GO?
COME ON, GUYS--
I WILL.
HISAO AND I--- I LOVED HIM. I LOVED HIM VERY MUCH.
HE WAS THE KINDEST, MOST BEAUTIFUL SOUL, AND I--
I BETRAYED HIM. AND I HURT HIM. WHEN HE NEEDED ME THE MOST. I USED OUR LOVE AS A WEAPON AND I--AND NOW I KEEP--
--I KEEP TELLING HIM, 'I'M SO SORRY, I'M SO SORRY--'
--AND I CAN'T STOP.
I KEEP TRYING TO GO BACK, I KEEP TRYING TO MAKE IT RIGHT--BUT HE NEVER ANSWERS--
--AND I KNOW SHE'S RIGHT...I KNOW HE DOESN'T HEAR ME--

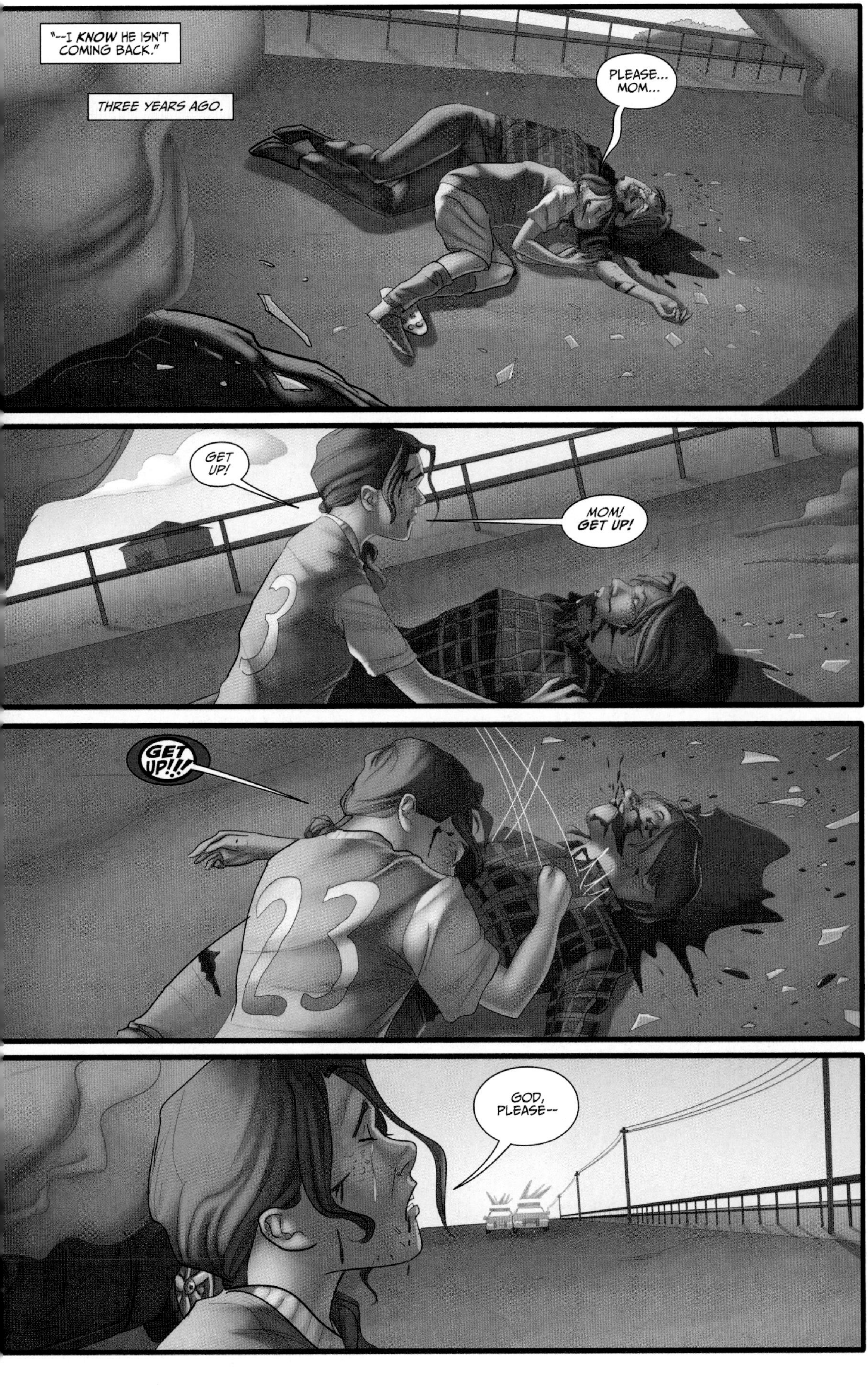
"--I *KNOW* HE ISN'T COMING BACK."
THREE YEARS AGO.
PLEASE... MOM...
GET UP!
MOM! GET UP!
GET UP!!!
GOD, PLEASE--

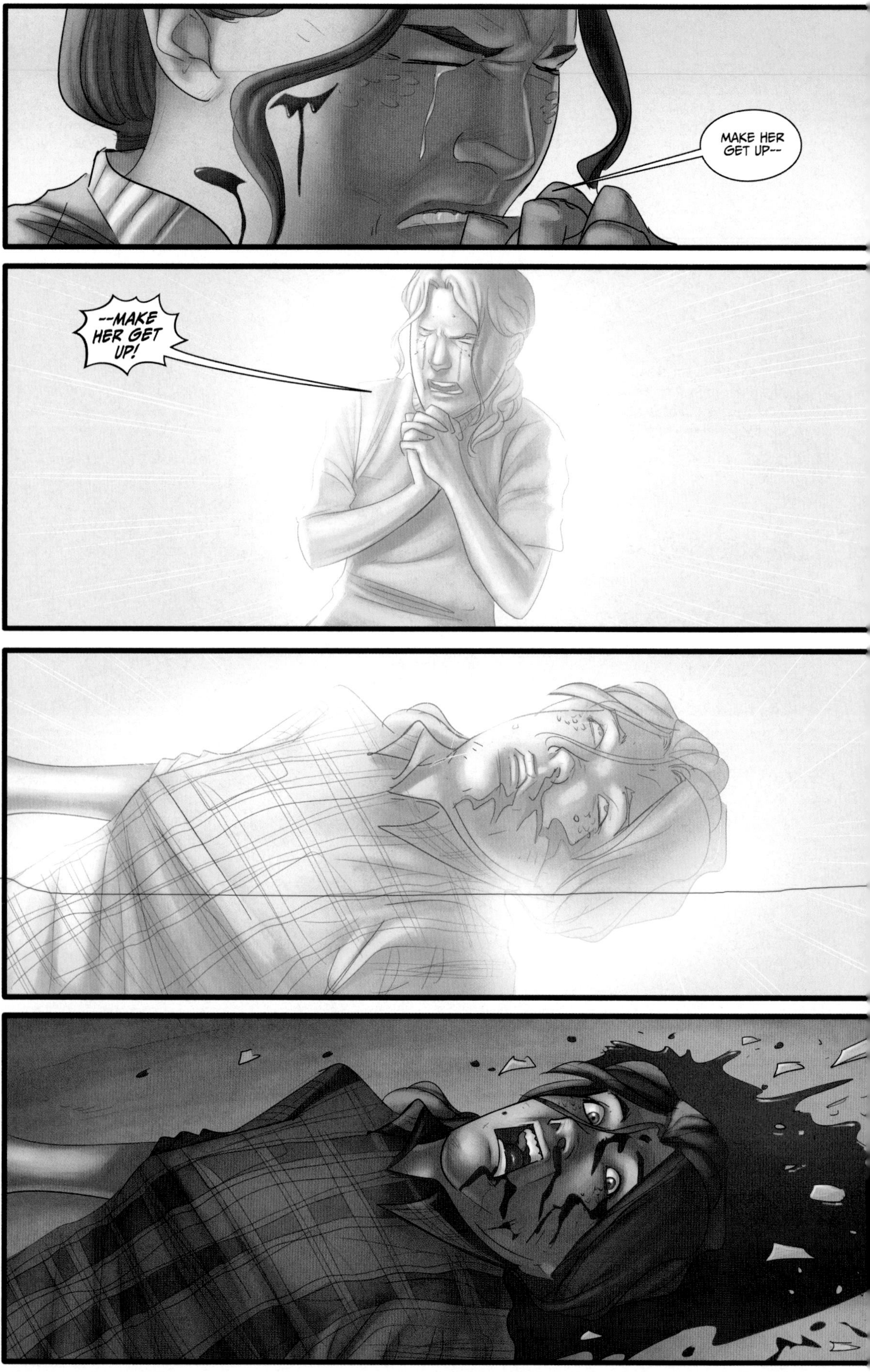
MAKE HER GET UP--
--MAKE HER GET UP!

extras

Morning Glories covers have showcased a startling array of artistic talent. Issues #28 & #29 each had 8 variant covers.

28

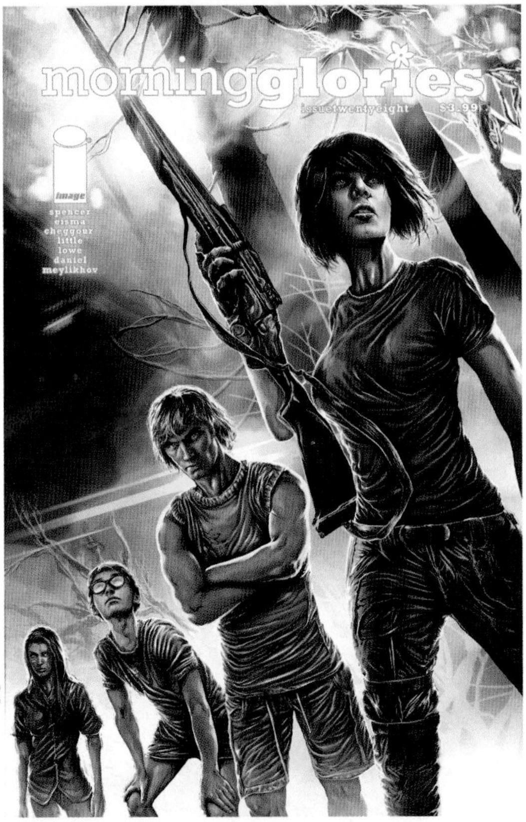
morningglories
issuetwentyeight $3.99
image
spencer
eisma
cheggour
little
lowe
daniel
meylikhov

Mehdi Cheggour

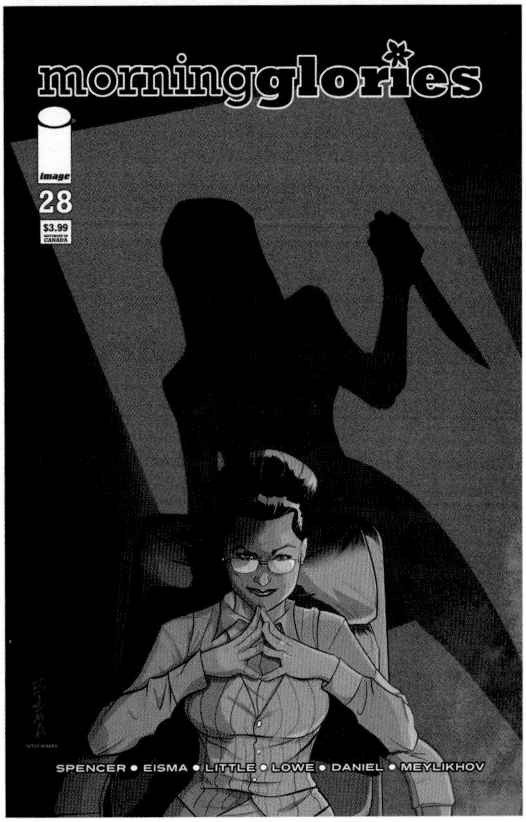
morningglories
image
28
$3.99
SPENCER • EISMA • LITTLE • LOWE • DANIEL • MEYLIKHOV

Joe Eisma

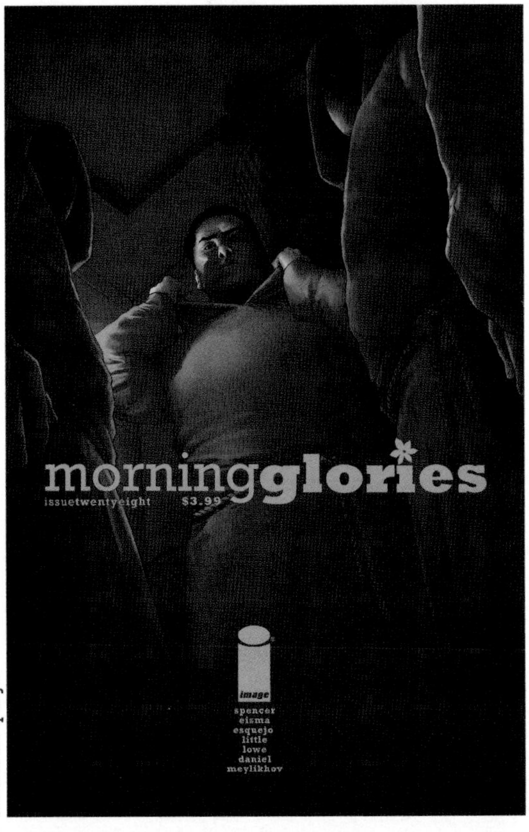
morningglories
issuetwentyeight $3.99
image
spencer
eisma
esquejo
little
lowe
daniel
meylikhov

Rodin Esquejo

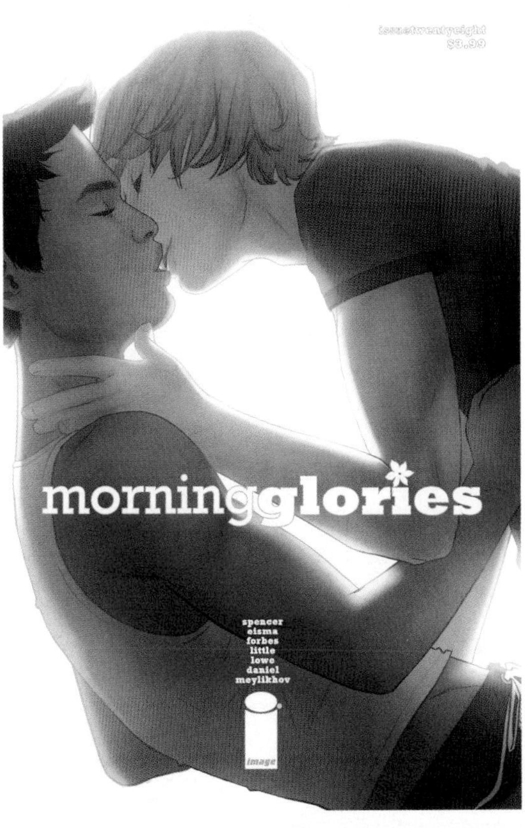
issuetwentyeight
$3.99
morningglories
spencer
eisma
forbes
little
lowe
daniel
meylikhov
image

W.Scott Forbes

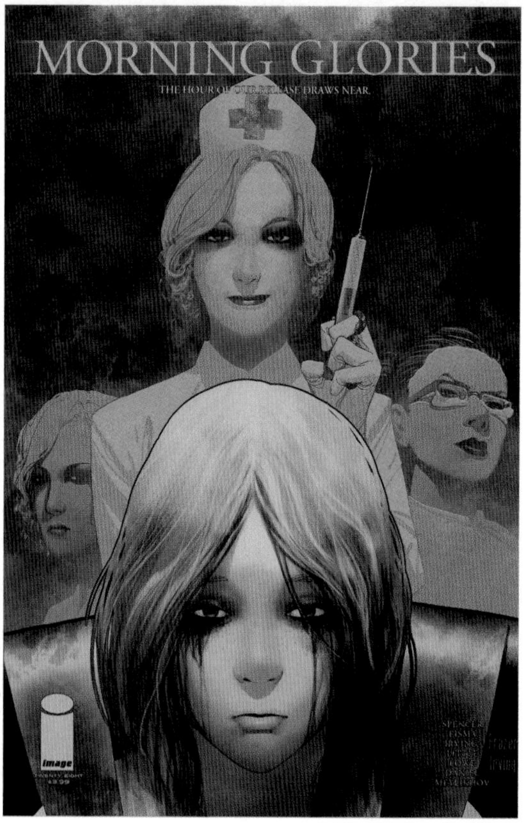
MORNING GLORIES

Frazer Irving

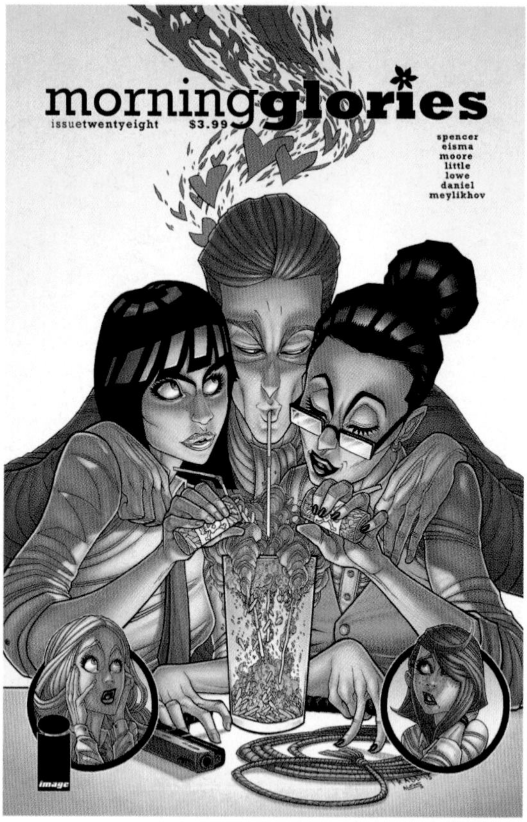
morningglories
issuetwentyeight $3.99
spencer
eisma
moore
little
lowe
daniel
meylikhov

Tradd Moore

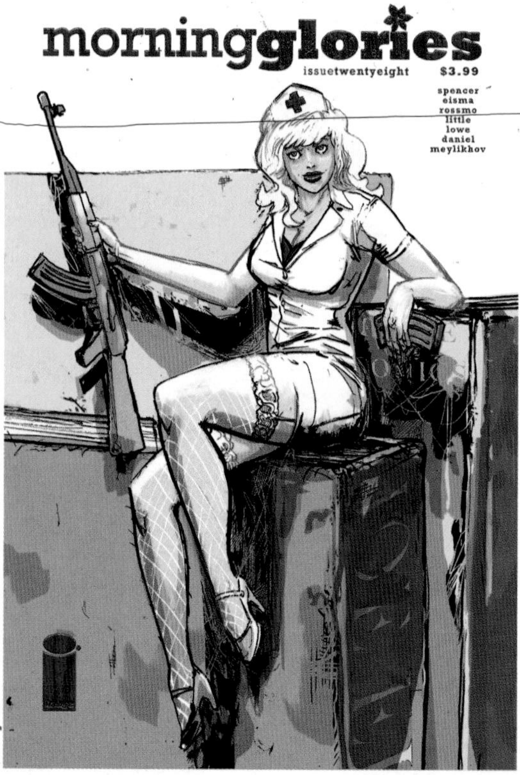
morningglories
issuetwentyeight $3.99
spencer
eisma
rossmo
little
lowe
daniel
meylikhov

Riley Rossmo

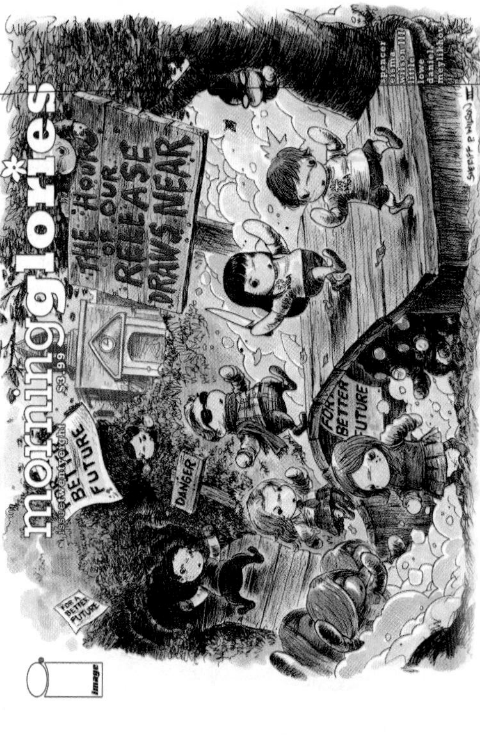
morningglories
$3.99
THE HOUR OF OUR RELEASE DRAWS NEAR
BETTER FUTURE
DANGER
FOR A BETTER FUTURE

Charles Wilson III

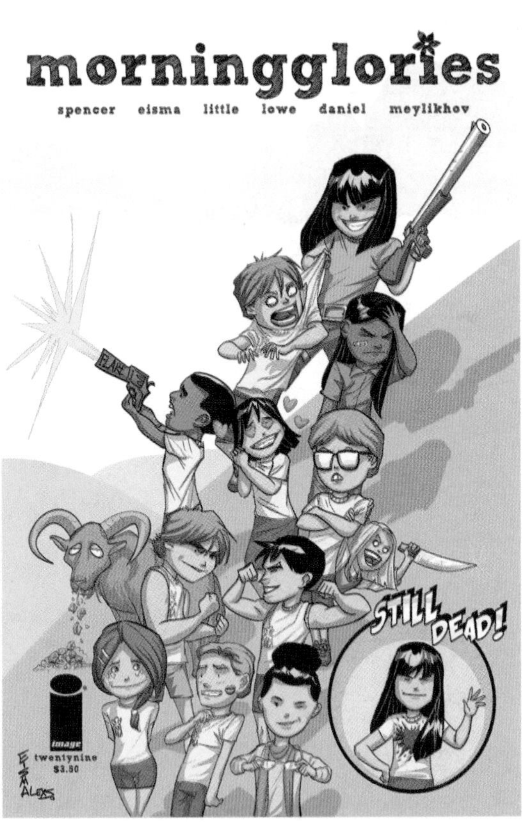
morningglories
spencer eisma little lowe daniel meylikhov
STILL DEAD!
image
twentynine
$3.90

Joe Eisma

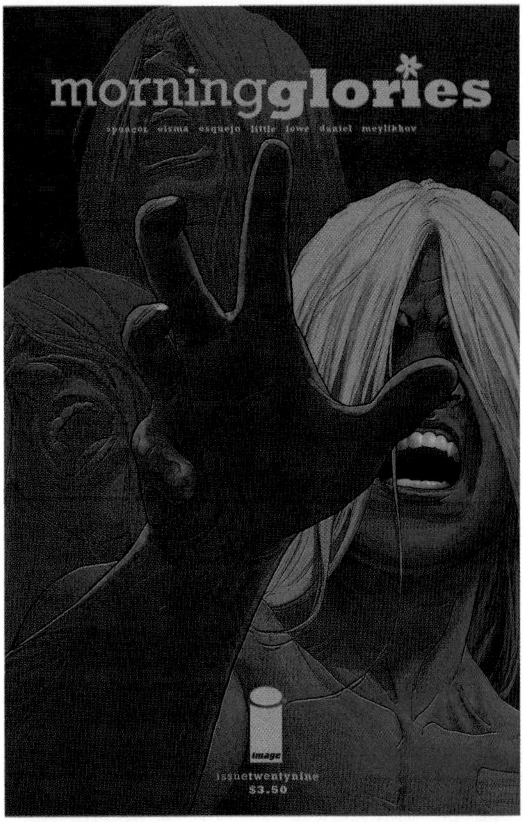
morningglories
spencer eisma esquejo little lowe daniel meylikhov
image
issuetwentynine
$3.50

Rodin Esquejo

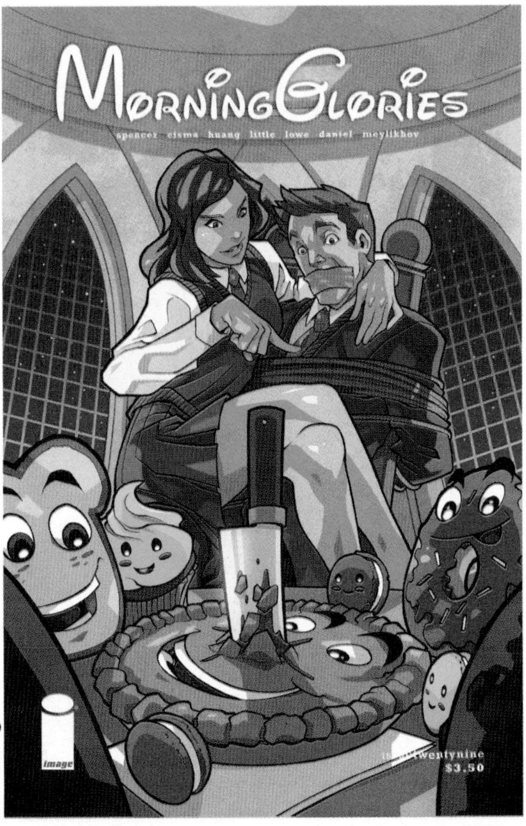
MorningGlories
spencer eisma huang little lowe daniel meylikhov
image
$3.50

Ed Huang

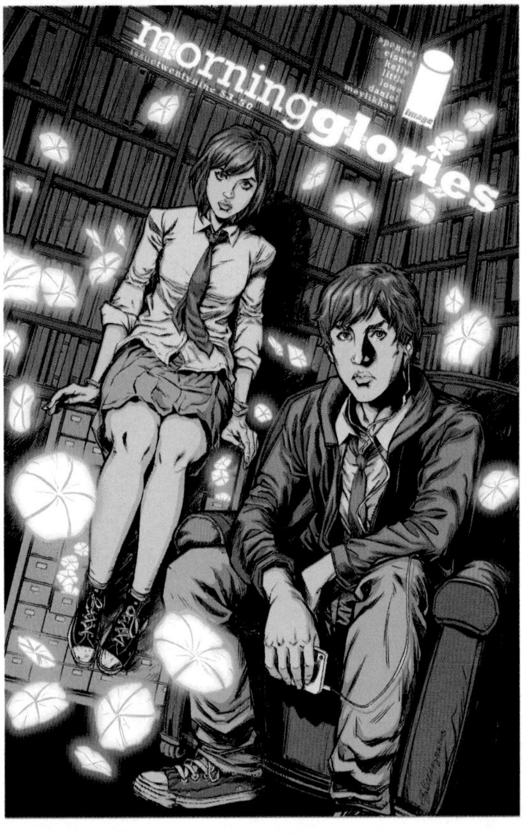
morningglories
spencer
eisma
kelly
little
lowe
daniel
meylikhov
image

Ryan Kelly

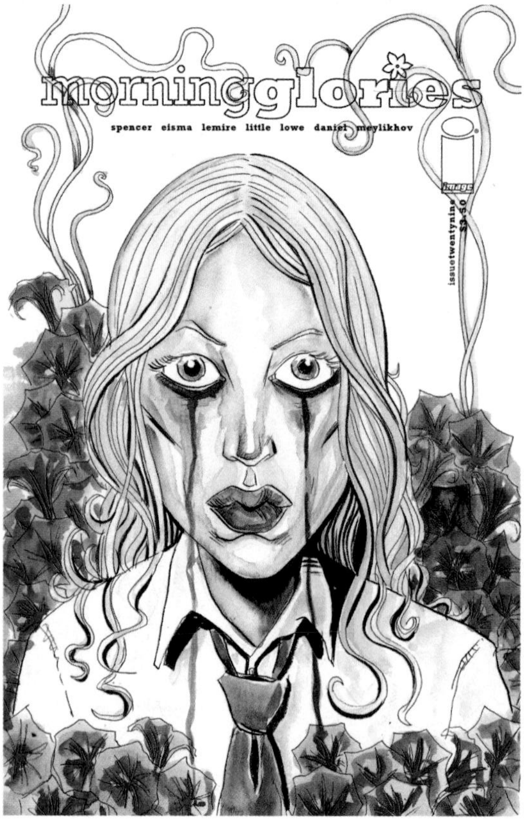
morningglories
spencer eisma lemire little lowe daniel meylikhov
image
issuetwentynine
$3.50
Jeff Lemire

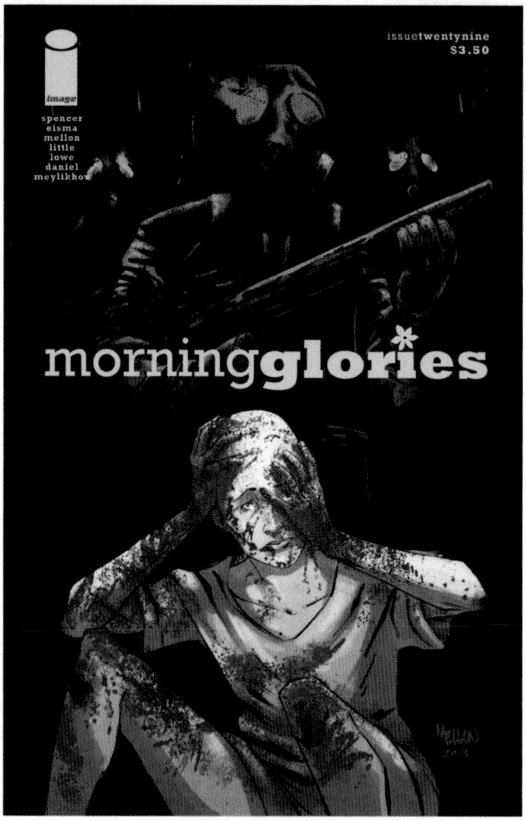
issuetwentynine
$3.50
image
spencer
eisma
mellon
little
lowe
daniel
meylikhov
morningglories
Kevin Mellon

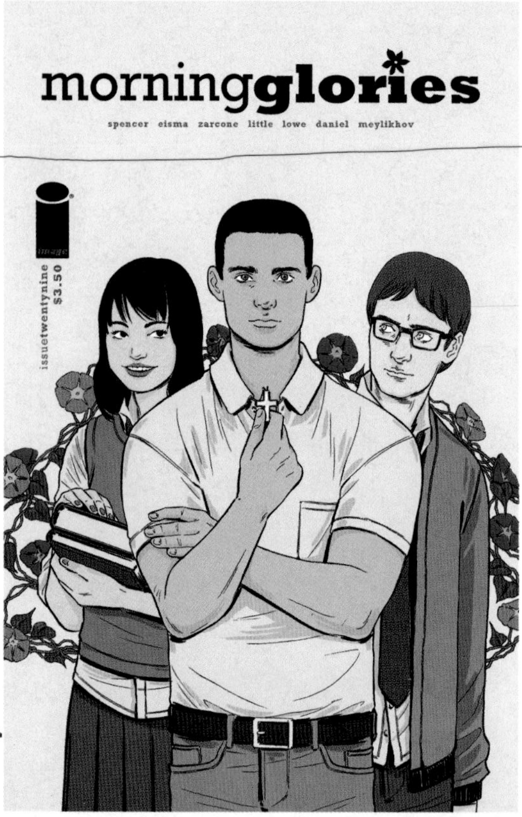
morningglories
spencer eisma zarcone little lowe daniel meylikhov
image
issuetwentynine
$3.50
Marley Zarcone

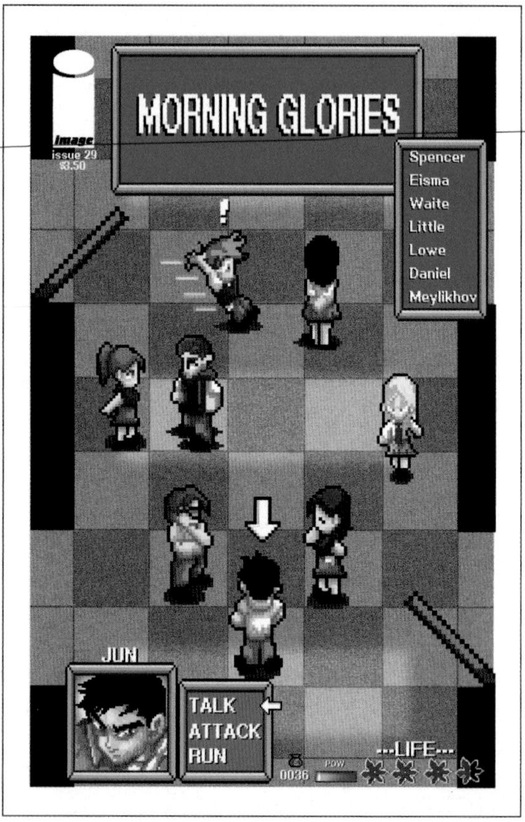
image
issue 29
$3.50
MORNING GLORIES
Spencer
Eisma
Waite
Little
Lowe
Daniel
Meylikhov
!
JUN
TALK
ATTACK
RUN
0036
POW
---LIFE---
Matthew Waite

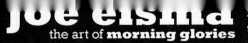

joe eisma
the art of **morning glories**

Morning Glories artist Joe Eisma shares a look into the creative process for crafting interior story pages.

KIDS
FIRE
BROKEN PIECES
Chains

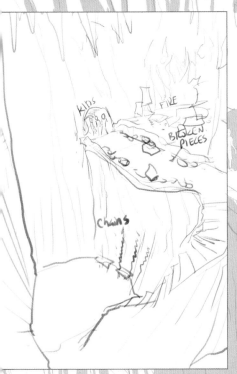

thumbnail
The key elements of the panel are mapped out as the composition of the page takes form.

inks
In this example from Morning Glories, Issue #13, page 22 - Joe has elected to include grey tones to indicate shadow for colorist Alex Sollazzo.

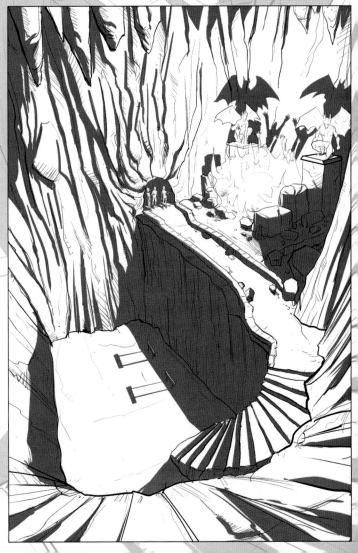

issue #17 - page 15.

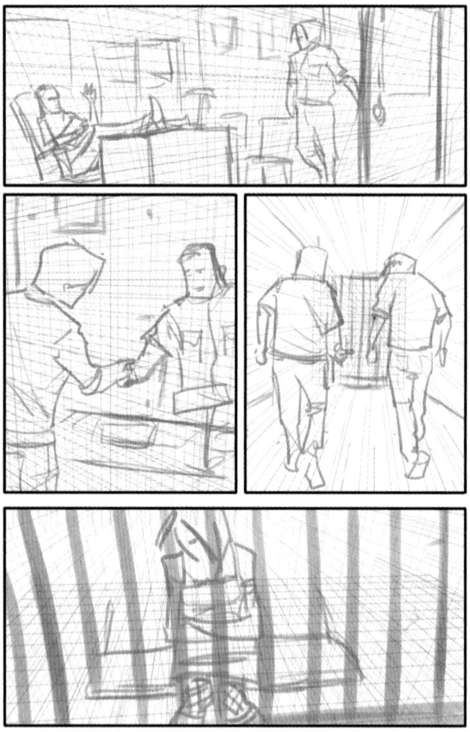

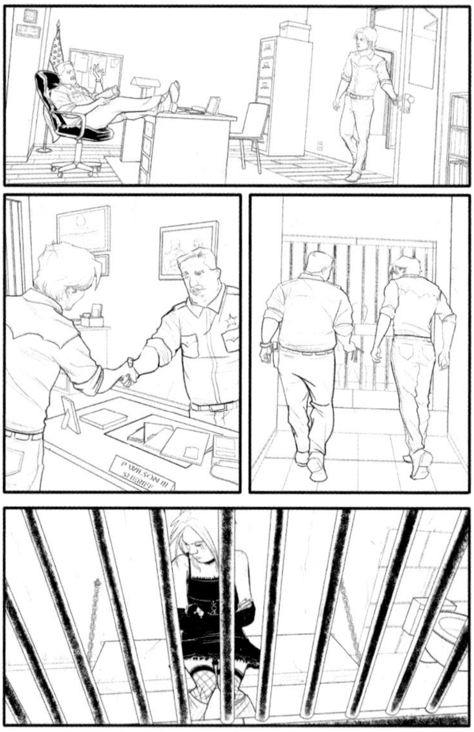

issue #18 - page 4.

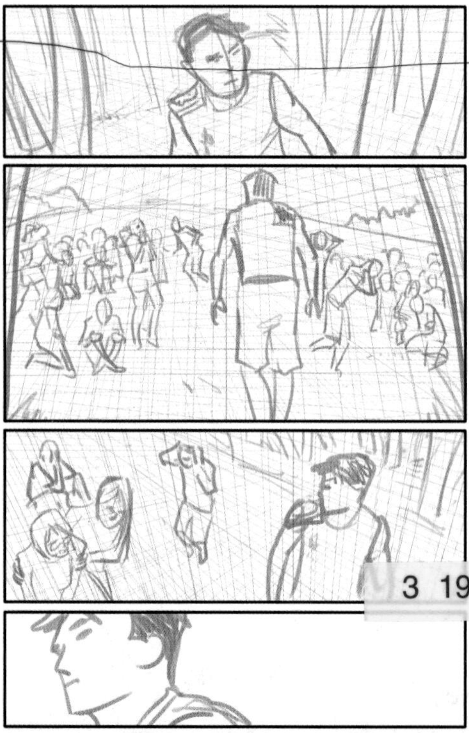

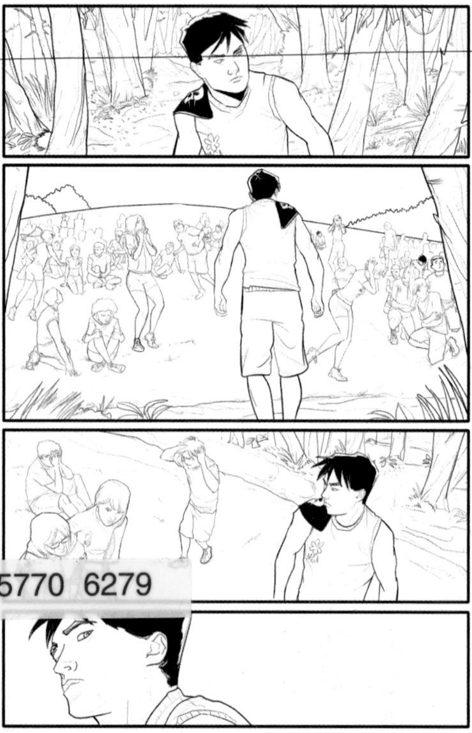